RIDING THE WINDHORSE

Manic-Depressive Disorder and the Quest for Wholeness

Robert S. Corrington

Hamilton Books
an imprint of
University Press of America,® Inc.
Lanham · Boulder · New York · Toronto · Oxford

Copyright © 2003 by
Hamilton Books
4501 Forbes Boulevard
Suite 200
Lanham, Maryland 20706
UPA Acquisitions Department (301) 459-3366

PO Box 317
Oxford
OX2 9RU, UK

All rights reserved
Printed in the United States of America
British Library Cataloging in Publication Information Available

ISBN 0-7618-2619-X (paperback : alk. ppr.)

∞™ The paper used in this publication meets the minimum
requirements of American National Standard for Information
Sciences—Permanence of Paper for Printed Library Materials,
ANSI Z39.48—1984

I DEDICATE THIS WORK
TO MY COLLEAGUES AT
DREW UNIVERSITY

TABLE OF CONTENTS

Preface   VII

Acknowledgments   XI

1. A Life's Journey and Its Dreamscape   1
   A.   A Life's Journey   8
   B.   A Dreamscape   40

2. Body and Soul — Medical and Psychological Vistas   55
   A.   Medical Vistas   58
   B.   Psychological Vistas   82

3. Creativity and Genius in Manic-Depression   103
   A. Creativity as Manifest in:
      Products, Processes, and Communities   104
   B. Genius and the *Not Yet*   111
   C. Two Case Studies of Manic-Depressive Genius:
      Newton and Sri Ramakrishna   127
    c.a.   Isaac Newton: Cosmology and Divinization   129
    c.b.   Sri Ramakrishna: Divine Energy   149

4. Intimations of Wholeness   167
   A. Spirituality, Sacred Folds, and Intervals   172
   B. Creative Distancing and Communal Testing   177
   C. Individuation and the Spirits   183

Appendix: My Passage from Panentheism to Pantheism   193

Endnotes   217

Bibliography   231

Index – Names   238
Index – Subject   241

PREFACE

Writing this book has been a great emotional and intellectual challenge, not least because I have been forced to confront a great deal about my own mental illness and about how it must look to others. No one likes peering into what C.G. Jung called the shadow side of the self, that side which always seems to intrude and overturn whatever hard won stability we may have at any given moment. In the case of an illness as severe as manic-depression, this intrusion can come with overwhelming force and shatter the boundaries of the psyche. This is an experience I have lived through over and over again and seen played out in my own extended family.

Yet at the same time, this most uncanny of psychic guests can propel the individual to acts of creativity and boundary transgression that are not available to those who do not have the disease. Part of my concern in writing this book is to make sense of this paradox and with finding some means for living with its moral ambiguities.

Manic-depressive disorder is far more common than many suspect, with one person out of a hundred having some form of the disease. Consequently, anyone reading this book is likely to either have the disorder or know someone who does. Its prevalence in the general population and its highly disruptive power are facts that force us to take a fresh look at what this uncanny disease is and how it has affected personal and collective history. I argue, following the important insights of Kay Redfield Jamison, D. Jablow Hershman, Julian Lieb and others, that manic-depressive disorder is profoundly embedded in the phenomenon of genius and may be a necessary condition for many forms of genius level productivity. Consequently, as I also argue, manic-depressive disorder, or bi-polar disorder as it is known in the medical world, has a value for the human species as a whole but may be destructive of its individual carrier.

I decided to write this book, my ninth, for deeply personal reasons. I needed to make sense of what has happened in my life and to that of close family members. Further, I wanted to find out everything I could about how to survive a major mental illness and about the positive aspects of a disorder that has such numbing depths and such searing heights. My research has taken me to many strange places and has intersected with the lives of courageous manic-depressive, both living and long gone. In the latter category I have taken great comfort from the fact that such people as Virginia Wolf, Sir Isaac Newton, Samuel Taylor Coleridge, William, Lord Byron, Charles Dickens, Vincent Van Gogh, Sri Ramakrishna, Ludwig Beethoven, Joan of Arc (perhaps), and Charles Sanders Peirce all suffered from their own deeply personal forms of manic-depressive disorder. As a way of honoring their lives and their suffering I have chosen two culturally diverse figures for detailed treatment: Newton and Sri Ramakrishna. Their contributions to physics and religious mysticism have greatly added to the stock of human wisdom and knowledge and neither of these individuals could have accomplished what they did without the disease that coursed through their lives.

The image I have chosen for the title of this book is taken from Tibetan Buddhism and refers to the psychic horse on which we ride in order to deal with the powerful emotional currents that surge through us. The late Buddhist philosopher Chögyam Trungpa developed it:

> Windhorse is a translation of the Tibetan *lungta*. Lung means "wind" and *ta* means "horse." Invoking secret *drala* is the experience of raising Windhorse, raising a wind of delight and power and riding on, or conquering, that energy. Such wind can come with great force, like a typhoon that can blow down trees and buildings and create huge waves in the water. The personal experience of this wind comes as a feeling of being completely and powerfully in the present.
> The horse aspect is that, in spite of the power of this great wind, you also feel stability. You are never swayed by the confusion of life, never swayed by excitement or depression.1

The *drala* is the energy that seems to come from a source outside of the self and can decenter and confound the ego. Learning how to live with this energy, since it can never be completely destroyed or tamed, is part of the wisdom that is learned through riding the Windhorse. I have found no better image than that of this high-flying powerful steed that feels the surge of *drala* in the upward draft of mania, and yet also feels the plunging down drafts of those shattering depressions that seem to choke out all life from the soul.

Learning to ride the Windhorse through the currents of manic-depressive disorder is the route to wholeness. It is my strong belief that with proper medical care and a good therapeutic relationship it is possible to find some form of wholeness even with a disease that can produce psychotic features such as hallucinations, suicide attempts, psychic inflation, and uncontrolled forms of acting out (financially, sexually, socially). While there is currently no cure for manic-depression, and while it is a progressive disease, especially if left untreated, there are many available tools for restabilizing the self and for finding deeper meanings in the mood swings that will always be prevalent even with medication.

But in saying this I do not want to romanticize an illness that still claims many lives through suicide and that takes a terrible toll on families and friends. Any serious understanding of the concept of wholeness must also understand what it costs and what it takes to find it.

It is my hope that this book, the result of a number of years of research and reflection, will be of value to fellow sufferers as well as professionals who are called upon to treat manic-depression. At the same time I also hope that scholars will find something of value in my case studies of Newton and Sri Ramakrishna.

I study these paradigmatic individuals not in order to "pathologize" them but to show how their courage and deep suffering entwined to produce epoch making works and visions. They produced what they did not *in spite* of their manic-depressive disorder, but *with* and *through* it. From my perspective there is an uncanny form of grace in this process, one that should be of as much interest to theologians as to psychologists. Again I want to stress my conviction that they would not have accomplished what they did had they been "normal."

Finally, I want to say a word directly to those of you who know the demons and angels of manic-depressive disorder in a deeply personal way. I have seen lives ruined and I have seen lives transfigured by manic-depression. With you I have experienced those blinding moments of sheer lucidity in which the world seemed to open up its deepest and most closely guarded secrets. And with you I have experienced those moments when time froze in its tracks and the world turned to gray on gray and all meaning drained away into a psychic black hole. With you I have considered suicide, and with you I have felt like a god incarnate.

    And with many of you I live in mourning for a self that has been taken away by medication, a self that still beckons to me even though I know I cannot bring it back. And, in the end, with you I have struggled to find a wholeness that will not be eroded by the winds of this disease. This book is my response to what genetic fate has handed me. I hope that you, of all my readers, will find something empowering in what follows.

ACKNOWLEDGMENTS

I owe a debt of gratitude to a number of people who have helped me with this book, either directly with the text itself, or with helping to make my life more fully livable. First, I owe an ongoing debt of gratitude to Dr. Karen Prentiss who has helped me to sharpen my understanding of Hinduism, Vedanta, and the life of Sri Ramakrishna. Secondly, Dr. Kathryn Kimball has been both a dear friend and has helped me to deepen my understanding of manic-depressive disorder, especially in the case of one of her subject-specialties, Samuel Taylor Coleridge. Thirdly, I remain in debt to my friend Dr. Carl Fulwiler whose integrated work in psychiatry and neuroscience has been an inspiration. Fourthly, I want to thank Sigridur Gudmarsdottir who helped make this book better and clearer than it would otherwise be. Fifthly, I am especially grateful for the work of Iljoon Park, translator of another of my books, for his difficult job of formatting this book. Also, I wish to thank the editors of *The American Journal of Theology and Philosophy* for granting permission for me to reprint my article "My Passage from Panentheism to Pantheism," which appeared in the May 2002 issue (Vol.23 No.2). Finally, I want to thank my wife Sara Henry-Corrington whose presence, power of mind, and compassion has been invaluable.

CHAPTER ONE: A LIFE'S JOURNEY AND ITS DREAMSCAPE

I can be walking on solid terrain and suddenly find that I am driven sideways by ferocious winds and inexplicable pulsations that seem to threaten immediate disaster. I was reminded of this when I attended a meeting of the American Academy of Religion some years ago. I was on the program where I was to read a paper on the nature of the philosophical movement known as pragmatism, which is a distinctly American contribution to world philosophy. On the opening night of the conference, I was wandering alone in the hotel looking for friends who could help me deal with the intense anxiety that comes with an academic meeting, especially one involving thousands of participants, each fiercely competitive in his or her own way. As the evening wore on I did what no manic-depressive is ever supposed to do; I started to drink alcohol to drown the anxiety of my isolation. The combination of lithium (which I was then taking) and alcohol intensifies and synergizes the effects of each, preparing a strong potion that can erupt in a variety of ways. Bumping into someone from my past, a person who always causes me immense anxiety didn't help. The next thing I remember is saying good-bye to her and going to the hotel bar where I had a wonderful conversation with some younger scholars. After they left, perhaps around midnight, everything more or less went blank. The only thing I remember is that a very strong man grabbed me and asked me to leave the bar immediately in no uncertain terms. Fortunately, I left with no argument or fuss, perhaps sensing that I had crossed some invisible line, at least, invisible to me at the time. I even remember being strangely thankful for this forceful presence, giving me a boundary when I obviously needed one.

What happened? Who knew, and, what is more, who knows now? What did I say or do? Will I encounter any of the bar patrons at a future meeting? Will anything be said? Do I even want to know? Is this amnesia that goes with manic-depressive disorder a blessing in disguise? The next morning I left for home to lick my wounds and to talk to my Jungian psychoanalyst. He was reassuring in a variety of ways, pointing out that I had not destroyed the world or my career, and like the person who falls off the horse, I must return to the hotel and read my paper. It took most of the courage I had to drive back and read my paper the next afternoon before an audience of around 50 people, a few of whom, perhaps, had seen me in my recent manic phase. Much to my relief, the paper went well and fortunately several people who have read my work came up afterward to congratulate me. So, my analyst was right, — I needed to get back into the post-manic world and find that I could still function, even on a highly professional level. Yet it all seemed to be some kind of dream, a somewhat thinner reality than normal. My paper and my manic episode blended together, each canceling the reality of the other. Was the conference a draw or did the more productive moment win out? Was there a deeper logic connecting the inner logic of the paper and the episode that remains outside of memory and its searing light? Ironically, part of my paper dealt with the connection between the philosopher Charles Sanders Peirce's (1839-1914) manic-depressive disorder and his own philosophical edifice. For a few people in the audience, or so I assumed, this connection between my paper and my episode must have been obvious.

But what of the inevitable crash that follows an inflated state, whether aided by alcohol (or some other substance) or not? For several days I was in a deeply suicidal mood. My self-image had once again been shattered. I had failed to live up to the demands of the profession, where, in my ego ideal and superego, I had to be both genius and saint at the same time. For people who are not manic-depressive, it is almost impossible to imagine the depth of shame that can envelop one after a public manic attack.

As all manic-depressives come to realize, the manic phase, however craved like a drug, is far more feared in the long run than the depressive phase. The depressive phase rarely brings public embarrassment, while the manic phase almost always will. Of course, there is rarely such a thing as a pure manic or pure depressed stage; they are usually mixed together in a kind of swirling cloud, making it difficult to separate the states in any clear and distinct way, even if one will partially dominate.

The attack brought back a larger issue for me. Should I leave the academic profession, which has seemed to become (with its political correctness) almost hyper-moral, perhaps puritanical, in terms of the life and behavior of its members? Perhaps acting and playwriting, two long-term interests of mine, could free me from the professorial super-ego.

After all, if there was ever a world tailor-made for manic-depressives it is that of the theater. Cheat on your medication, have an occasional blow out, dazzle and impress, but the world will not end. Be brilliant, charming, seductive, live on the edges of language, create grand illusions that transfix those around you, and you will be free to live on the Windhorse of your condition. Was this another grand delusion of the manic mind? Perhaps. But, again, one is never sure. If there is one principle that I have learned over the 30 some-odd years of my condition it is that manic-depressives cannot read the signs. We sometimes cannot know what signal is actually being sent to us, what message is really trying to reach through our depressive, paranoid, or manic network of signs. Is someone really in love with me, or is it only the way the light shines in her eyes at the moment? Is someone really so envious of me that they want me out of the way, or are they merely reminding me of some of the boundaries of the ego? For someone who has written nine books and fifty articles, the envy issue is not an "academic" question, it can have real bite. How does one know? Where is the stable grid of meaning that can weight the evidence for us? It seems forever out of reach, on the far horizon where we will also find our true selves, the self that lies beneath all of the fire storms of life and that shines forth in all of its wholeness.

In philosophical terms, this is the problem of hermeneutics. The term "hermeneutics" derives from Greek origins and is analogous to the Latin term "interpretation." The discipline of hermeneutics is concerned with finding the principles by which we interpret something. Historically, philosophical hermeneutics developed in the early nineteenth century as a way of aiding scholars in biblical interpretation. As the Bible came more and more to be seen as a human document with human authors and their all-too-human needs, scholars sought to regain access to this primal text in ways that would let its deeper and truer meanings emerge. How, for example, do we understand the world of Job or the world of St. Paul? A well-developed hermeneutic framework will bring the text back to us in new and compelling ways. Or so went the thinking. As hermeneutics evolved, it was used to cover all texts and all forms of human linguistic expression. In the twentieth century hermeneutics has been expanded to deal with almost anything whatsoever, from texts, to persons, to historical events, to works or art, to gardening, and to any human contrivance.

How does this philosophical study of interpretation relate to issues in manic-depression? Like any interpreter, the manic-depressive is trying to sort through false signals to get to the real. Of course, for philosophers, the term "real" is fraught with difficulties. In the current philosophical climate of postmodernism, the concept of reality, or of the real, is banished to the imperial thought of the past. Our world, so this dogma goes, is so filled with signs and symbols that it is impossible in principle to get through them to anything like a true structure or true reality.

There are strong philosophical grounds, however, for rejecting the pessimism of postmodern views on hermeneutics, and these will emerge as our story unfolds. For our purposes, it still makes sense to talk of signs and symbols as retaining validity, even though we remain caught in the dilemma of determining just which signs are valid and in which way. Peirce argued that signs are always about both other signs *and* partially hidden objects. The term "object" refers to anything whatsoever, from a solid space-time particular, to a poetic contrivance, to a possibility, to an empire, to a puff of smoke, to a gesture, or to anything that can be pointed to by human beings. What we are seeking are those dimly grasped objects that promise to show us the way toward a true understanding of the world.

That being said, how does anyone, let alone a manic-depressive, get to the real, to the domain of objects? It almost seems as if objects have their own desire to hide from view, to play a kind of ironic game with the self so that they only let part of their reality become available. In the long and painful aftermath of a manic attack, it seems as if no truth can come to light from the debris that surrounds the self. Shifting sands make walking difficult, and strong winds keep the atmosphere filled with dust storms that cloud vision and corrode morale. I am persuaded that the danger of suicide, a constant temptation for manic-depressives, is greatest during this period of hermeneutic confusion in which the signs lead everywhere and nowhere at once. The self and its world are in a deep eclipse. Like the comforters of Job, one's friends often unwittingly pour salt on the sores that seem to remain open no matter how much time has passed.

In fact, thoughts of suicide are rarely a matter of a simple exit from a painful situation. It is as if suicide can be personified as a deep voice of wisdom, telling the self with an uncanny logic that all other roads are blocked and that suicide represents a rational and, strange as it may sound, healing road toward the whole self that seems forever out of reach. In the profound self-loathing and shame that come from loosing control of the self and its signs, suicide represents a still-point of clarity and fulfillment. Does this romanticize suicide and take away its tragic reality? No. It merely acknowledges that there are inner psychological steps that lead to the brink of suicide, and that these steps, to the mind of a manic-depressive, are more logical than anything else that presents itself at the moment. Is suicide then some kind of higher logic? No. The power of suicide, as a personified voice of "reason," is a power that comes from the most drastic misreading of the signs. We have come around full cycle, thus entering what philosophers call the hermeneutic circle. Suicide represents a totalizing hermeneutic system, a model of interpretation that swallows up everything in its path. Put in stark terms, the potential suicide tragically misreads the signs and has no external signs that could provide an alternative reading to the situation. The choice seems to be death or death, only the means must be selected.

The thought always remains in the recesses of the mind: when will the inevitable earthquake return, and how might my own unconscious conspire to bring it about? There is insufficient analysis in the bi-polar medical literature concerning the intense dialectic between consciousness and the unconscious that always is part of the changes in brain and enzyme activity responsible for extreme mood swings. Perhaps this stems from the recurrent hostility between medical and psychoanalytic models of the cause of manic-depressive disorder. There are, of course, a few misguided psychoanalysts who attempt to deny chemical treatment to their patients, assuming that their difficulties can be traced to antecedent childhood and adolescent conditions. Yet it does not follow that an understanding of the unconscious is incompatible with an understanding of the chemical and genetic aspects of this disorder. In fact, many medical and psychological practitioners have become more sensitive to the reality of triggers in the current environment of the patient, triggers that have their connection with unconscious complexes of great power and scope. A significant part of living with this genetic disorder is in finding means for avoiding trigger situations, or, where this is impossible, in finding buffers (combined with possible medications) that lessen their impact, such as finding trusted traveling companions with a full knowledge of one's form of manic-depression.

What do I mean by the concept of a "trigger?" The idea is really quite simple. In my unconscious psyche I have a number of complexes that have strong centers of feeling. In fact, the Swiss psychologist C.G. Jung referred to them as "feeling-toned complexes" that are like small planets with their own gravitational field. For example, I can have a power complex that is activated whenever I confront someone with greater power than my own. Whether they actually have this power is often a vexing issue. The important thing is that in projecting my complex on to them I assume that they do. For most people, this trigger situation can be dealt with, even if it proves to be painful. But suppose I have manic-depressive disorder in which the boundaries between a projection and the reality of its object are impossible to gauge. I run the risk of being thrown into a severe depression because in my mind I am reduced to a mere nothing. Again, manic-depressives cannot read the signs. It is all or nothing, and nothing is done by halves!

Once you know your complexes, at least insofar as this is incompletely possible, you can imagine those situations in which they are most likely to be touched by outer reality. Then the task becomes one of navigation around the shoals that threaten shipwreck. It must be remembered that there is no cure for manic-depressive disorder; there are only an endless series of tactical moves around possible points of trouble. Lithium is an immense aid in this process (along with other medications like Tegretol and Depakote), although it is rarely as magical as the medical establishment often wishes us to believe.

The problem comes when our own unconscious, ever itching to activate and act out its complexes, puts us into situations that we consciously know will be trouble. We must acknowledge that the self is often divided and at war with itself. How many manic-depressives have stood with drink in hand secretly smiling at the prospects about to unfold, even while knowing full well that the pay back may be much greater than the hoped-for manic pleasures. Close to 50% of patients on lithium (or other anti-mania and anti-depression drugs) stop taking their medication. This basic fact has convinced me that proper treatment requires both medicine and intense depth work with the psyche, which ultimately helps with drug compliance. The foundational goal of psychoanalysis is to help consciousness negotiate with the cunning of the unconscious so that personal and inter-personal disasters can be avoided.

Thus, to be a manic-depressive is to constantly work to stay in remission, remembering that we are living with a disorder that is far greater than the conscious ego. In the manic state we enter into a reality that Jung calls "psychic inflation" in which we are god-like. There are no earthly boundaries that can frustrate the expanding universe of a true mania. Gravity is overcome and the heavens are as close as our fingertips. The unconscious, much of it collective and universal, pours into our conscious mind, giving it the illusion that it is the center of the universe. We dazzle ourselves, and others, insofar as they can or want to follow us, and even put God on notice, namely, that we have assumed the role of ruler of the world, and any interference will not be tolerated. Anyone who has had this experience will know exactly what I mean, while anyone who has not will be deeply puzzled by such inflated language. In one of my own manic highs I was convinced that I could cure all homeless people of their illnesses. I roamed the streets of Berkeley, California dispensing such cures until the early morning hours.

In the rest of this chapter, my own case study, I want to correlate personal history with the concepts that I have begun to develop. This entails integrating the course of my rather typical illness with some psychological and philosophical concepts that show its inner and outer meaning. We are lacking in a detailed philosophical study of the hermeneutic problems of manic-depression, and this has often meant that we have a truncated understanding of the struggles of the psyche with and against itself as it tries to find wholeness. Like Jung, whose presence will be felt in what follows, I am persuaded that in the midst of all of the minor and major disasters of this disorder there is an unquenchable hunger for wholeness that gathers in and transforms the poisoned fruits of mania and extreme depression. In the individuation process, that is, the movement toward wholeness in time, the fruits of this disorder are transfigured into healing realities that can nurture and stabilize the self. Fortunately, while some manic-depressives do commit suicide, most do not. This fact gives us some clues as to the power of individuation even against a psychosis as powerful as this one. Just as we can have a theology of hope, so too can we have a psychology of hope, a hope that withstands even the greatest storms and that outlasts the greatest personal and inter-personal suffering.

A. A LIFE'S JOURNEY

My story begins, as is so often the case, with my mother, Lois Lee. She grew up in rural South Dakota, struggling with her impoverished family circumstances. After marrying my father Murlan, they moved to Ohio where my father focused on his graduate studies in mathematical physics. She quickly showed immense talent, in acting, writing, and in developing her own radio program in Columbus. She often gave dramatic readings of various plays and envisioned a much larger career for herself on stage and in film. At the time, this range of interests seemed appropriate, and there were few hints of an impending disaster.

Circumstances brought my mother, father, and sister to New Jersey where my father had obtained work in advanced research at the RCA Corporation. He decided that an academic career was not financially viable, this at the tail end of the 1930s depression. He thought that industry held greater prospects. My mother acted in the local theater and continuing to dream of better things.[1] For anyone who has studied acting and come under its uncanny spell, this aspiration is perfectly normal.

The major alteration in the situation came when I was born in 1950. Shortly after giving birth, my mother sank into a postpartum psychosis that was unrelenting in its power. After a short period of time, she began to show irrational forms of behavior and her delusions of grandeur began to move from the exaggerated to the manic. Her manias were marked by extreme violence in which she would smash cars, furniture, and, on occasion, physically attack the people around her. As her condition worsened, she even attempted to try to kill her infant son—me—by various means. Her great delusion was that she wanted to move immediately to Hollywood to assume the mantle of the great actress.

She would sink into depressions during which she would lock the doors of the house so that my sister and I could not get in. I wandered the streets, while my sister Joann, who was thirteen years older than I was, would sit on the porch after school waiting for my father to come home from work. Sometimes my mother would manifest the other extreme of mania, perhaps being a rapid cycler, and rant and rave on the other side of the locked door. She would enact scenes from plays, totally oblivious to the fact that her two children were stranded outside in whatever weather. She never worried about feeding us, but fortunately we were able to get food from a neighbor. My sister reports that once my mother flew into a rage during which she had a violent fight with my father. Joann rushed over to my crib to rescue me but my tiny fingers dug so hard into her skin that she dropped me and fled the house. She eventually ended up in Philadelphia where she wandered the streets in a state of intense anxiety. In another incident, which I heard reported in the court hearing in which I was officially adopted by my step-mother, my mother came at me with a knife. My sister stepped in between my mother and me and took several blows from the knife. The cuts were not life threatening, but after that incident, my sister strapped a knife to her leg so that she would always have protection against our mother's unpredictable assaults.

My sister, being in her vulnerable teen-age years, was dealt a heavy blow by this family tragedy. She quickly sank into a form of schizophrenia, or more likely, schizoaffective disorder, which is both a mind and mood disorder. She spent many of her teen years on the run from the horrors of the home situation. The physical and psychological violence to which we were both exposed was far too much for any psychic system, let alone ones as genetically loaded as ours were.

My sister's subsequent years were marked by tragedy. Her psychotic illness was treated with the rather brutal drugs of the 50's and 60's, and she continued to wander the streets whenever her inner voices drove her. Delusions of an apocalypse alternated with the idea that she was a great singer. She often thought she was Judy Garland and would sing at the top of her voice under bridges where she could get the echo effect she desired. This alternated with innumerable stays in mental hospitals and jail cells, but she would always check herself out after the legal limits for enforced treatment had passed.

She also subsequently suffered from tardive dyskinesia, a condition brought on by brutally powerful tranquilizers, which manifested itself in constant circular movements of her hands and mouth. The muscular spasms in her mouth became so strong that they broke her false teeth. The astonishing thing is that she went through all of this with intelligence, humor, and an almost total absence of complaint.

It is clear that the marriage between my mother and father could not survive the open wound produced both my mother's disease and by my sister's illness. As a condition of the divorce, my mother moved to Florida where she enrolled in a college to study acting full-time. Shortly after her move she went into an extreme and violent manic episode in which she smashed everything within reach inside a campus laboratory. Two police officers arrived to subdue her, which drove her into even deeper rage. She smashed a large plate glass window and tried to kill the officers with a big shard of glass. They could only stop her by shoving her large body (she weighed over 300 pounds) against a wall with a couch.[2] She was disarmed, arrested and sent to jail where she was put in solitary confinement without any clothes. From there she went to county jail for a number of months. Subsequently she was transferred to a mental hospital. For the rest of her life she went from one hospital to another, ending up in a halfway house that provided some relief from her suffering.

The treatment for the mentally ill in the 50's was often as barbaric as the Hollywood stereotypes. Cold cells with no clothes, strong electric shock treatments, and mind-numbing tranquilizers that left permanent reminders—like tardive dyskinesia. When I think of what my mother underwent in this period, I am reminded of the 1795 engraving of the Babylonian king Nebuchadnezzar done by William Blake. The powerful king is depicted humbled and crawling on his hands and knees in a cave of ignorance. Blake's image comes from the book of Daniel 4:33 which describes how the king, ". . . was driven from men, and did eat grass as oxen . . ."

At the time, such behavior was almost always diagnosed as a form of paranoid schizophrenia. Rarely was the diagnosis of manic-depressive disorder given, even when the profile was classical, as in her case. This medical blindness has been well documented, especially in comparisons between British and American frequencies of manic-depressive diagnosis.[3] We now know that both forms of psychosis, thought and mood, can share traits such as paranoia, hallucinations, and delusions of grandeur. Tragically, even if my mother had been given the correct diagnosis, she would have had to wait twenty years before lithium became available. In a fairly obvious sense, she was doomed to a life of utter misery.

I have no doubt that I inherited manic-depressive disorder from my mother, a fairly common genetic link. One of my cousins has the disease and there is strong suspicion that my paternal grandfather was also stricken. Unfortunately, my mother's inaccurate diagnosis prevented me from getting the treatment I needed when the first signs of my illness manifested themselves. In fact, the very concept of manic-depressive disorder was one that the family had not even heard about, such being the vagaries of diagnosis. My father worked heroically with all of the forms of treatment then available but had to give up on my mother after several years of struggle.

While my mother was in jail in Florida, my father decided to move out of our house into a small apartment. He had the good fortune of having one of his brothers and his family living in the area so that he could ask them to move into the house and raise me for a year while he started to rebuild his life. I have no doubt that this year with my aunt and uncle and my two cousins had a dramatic and positive effect on my vulnerable psyche. My aunt had a very clear sense of what I had gone through and gave me my first, and still paradigmatic, experience of the positive side of the maternal. I vividly remember what it was like to get warm meals for a change, and to have the benefits of two fathers and two male "siblings."

My father starting dating a woman from his office at RCA and the moment came when I was to be introduced to her. I experienced an utter confusion of emotions as I was compelled to face the prospect of letting go of my aunt for an unknown quantity that I dimly sensed could not be trusted. When the dreaded moment came, I walked into her home with my father and for some deep unconscious reason all of my fear and anxiety focused on her Siamese cat (a kind of evil transitional object). I started to cry out in terror that the cat was dangerous and that it was going to attack me. My mother-to-be and my father did their best to comprehend my bizarre behavior, but their attitude quickly changed from one of humor to that of anger. At that moment something in my mind clicked and I knew that this whole business was going to be wrenching.

It is probably fair to say that my stepmother Isabel was simply not equipped to take on a profoundly wounded child and to raise me in the way my aunt had. She just did not have the maternal instinct, and even at the tender age of eight or nine I knew this. Our subsequent relationship was always fraught with great tension and her moralizing temperament, combined, I later found out, with alcoholism, drove me even further away from the treacherous maternal ground. When she was drunk, which was almost every night in her later years, she would savagely attack me in the vilest language imaginable, and did everything in her power to undermine any sense of my self worth. She was insanely jealous of any of my male or female friends and would move quickly to end any relationship that was a threat to her. I remember one incident in which she drove her car, probably drunk, across town at a blinding speed, coming to a screeching halt in front of a friend's house, demanding that I return home at once. Unfortunately, my father sometimes got caught up in her madness and would call the parents of a potential girl friend in an effort to break off the relationship.

I am sure that my stepmother had frustrations of her own. She had gone to college to pursue a career as a fashion designer, but economic realities, not to mention the patriarchal culture of her era, forced her to give up her plans and obtain work as a secretary. But her behavior toward me was far worse than anyone in the larger family ever realized, and it is with great anger and bitterness that I look back on this entire period. Tragically, her addiction to cigarettes cost her life when she was still in her sixties. I remember feeling little remorse at her death, other than a strong feeling of sympathy for my father. But as the events surrounding the funeral drew to a close, my father was able to reveal some of his own bitterness about the situation, and that brought us a little bit closer.

My own genetic clock started ticking in the womb. The alarm went off, heard by no one, when I was around nine or ten and was manifest by hypomanic energy, intense flirtation (which earned me the name of "lover boy"), and attention deficit disorder, which accompanies early onset manic-depression. Later in high school I started to develop extreme forms of anxiety and depression, with an occasional hypo-manic high that gave me my own delusions of grandeur. I was to become America's greatest writer, creating both poetry and novels. I sent some of my poems to the fantasy writer Ray Bradbury in hopes of getting his imprimatur. He was very kind in his reply, but this didn't provide the full evidence I craved. Sensing trouble, my father sent me to therapists, psychiatrists, general practitioners, and internists. I was given EKG, EEG, glucose tolerance, and other tests to little avail. At the conclusion of all of the tests and analyses I was put on Valium and the anti-convulsant Dilantin (my sister suffered from epilepsy so they were being extra cautious). None of the prescribed treatments seemed to help. Eventually I stopped taking any medication and learned to struggle on my own.

Along with the mood swings characteristic of this disorder are periods of irritability and anger that are disconnected from environmental realities. I sought to channel this immense negative energy in track and boxing. Unfortunately a severe shin splint injury ended my participation in track, while a partially collapsed lung made boxing impossible. I was brutally reminded of death when an inept physician in the hospital told me that my lungs could both collapse at any time in my life and that I would have no chance of survival. I was seventeen when I heard this. Fortunately, another doctor corrected this ridiculous diagnosis, and I was able to envision something like a future. However, I must admit that when I feel any pain connected with my lungs, the old terror comes back.

I early on saw death as a companion. The terrifying infanticidal rage of my mother entered into my very marrow, making it impossible for me to trust the world. Add the real or alleged physical condition to this early material and the psychic plot is ripe for an overarching sense of death on the horizon. I am persuaded that a predisposition to manic-depressive disorder can be accelerated by intense and traumatic experiences that, in turn, give the disorder a unique personal flavor. Each person has his or her unique complexes that help to trigger the general features of the disorder and are manifest in its shape.

Life in college brought with it the well-known remedy of self-medication. In my case, this meant alcohol, which I had studiously avoided until then. I did smoke some pot but experienced such intense forms of paranoia that I couldn't continue after a few months. Now I am extremely grateful that I stayed away from yet harder drugs, no small feat at the time. All the while, I knew something was wrong, but I couldn't put my finger on it. Within the family lore was the understandable fear of any form of mental illness, and I spent much of my time deathly afraid that I would end up like my mother. So I carried on and pursued my studies. One of the strange benefits of manic-depressive disorder, when it is manifest in its milder guise, is that it enhances the life of the mind. I decided to major in the most difficult of the humanities, philosophy, where the intellectual demands would tax me and test my mettle.

Fortunately, I was allowed to pursue my heart's desire, even though philosophy is not often thought of as a major leading to anything like an income. I received excellent training at Temple University in at least a few of the aspects of this vast field, and honor my teachers for their brilliance and expertise. Yet, I also went my own way. The British analytic tradition taught there held few charms for me, but I quickly discovered the Continental existentialists. Heidegger became my central figure, and I remember struggling until I had mastered his major work Being and Time. One of the things that attracted me to Being and Time was its emphasis on the centrality of being-toward-death as the basic heart beat of the human process. In recognizing that all of our projects, all of our anticipations, and all of our forms of resoluteness pointed toward the ultimate possibility of no longer being at all, Heidegger exhibited the depth logic of what it is to be human. This was something that I could instinctively understand.

Of course, this intense study did not take place in a vacuum. My depressions continued to plague me, and I would go days without shaving, or without contributing anything to class discussion. I had no idea that I was depressed in anything like a clinical sense. I simply assumed that I was probing into the shadow side of the world along with the existentialists. One of the intense dangers and delights of philosophy is that it tends to be omnivorous, speaking about whatever is in whatever way. The idea that there could be a discourse outside of, and even equal to, philosophy was something that I rejected as philistine. Consequently, any mood changes, or any sense of irritability were encompassed within a philosophical understanding—namely, as a form of my own unique being-in-the-world. In other words, there was no place in my intellectual world for a concept of the pathological.

Whenever there were setbacks in my intellectual journey, say a slightly lower grade in a course, I fell back on a manic sense of my own unique gifts, what I call my genius myth. Everyone around me who had academic talent was merely brilliant, while I belonged to a different order of creature. Needless to say, this view didn't always make me popular, especially when I did do well in course material. I read voraciously, and, when the conditions were right, could hold forth and captivate those around me. When my depressions were in force, I could barely read the simplest prose—and had to use wit to escape being found out. Yet, again, I didn't understand any of this in psychological terms. The family abjection and fear of madness still kept me from finding the right understanding of the situation.

As I look back on my early 20s, I am astonished that I negotiated the unfolding power of this disorder as well as I did. I have always been cursed with what I call my super-ego from hell that kept me working in spite of a psyche that was erupting and dissolving in innumerable ways. I was able to graduate *cum laude* in 1973 with my degree in philosophy, never suspecting that I was headed into yet deeper psychological waters. I did some graduate studies part-time but had little heart for the enterprise. I later withdrew and worked various less than glamorous jobs in order to raise money for a move to Europe. My thought at the time was that I would move to the Continent, perhaps the Netherlands, and write the great books that I knew were in me. Such being the nature of manic delusion it never occurred to me that the Dutch Government might not have any interest in giving me residency status.

     My first wife, a gifted painter, and I did move to Europe in the hopes of setting up a much richer life than we could find in America. This was in the mid-70s, and I was in an anti-American mood. I thought that Europe would recognize my genius and grant me special privileges.

     After finding a small apartment in Amsterdam, I proceeded to write the great work, or so I thought. At the same time, in the grip of my genius myth, I put posters up all over Amsterdam offering lectures in English for a small fee. I had already gone to the universities and churches offering my services to no avail. Of course, no one came to my lectures, and I was thrown into a depression. The noble experiment ended after four months and we returned to New York. Hindsight gives you that uncanny sense that all of these manic activities went on without any sense of their utter futility.

     By happy chance, we discovered a small slightly new-age center, The Center for Cultural Awareness in southern New Jersey, where we could both live and I could give lectures. Everything was hand to mouth. If I had a good crowd for a lecture, we could get a few days worth of groceries. This was an idyllic situation at first, as there were two other people living in the house who actually ran the center. We all became close friends. Yet once again the old demons started to appear. I would have intense crying episodes for no reason, which disconcerting behavior caused everyone to withdraw. I remember when all four of us went to the racetrack to bet our modest sums on the horses. I won the princely sum of around $20 and thought, in my inflated idea of self, that I had mastered the art of picking horses. There was a feeling of almost divine intuition in which I could never lose. Gambling is one of the many delightful vices so beloved by manic-depressives. For some reason, this vice has only held a minimal charm for me. Yet I vividly remember the special flavor of that manic inflation.

The four of us at the center drifted apart, and my wife and I felt the need to move on. In the back of my mind was the still unresolved issue of graduate school. I concluded that without a Ph.D. my work, such as it was at the time, would not get a hearing. A subsequent search of prospects brought me to Drew University where I could work in philosophy, psychology, and theology simultaneously. I wanted an interdisciplinary setting because, after my earlier period of philosophical exclusivity, I felt choked by being forced to live totally in one discipline. Like my mother, who transgressed social and personal boundaries in her mood swings, I felt that boundaries must be crossed, not worshiped. So at the age of twenty-seven, after bidding Europe and the cultural center adieu, I commenced the arduous task of getting a Ph.D.

My wife and I set up shop at this beautiful and intellectually thriving campus in northern New Jersey. It has a long tradition of distinguished graduate work, going back to the early part of the twentieth century, appealing to more creative and less discipline-bound graduate students. Perhaps for the first time in my life I felt at home. I was able to discuss Heidegger, Jung, Tillich, Emerson, Schleiermacher, Wittgenstein, Husserl, and issues in comparative religion with great intensity. The faculty expected excellence but gave students a free rein to design their course work and their comprehensive examinations. Everyone had to pass the French and German exams, as well as complete two years of course work. At long last I could unleash my mind and cross over any boundary that stood in my way. This cross discipline material had depth, unlike so much of the analytic philosophy of my undergraduate days, and was still unfolding. It also had relevance outside of the academy because it had implications for social change and personal growth.

As before, this initial enthusiasm soon gave way to darker rhythms in my psyche. I grew profoundly restless in my marriage, divorced, and soon remarried. I experienced the old manic attacks again, proclaiming my genius and probed into the ideas of Plato, Heidegger, and Hegel as if I were fully their equal. Sometimes, when I drank, I would get irritable at a party and come very close to a fist fight, for reasons that were probably inane, and that have long since fled from memory. Yet I did exceedingly well in course work and on my comprehensive exams, and managed to get my first degree, the MPhil, with distinction. I think that manic-depressives often do better in graduate school than in undergraduate school because of the greater degree of freedom and self-direction. This enabled me to go with the rhythms of my depressions and to match my hypo-manic states within the academic models that can so well resonate with them.

Not surprisingly, issues in hermeneutics began to fascinate me. Instinctively I knew that I was not generally a good reader of others or of my own internal states. How could I miss the mark so often? How could I get past my own fierce projections and find the philosopher's stone that would give me wholeness and some sense of the real? I suspected that hermeneutic theory could bring me closer to something I dimly sensed to be there. Consequently, I chose as my dissertation topic the hermeneutics of Josiah Royce (1855-1916), the great absolute idealist at Harvard, who had also worked with Peirce. In writing about Royce, and contrasting his position with earlier nineteenth century views, I came to understand that all genuine interpretation takes place in a community of interpreters that has as its role the filtering of signs and symbols so that some genuine meanings can emerge.

On one level, the dissertation was a scholarly project that aimed at resurrecting a little known American tradition that could become competitive with Continental thought. On another level, it seemed to be an effort to find my way past projections and complexes toward the genuine heart and face of the Other. Royce gave me some needed clues about how I might enter into the contrasts and identities that connect me with another person, or, by extension, my own unconscious. Here was the beginning of a continuing project that tied together philosophy and depth psychology around the needs and vagaries of my still unnamed manic-depressive disorder.

In 1982, with the completion of my Ph.D., the search for a job began. My five years in graduate school seasoned and enriched me. I had been able to teach at several local universities and sharpen my pedagogical skills. But the issue of academic employment loomed large. At that time the job market was at low ebb. Hundreds of people would apply for each opening, which was always filled through a national search. How on earth was one supposed to get a job in this climate?

One of the gifts of manic-depressive disorder is manifest in its hypo-manic phases in which high creativity can goad the psyche into meaningful work. I published five articles while still in graduate school, and one of them came to the attention of the well-known philosophy department of Penn State University (main campus). This, combined with the recommendation of a friend, led to my being invited to interview for a one-year position. For whatever reason, I got the job and commenced a very different kind of life. The one-year position was to be converted to a tenure-track one, thus requiring another national search. I was, of course, the inside candidate. However, this "privilege" brought few rewards. I have never, before or since, been under such intense psychological pressure. In my mind, I had to be the best at everything: teaching, writing and publishing, departmental politics, university politics, etc. It was clear that the department was unsure of the job description or about how to fill it. I felt like I was competing for a moving target.

After an initial shock, in which someone else was envisioned for the position, I received the appointment. Now the publish or perish race could begin in earnest. Would my hypo-manic states be forthcoming, or would I be held captive to depression? Of course, I did not use these names at the time, but I was caught in the grip of an immense fear that I would not produce enough to satisfy the various tenure committees. Out of the blue I received a letter from an editor who was very interested in my dissertation. Would I like to consider publishing it in a series? The series editor sent the dissertation to the publisher who rejected it flat, saying that it was obviously a dissertation and needed to be rewritten. I did not disagree with this, and the editor and I worked out a plan for a revised manuscript. After several months of intense work, the book went to the publisher and the outside reviewer strongly recommended publication. So my public career was now launched.[4]

Throughout this intense period, I continued to self-medicate, to use the euphemistic phrase. At one point I had such a bad manic attack under the influence of alcohol that I gave up all use of this drug for three years. At the time, alcohol was being widely used by students and faculty, so my behavior was within the norm, except, of course, that I was especially vulnerable to even small amounts. The dark logic of this drug for the manic-depressive is that one or two drinks can lift one out of a depression and produce a feeling of self-acceptance that can last for an hour or more. However, the disorder demands more toxin to continue its uncanny work, and the so-called "will" may not be in a position to slow down consumption. This struggle early on convinced me that the Christian doctrine of "original sin" is psychologically profound. Or, in the terminology of Tillich, that we are estranged from the ground and root of our own being, and this estrangement is not a product of human freedom. Manic-depressive disorder carries its own form of estrangement, and no approach can work that does not understand that the disease has nothing to do with human freedom and its use or misuse.

Teaching at a state university has its own challenges. One day a professor of philosophy might have a class of 190 students studying, with great resistance, Business Ethics. Wearing a microphone and entertaining a hostile audience is not the ideal dream of the young assistant professor. On another day one may have a graduate seminar with seven students. While the former challenge is to keep things moving between examinations, the latter is to deal with cutting edge ideas and the transferences and complexes that continue to enter into the material. Graduate teaching, which is my preferred and now almost exclusive mode, is laden with fascinating psychological undercurrents. At the same time it propels you to the boundaries of your disciplines so that you cannot afford to repeat earlier work. I am persuaded that the so-called conflict between teaching and research is an artificial construct. In publishing books and articles, I become a much better teacher, while in teaching I can try out nascent forms of my philosophical perspective and gauge their fruitfulness before publication.

Philosophy is somewhat unique among academic disciplines in that its primary goal is to generate and propagate perspectives that have a deeply personal stamp. As one friend once put it to me in his typical exaggeration, "There can be only one philosopher." By this he meant that a philosophical perspective attempts to be encompassing and pervasive. In its worst manifestation this means that all other perspectives must be false, or mere fragments of one's own. At its best this means that one's perspective has a richness and scope that can compel assent without drowning criticism. The purpose behind writing foundational works is thus to ignite a community and to have that community articulate and reshape that very perspective. Given this ancient model, it is no wonder that many philosophers work best with graduate teaching. Is this a kind of high-level narcissism? I think that it often is, but again, at its best, a rich philosophical framework transcends its antecedent psychological conditions.

In the mid 80's the issue of having children came up for my second wife and me. Now was the time to do so, regardless of any professional insecurity, and who, after all, is free of all job worries. However, it became evident after a while that something was wrong.

We both started that long series of humiliating tests that people in this position know so well. Working with the appropriate medical specialists, we learned that the problem was on my side. I will never forget that moment in the doctor's office when he informed me that I was infertile and that my case was so bad that little if anything could be done. We decided that I should take the drug Clomid for a six-month period, even though there was some risk of liver problems associated with the experimental use of the drug. After six months, my test results were as bad as ever. I had to face the reality of the death of my biological future.

At the time, with all of the other things going on in my life, I seemed to handle this brutal fact rather well. What I didn't realize then was that I slowly began to transfer that procreative energy onto my work. If my literal sperm was dead, perhaps my mental and spiritual sperm was not. There is in fact a strong medieval precedent for thinking this way, namely, the link between the spirit and a kind of higher sperm, i.e., the "pneumos spermatikos." I would use words to fructify the womb of the spirit. My books would be my children though this might have happened in any case.

There is another, much more complex issue involved in my infertility. At that time I had not yet studied manic-depressive disorder, and certainly never envisioned that I had the disease. I did not know that the disorder is genetically transmitted. Consequently, I did not realize that by being fertile I would run the risk of bringing another manic-depressive into the world. As our knowledge of genetic codes increases, we may be able to test for the manic-depressive gene, and thereby force the question, however horrid, of the termination of pregnancy when the gene is found. I have been on both sides of this issue many times. Some times I think that an abortion should be considered under such conditions, while at other times I think that timely information about a possible tendency to the disorder can help parents find proper treatment should their child manifest symptoms in his or her teen years. For the most part, as painful as it is, I am now thankful that I am infertile. Yet I still look at children with some longing. Mine would be around eighteen by now.

Along with my teaching, writing, paper presentations at conferences, and the usual onerous committee work, I, along with thousands of others, was becoming aware of the frightful situation in South Africa. For universities, the issue had become focused, with almost blinding intensity, on the problem of divestment. Like many other large institutions, Penn State held stock in several companies that continued doing business in South Africa. A divestment campaign began to compel the university to sell these stocks so that a strong signal could be sent to the government in Pretoria. I watched from the sidelines as student leaders began to generate support from among other students, efforts that culminated in a shantytown built in front of the administration building. Since I was without tenure, I remained cautious about entering into such a struggle, correctly sensing that the university would not give in without a fierce fight.

My life changed, in ways that I still feel, in October 1984 when I went to hear Bishop Desmond Tutu give a sermon/lecture on conditions in South Africa. This was right after the Nobel Committee announced that he was their recipient of the Peace Prize and before he was elevated to his current position as an Archbishop in the Anglican Church. The New Jersey church was filled to capacity and television cameras were everywhere. The atmosphere was one of intense expectation. What would he say, and how would we all be challenged? We were not disappointed. He gave us a moving description of the horrors of apartheid and of the role of the church in helping with its removal. He told us that if he came out for divestment he would be subject to arrest and a prison term. So he did an end run around the South African law and presented the arguments that might lead one to favor divestment.

Part way through his sermon his voice suddenly grew quiet and you could see a deep transformation working its way through his body. His arms floated upward, his eyes closed, and he entered into an altered state that can best be described as mystical, that is, one that was living directly out of the spirit. He spoke of the power of the Eucharist as a social force that could change communities. Most of us had come out of a prophetic tradition that, like Martin Luther King, Jr., stressed the Word. To hear of the Eucharist was a new and moving experience. One could almost taste the healing revolution to come.

I returned to Penn State with my mind not quite made up about divestment and social activism. But the scales had tilted. It took over a year before I was ready to take the plunge. Against the advice of my colleagues, one of whom said I had a "death wish," I entered into the divestment fray, little realizing what it would cost me. Here the issues become especially vexing. How much of my work with the divestment fight came out of a genuine concern for justice, and how much was driven by my need to enter into an intense experience and commitment as a way past my depressions? To this day I have not sorted out these dimensions, and I doubt that I ever will. Even pathologies like manic-depressive disorder can have positive fruits. Perhaps without the disorder I would not have had the courage to stand up in a very public way and become a target. And perhaps without this disorder I would still be at Penn State.

My participation started out slowly. A graduate student friend of mind, with a lot of protest and street time behind him, became my mentor. Foucault shaped his own political theory, and he had little sympathy for grand liberal or left wing dreams. My approach came from the Christian liberal and prophetic tradition so that on the surface we had little convergence in views. Yet we found much common ground in our tactical decisions and in the symbolic and public aspects of the protest.

Early in 1986, I, along with another professor, called for a general faculty fast. We were to give up all food for three days and to staff a table in front of the administration building. We handed out fact sheets, complete with the obligatory scholarly footnotes. The initial fast brought out about sixty-five professors, more than I expected in a conservative environment. The local newspapers came out and the wire services soon came on board. I became adept at the mini-interview and was quoted across the country.

I chose the tactic of fasting because of the work of Gandhi. To fast is to humble one's self first, to find, in effect, the Afrikaner within (a must for white liberals), while putting creative and non-violent pressure on the establishment. I did not realize how immediate and how strong the response would be on both sides. Fasting calls many of our connections into question, food being one of the strongest symbols we know. Yet even here some ambiguity enters. It was much later that I realized that manic-depressives often engage in strange experiments with eating patterns. A fast is not uncommon when mood changes are at work. Was my fasting a form of spiritual protest, or was it part of an unconscious manic wish? Was my colleague right after all; namely, that I had a death wish? These issues remain impossible to resolve. In such situations I rely on pragmatism, which asks: are the fruits good for the self and its communities? If so, the action is right. Unfortunately, pragmatism is less helpful discerning motives and with probing into the workings of the unconscious.

I made new faculty friends, and lost some old ones. Professors in their classrooms sometimes ridiculed my work; while at other times I became the object of positive projections, a kind of political transference. Other activities followed: teach-ins, marches, guest speakers who were victims of apartheid, candle light vigils for the deaths in Soweto, etc. In one especially symbolic act, I suggested that faculty, staff, and students surround the administration building and link arms. The idea caught on immediately. I vividly remember standing in the rain as nervous administrators peered out the windows at this highly disciplined group. We broke up without incident.

The following year brought everything to a head. Several of the leaders agreed, at my suggestion, to hold a seven day fast that would put the maximal amount of pressure on the administration. This was our go-for-broke move. And this time we were going to be prepared for come what may. The first thing needed was a vote of affirmation from the Faculty Senate. This we got. The second was to see that the news organizations would be present. This we got in abundance. Partway through the fast we heard the sound of a helicopter coming in for a landing. It was from a major NBC affiliate and was ready to do a serious piece on the whole divestment campaign at this university. Along with other faculty and student leaders, I was interviewed. Part of my class was even taped (we insisted that all fasters fulfill their contractual obligations to the university). One of the beautiful ironies of the situation was that I was filmed lecturing on reverse discrimination while fasting for South Africa! But what is a protest without some irony? The film went out across the country. I remember being awakened by a phone call at around 7 a.m. My mother-in-law shouted into the receiver that I was on national TV. What a shock this produced, exacerbated by the fact that I was in my fourth day without food.

The leaders of the fast had a wonderful meal at the conclusion of our seventh day. All we had was soup, not wishing to injure our taxed systems, but the fellowship was glorious. Had we succeeded? What had been accomplished? And were we near the end of our journey? It was obvious within a short time that the administration had been deeply wounded by the fast. For the first time, or so we thought, they were on the defensive. This second fast had around ninety participants willing to sign a petition that was published in the campus paper. Our movement was growing in strength and in moral authority.

It was in the middle of this fast that several of us met with a high official of the South African government. There is little doubt in my mind that their government closely monitored us. So-called South African "tourists" came to photograph us as our fast table, etc. The official turned red in the face and started sputtering about all of the Communists in the ANC. Our counter arguments were to no avail (even if he was technically right). For me this was an experience of worlds colliding.

After the fast, things got a little less civil. Students, frustrated with faculty efforts, decided to storm a trustees meeting, a tactic to which I was opposed, even though I lent a kind of distanced support. After all of these tactics, after all of the hundreds of surplus hours spent, after all of the sacrifices made, the irony is that divestment didn't come until a new Governor entered the state house and demanded that the university divest. He had a stick that we didn't; he could cut off state funding. Divestment came in September of 1987, with the trustees claiming credit. Thus ended the great experiment in which many lives were deeply transformed and many non-participants were left to wonder over their own lack of courage.[5]

For me, this remains the great moral experiment of my life. The issues were clear, the necessity for a decision equally clear, and the effect of the decision was one that did have a positive effect on life in South Africa. Yet I was left with a somewhat hollow feeling, sensing that there might still be a personal price to pay. In the meantime, I continued to publish and to dream of grand things on the horizon. My second book was unfolding, a kind of prolegomenon to a larger metaphysical enterprise, and there were some reasons for hope. I noticed, however, that there was a certain coldness creeping into my relations with the department. Was I being paranoid (not an academic question for a manic-depressive)? How would my tenure struggle go after all of this highly public activity, much of which surely embarrassed the higher officials in the university?

When the moment of truth came, no grounds were given for my denial of tenure. I simply received a brief form letter in my mailbox telling me that the university would no longer need my services. There is a difference between being laid off in a white-collar job and being denied tenure. People can be laid off without stigma, whereas someone denied tenure could be tainted for the rest of his or her career. In addition, given how small and homogenous an academic field is, word spreads quickly when bad news comes. Within days I received phone calls from colleagues who all expressed astonishment. People who wrote strong letters of recommendation for me were outraged, while friends couldn't believe that such a thing was even possible. Fortunately, anyone who knew the situation well understood that I had been dealt a profoundly unjust blow.

Looking back after over a decade later I am compelled to wonder what role my disorder played in the tenure decision over and above the political issues surrounding divestment. Perhaps I remain in denial of some aspects of my interaction with colleagues that were also at play in rendering the final decision about my tenure status. Honestly forces me to take my pre-diagnosis behavior into consideration even when it might be painful in retrospect to do so. For me this remains an open question.

In such cases, the person denied tenure has another year of employment while he or she looks for another position. The stigma of being denied tenure can, of course, hurt the job-seeking process. One interviewing team wanted to know what I had done wrong to be denied tenure. After all, they saw my VITA and my letters of recommendation and couldn't connect the two disparate realities. I was able to find another, somewhat tenuous job, at the College of William and Mary before my final year was over. This enabled me to leave the university a semester early, and begin to put all of this pain behind me, or so I thought. To this day I have vivid nightmares about life at Penn State, and I often wake up in a panic wondering what I did wrong. The dreams usually involve displacement, humiliation, and exile.

One of the most painful ironies of this period took place when I was driving to my new job. The car radio was on, it was in December of 1989, and I heard an announcer say that Archbishop Desmond Tutu was going to give a major address at the university that had just cast me adrift! He would not speak at Penn State in past years because it had not yet divested. Of course, the administration took full credit for his appearance.

My wife and I joined the faculty of this architecturally beautiful university in Virginia—the philosophy department, for example, was housed in a Christopher Wren building. Even though the philosophy department there could only give me an adjunct position (which meant that I took a drastic cut in pay and a loss of all benefits) I was treated with great civility and respect. Never before had I encountered colleagues who were so interested in my work, and who understood what it took to work together as a department. My time at William and Mary will always remain one of my fondest memories. On the darker side, my second marriage was in trouble, partly because of my manic-depression, and it became clear to both of us that we would not continue as a couple. Once again self-medication became part of my world as I struggled against the deepening power of my disorder. It can't be stressed enough that manic-depressive disorder is a progressive disease. When it is untreated, or treated through home remedies such as alcohol, it begins to spiral out of control. Thoughts of suicide alternated with delusions of grandeur. Yet, again, my imperial ego ideal kept me at work. I completed my second book and started on the process of finding a publisher. Because of the unusual metaphysical framework of the book, my own perspective of "ecstatic naturalism," several academic presses turned it down as not fitting in with established schools of thought. Fortunately, Fordham University Press was enthusiastic about the book and published it with only the most minor revisions, an experience that has now repeated itself with other publishers.[6]

Mid-way through the spring 1990 semester, I saw an ad in the American Academy of Religion job listings. It was for a position in philosophy and theology at my old graduate school at Drew University. Should I apply? Would they hire one of their own? Could I work in a setting that was deeply theological? And, finally, could I return to a place where so much intensity and manic living had occurred? These thoughts raced through my mind with tremendous force. In a matter of minutes I made up my mind to send my VITA and see if I was in the competitive ballpark. The position entailed graduate and seminary teaching, with no undergraduate courses. This appealed strongly to me.

I was put on the short list, which usually has three or four names, and asked to drive up for an interview. It was certainly not old homecoming week. I was put through my paces and given the most thorough and intense interview I had ever experienced. Two deans, several faculty members, and students from both the graduate and theological schools asked me a series of questions. My manuscript material was quoted and I had to defend my work. One can imagine how strange the entire process felt. I returned to Virginia with little assurance that things were "in the bag." A week or so later, the Dean of the theological school called, offering me the position. I practically shouted, "yes" into the phone. The salary was even civilized, much better than what the state university paid me, and it would be good to get benefits again.

My wife was offered a tenure-track job in the South, which meant we had to finally face the moment of decision. She took the job, which was the only sane possibility, but then we knew it was time to call it quits for other reasons. In my more humorous moments, I think that universities should provide professor-couples with jobs for each, as the prospects of two academics teaching at the same institution are near zero. But the problem is simple: no department is going to accept a spouse, as is, when they would much prefer to have their own national search for a new person. Perhaps a professor should only get married after tenure.

Returning home, especially as a real person with a salary, was an exhilarating experience. I quickly adjusted to the teaching and found myself writing at an almost fevered pitch. My third book unfolded with great assurance.[7] A fourth and fifth followed shortly after, although the fifth book, on the self, was interrupted by a series of mood swings.[8] I thrived on graduate teaching, feeling that I had at long last found my niche in the world. My depressions lifted for a while and I did not have to fight against myself to move forward. I soon found myself spending time with a woman on the faculty whose lectures I had attended ten years before when I was a graduate student. The mutual attraction quickly flowered, under the watchful eye of my colleagues, who were quietly affirming. Everything now seemed to be falling into place.

Alas, the situation once again started to shift. Even with personal and professional security and happiness, the underlying disorder insisted on getting its due. My depressions started to return and the manic highs became more and more intense. I remember one evening, following another (non-political) fast, in which everything started to unravel for what seemed like the hundredth time (there was no alcohol involved). I was watching a movie on TV when my mind started to race. Suddenly I knew that I was destined to quit my job as a "mere" professor and become the greatest playwright since Shakespeare. I was to move to England and live with the great film director Stanley Kubrick (my favorite) and we would put my plays on stage and film. I kept muttering something about being the reincarnation of Tennessee Williams, and that I would be able to write in every possible genre. I frantically went through my artifacts in the basement, bringing the symbolic ones upstairs and arranging them in a great semi-circle. Every book, object, or paper had some deep cosmic meaning pointing to my eventual triumph. This was my ultimate hermeneutic circle! God had at least revealed to me what my mission was. If only the dull and hopelessly slow world would understand. I would enter into the great circle of ecstasy and be bathed by the healing currents of the ground of being.

In this experience I had shattered all of the boundaries that I thought were holding me back from my destiny. The vision had come in one violent burst of energy. It was time to announce it to the world and to start my new life. The decompression from this vision was almost as swift as the vision itself, but it left immense psychic debris in its wake. Yet there is a curious sense in which this vision was partially valid. I have since started writing plays and have had a reading of my first play that went very well. It is also the case that I remain restless about the perceived constraints of being a professor, like many of the most creative in the profession.

My long time interest in the thought and life of C.G. Jung led me to find a Jungian psychoanalyst with whom I could work through some of these issues. I was able to find someone with a similar academic background and who would thus honor the kind of work I was doing. In the Jungian world it is important to listen to dreams and their portents before entering into an analytic relationship. My analyst and I met five times, going over my dreams of this period with great care. After the trial period was over, we both knew that the psyche wanted us to enter into the transference and to start depth work with the unconscious. Subsequently I worked for several years with another Jungian psychoanalyst, a deeply gifted and intuitive woman, to open up the contra-sexual aspects of the unconscious. The dreams that continue to emerge from this ongoing analytic vessel remain among the most important touchstones in my life. Later, I will present a few of the more important dreams as they shed light on my manic-depressive disorder and its relation to psychic growth.

In therapy I dealt with the specific issue of job and career, trying to find a meaning contour for my movement toward a more encompassing sense of self. Yet the restless nature of my sense of profession remained. There is a perennial temptation for the manic-depressive, which is to impulsively quit one job for some dreamed of possibility on the edge of the horizon. So far I have been able to resist the temptation because of a strong awareness of the scarcity of alternative academic jobs, not to mention the scarcity of grand but vaguely defined jobs that somehow fall in one's lap from a benevolent deity. Yet there remains the curious restlessness of the disorder that shines a stark light on the real or alleged inadequacies of the present situation. Add to that the kind of paranoia or persecution anxiety that often accompanies manic-depression, and it is easy to see how a present job might appear to be deeply flawed and internally and externally under siege. After all, my colleagues might be against me, secretly desiring my removal from the institution. Again, how do you read the signs? How can you tell from an inflection or subtle gesture whether or not you have been "found out?" Deep down you suspect that you are not like your colleagues, and that they are the real professionals while you are clinging to your job by your fingernails.

Each manic episode brings with it a several week period of paranoia about one's future. Only the passage of time, not any change in objective behavior, can ease the pain of feeling under examination, under the watchful eye of the malevolent super-ego. But the fear and the anxiety do lift, and the signs return to normal. The world does not strike you dead for your monumental sins, any more than it was as intensely aware of them as you were. All resumes its regular rhythm until the next episode.

It may stretch the reader's credulity if I explain that there was yet one more near disaster in the offing that accelerated the trajectory of the disorder. It had to do with the conditions under which I was hired in 1990. The stated job description was for a two-year position to replace someone on official leave. At the time of my interview it was made clear to me that this person would not return and that the job would almost certainly turn into a permanent one. This would, of course, entail a second national search because the *nature* of the job would change. Consequently, I was prepared to settle in for the long haul.

All of this potential security was shattered when one of the deans called me in to inform me that the person on leave had decided to return after all. Unfortunately, this also turned out to be a year of a serious budget crisis, with no money envisioned for what would now be an added position, known as a faculty line. People outside of the university world do not often understand how mystical the word "line" can be to an academic. Any department or school has only so many faculty lines, and any one of them can easily be lost through retirement or someone transferring to another institution. Since these lines lead to tenure, the university is committing itself to perhaps a million or more dollars if it opens up a single new line. To *add* a line is thus almost unheard of, especially in the budget-conscious 90s. To take away lines is much more the norm.

When I heard this news, I cracked open in a way that I had never experienced before. I literally felt as if my inner skeletal system had broken and that I was now changed in some dark recess of my being. I was on the floor and felt a strong sharp snap, as if my spine had split in two. My wife Sara called a clerical friend very late at night, and he drove several miles to our house to help me with this experience of utter abandonment. In later therapy I came to realize that for me the university was truly the *alma mater*, a kind of great mother who would protect me. When it turned out that she had limitations of her own, I was profoundly shaken. It seems that I had developed a transference onto the institution itself.

For several months two deans and a host of other people worked valiantly behind the scenes to cobble together enough money to keep me on the faculty. My chances of landing another job in my mid-40s were slim and I knew that this was one of those determining moments, the repercussions of which could never be fully grasped. Finally, I got the word that things would turn out all right, and that I should prepare for a formal interview for the new tenure-track position. Of course, other scholars were brought in, and I was told that a real superstar could be hired if he or she had all of the right traits deemed valuable to the institution. My paper and interview went well this second time, and I was formally offered the position. One lesson derived from this experience is that it is dangerous to put too much transference energy into any person or institution. In my case, substitute mothers are always trouble!

The crisis connected with the disorder came to a head in February of 1994. A series of imagined rejections and slights, such as the experience just described, started to build into a grand crescendo in which I became convinced that my world was destined for a total collapse. One evening, after my wife had gone to bed, I fell into an intense mixed state in which irritability combined with profound sadness about my failures in the world. This mood came at the end of another one of my long fasts, so that my body was already in a vulnerable state. I began to experience a presence that my analyst and I labeled the "death mother" who entered into my consciousness and assumed a central position. She is an incarnation of my mother, but lives on a cosmic scale. She presented me with an entirely convincing scenario that said that I had finished with my life and work in this world and that I must return home to the true world. She did not speak with a literal voice, but as a kind of knowing presence. Every argument I raised against her she refuted with a deeper logic. She wanted me home so that my aborted life could be properly terminated.

Fortunately, I called a friend in the midst of this suicidal ideation and she urged me to contact a doctor who was known to her and who had experience in dealing with these thoughts and feelings. I vividly remember going to the office of this new doctor, ego bruised beyond recognition. He asked me what seemed like an endless series of questions, some about my family, some about my behavior (drinking, sexuality, sleeping patterns, etc.), and some about my medical history. At the end of the hour he looked at me with an almost sad expression and told me that I clearly had manic-depressive disorder (a term which I had heard before). The diagnosis made sense, although I was to enter into a long period of denial, assuming that I would be unique in the *way* I was manic-depressive. I was told that the disease has no cure but that it can be put in remission if I take lithium and refrain from alcohol and any other forms of self-medication. It was also made very clear to me that I was dealing with something of immense power that had to be taken with the utmost seriousness, especially since I had gone undiagnosed for over thirty years and the disease had had time to become stronger in my system.

I have never liked to give blood. I don't mind the pain, which is minimal, or even the rather large needles and containers. My primary objection is to giving something so deeply integral with my being over to total strangers. This is surely an atavistic feeling, yet its evolutionary roots should tell us something about our sensitivity to inner and outer boundaries and forms of transgression. This first post-diagnosis draining of blood made it possible to check a variety of internal organs and systems, making sure that there were no kidney, liver, or thyroid problems. Once the blood was drawn I was instructed to go to the drug store for the first bottle of the medication that I thought would be necessary for the rest of my life, barring any major advances in treatment. What a strange feeling to hand the small blue piece of paper to the druggist, a piece of paper linking me forever to a simple salt that supposedly could bring me out of the hell of this disorder and allow me some peace. It was an even stranger sensation to realize that I would now be defined by a psychosis rather than a more exotic existential despair.

The issue of denial is a basic one with this disorder. My philosophical training was not exactly open to a concept of unconscious resistance, since, for the philosopher, everything must be "up front" and available for examination and analysis. To accept that I could actively but unconsciously undermine the evidence staring me in the face was alien to my philosophic mind. And, of course, one can assume a unique status *within* a disorder, a status that frees one from the obligation of behaving like other sufferers. Thus, while I knew that my newfound psychiatrist was right, and that I had the lucky grace of receiving a major hermeneutic key to my life, the diagnosis was something that I still fought in a variety of ways. It must be remembered that for every manic-depressive diagnosed, one or more go through this hell without being diagnosed and coming under proper care. Add to this the above-mentioned fact that among those who *are* diagnosed, around half stop taking their medication, and it is easy to see the power of denial.

This is why the disorder is so profoundly ambiguous. There is a medication (or medications) that can push it into remission, but many do not learn of it, while many more refuse to stay on it. The reason for going off medication is actually fairly simple: one misses the manic or hypo-manic states. For some reason, the depressions are forgotten. Lithium, for example, can also produce weight gain, some dizziness, sleepiness, nausea, hand tremors, skin eruptions, and an unpleasant metallic taste in the mouth. To a physician, these side effects are quite minor compared to the benefits gained. Yet to someone who goes from riding the Windhorse to feeling like an underwater creature, the change is dramatic.

In my own case, I have usually been faithful in taking my medications (with one exception to be described later) and in getting my blood tests. Yet there are moments when the thought of taking my pills (now Depakote, Seroquel, and Wellbutrin) brings me close to tears. It is like being chained to something forever, and even if one is thankful, there is also the inevitable resentment. Looking at the various bottles of pills, I see my autonomy, and sense of self, taken away from me. I have a psychosis that is working against my stability and that "wishes" to grow stronger inside of me. Occasionally, I get the irrational feeling that if I stop my medication for a while and let the genie out of the bottle, the disorder will get its due and leave me alone after a manic episode. This is magical thinking and the results would be just the opposite. It is not like letting steam out of a boiler, but more like feeding a voracious animal with raw meat.

After receiving my diagnosis, which my first analyst strongly endorsed, even though he failed to make it himself, I still struggled with self-medication. Many an evening I would have a few drinks, and in typical manic fashion, get on the phone and talk the ear off of anyone who would listen. There is a deep need to communicate when in the grip of a hypo-manic state, and the phone gives the manic-depressive an entire universe to explore. Perhaps the phone company should give a manic-depressive discount because of the increased traffic. I marvel at the indulgence of friends when I look back at that period of activity. I was still in partial denial, assuming that I was a creative genius who *also* had mood swings to enhance my rich inner life. As I began to devour the literature on this disorder, starting with Kay Redfield Jamison's wonderful and epoch-making work, I found little portraits of myself that were quite disquieting. Here I was on page so and so of this or that book, exposed to the world. I was becoming a statistic with a predictable profile.

I continued to wrestle with the suicide demon, with my death mother within who wanted to take me away from the conscious world of the sisters. The issue of the sisters, especially for a Jungian, is a vexing one. In my own life, my sister often protected me from my mother's infanticidal rages. Sadly, she died quite suddenly at the age of sixty-two from a massive heart attack that was clearly facilitated by her difficult life earlier wandering the streets of Philadelphia. The local hospital had brutally discharged her after a quick and superficial examination on that day. She had gone to them for some help because of pain in her chest. She lived outside of the world that I knew and intersected with mine only rarely in her later years. She lived in a halfway house with her mother who died a few years before she did. She was cremated and buried in Haddonfield, New Jersey where she and I grew up together for the short period before she married and left home.

The sisters, known to Jungians as manifestations of the "anima," provide protection and affirmation. To Jung, for the biological male, there is a deep feminine archetype within which shapes all dealings with biological females. With the biological female, the contra-sexual archetype is called the "animus" and is projected onto biological males. It should be mentioned that Jung's understanding of the feminine is laden with patriarchal distortions and outright stupidities that cloud the issue of gender and the internal contra-sexual component within the psyche. Yet his categories can be reconstructed in a post-patriarchal world, should we be fortunate enough to enter into one, and used to illuminate how each gender deals with its opposite within. For me, this sense of the healing other within became projected onto the sister who would keep the death mother away. Of course, this projection had its origin in a real situation and derives its continuing power for me from my literal escape from death.

My personal mythology was thus forged with great intensity during this period. There is the death mother, the saving sister, and the distanced father. Older sisters protect, mothers wish to utterly annihilate, fathers hear about these things from the police. My sister learned to sleep with a WW II German bayonet, purchased at the local Army/Navy store, under her pillow.[9]

Understandably, my closest friends are often women, precisely because of my innate need to project the power of healing onto the anima. This is not to say that my female friends are mere blank slates upon which I can cast my projections, but that there is a deep resonance between the richness of their lives and my sense of incompletion without the presence of their contra-sexual wisdom. The obvious danger is that of idealizing the projection and missing the living breathing self with whom I am in relation. But honesty helps to separate the projection from the real. The sisters provide hope, and this hope is one of the essential needs of my life. Whenever I have had to pick up the pieces from yet another humiliating manic episode, or whenever depression has prepared a place for the return of the death mother, my female friends have been a strong and caring presence. They also appear in my dreams at the right time to help me with a real world transition or dilemma.

One of my worst experiences connected with the issue of medication came after I read a paper at a conference in Canada. Because of the recent severity of my mood swings, I was then compelled to take 1800 MGs of lithium a day. I could barely read a book and had many of the side effects mentioned above. So, taking matters into my own hands, I abruptly stopped taking *any* medication whatsoever, telling no one. For about a week or so I began to feel as if a great weight had been lifted from my body and that I might be able to live without this powerful drug in my blood stream. Then there was a dramatic sea change, and I began to plummet downward into a suicidal spiral that was worse than any I had ever experienced. Fortunately, I was scheduled for my regular check-up with my psychiatrist. He very quickly got wind of the situation, and when he found out that I had stopped the lithium, he got on the phone immediately to my wife and my analyst. I had never seen him act so forcefully and swiftly. He made his position absolutely clear: either I give him a complete guarantee that at least one person would be with me twenty-four hours a day, or I was to go into the hospital within the hour. He left me with no maneuvering room. It turned out that the former possibility was an option, so we averted the hospital stay. I was now on suicide watch.

We decided to make some changes in my medication; since there was no way I would ever go back to that high dose of lithium again. Fortunately, he could recommend a new anti-depressant known as Wellbutrin, a drug that is much safer for manic-depressives than Prozac in that it was less likely to trigger a manic episode. I was given a very small prescription of this new drug (so as not to tempt a suicide attempt) to be augmented with a lowered dose of lithium. The new regimen involved 150 mgs of Wellbutrin combined with 900 mgs of lithium. This combination was far better to live with, even though there were still mood swings to ride out. In fact, the most recent research indicates that even with medication, mood swings, some of them still severe, will always be part of the prognosis of this disease.

With all of this hard won wisdom, one could assume that I would be able to control the worst effects of the disease. However, I had not yet faced the most difficult aspect of the disease, the perennial problem of self-medication. As before my diagnosis, I continued to drink alcohol, especially when I was moving upward into a mixed or hypo-manic state. I almost never craved alcohol when depressed, but instinctively reached for a beer or a glass of wine when the psychic spirits were churning. By far, the worst experience of my life came from the deadly mixture of alcohol and medication.

I had gone to a party on campus and starting drinking along with the students. Unfortunately, I was unable to stop with one or two drinks. A post-party was quickly formed where there was more drinking, in this case, straight vodka. I kept downing drink after drink and became more and more manic, conveniently ignoring the fact that I had to read a scholarly paper the next afternoon. At 4:30 AM I walked home and crashed on the bed. I managed to present my paper the next day, and even did rather well with it, but immediately slipped into a terrifying depression. I convinced myself that I was a horrible person, a person with the mark of Cain on his brow, that I must end my life by hanging, like the biblical Judas. I had a plan very carefully worked out and was ready to act.

For some reason that may always remain a mystery to me, I summoned up the courage to tell my wife what my intentions were. We immediately decided that I should go to the emergency room of the local hospital to be put under observation. After leaving phone messages with my psychiatrist and analyst, we drove to the hospital. Because of the utter seriousness of my intent, I was put into an observation room overnight. I was stripped of my clothes and had to put on a hospital gown. My wife decided to return home and come back in the morning, as there was no appropriate place for her to wait. By far the worse moment came when the door slammed shut and the key was turned locking me in. I will never forget that sound as long as I live. The observation room was little more than the size of a large closet with a glaring fluorescent light and a TV camera watching my every move. In a matter of hours I had gone from reading what I thought was a brilliant paper to being locked in a cage like a deranged animal.

In the morning a very sensitive social worker and a somewhat abrupt doctor interviewed me. The social worker remembered me from before when I was hospitalized during a dangerous depression, and he treated me with respect, while the doctor, a woman who seemed to be rather new at psychiatric interviews, wanted to get to the facts straight away. Of course I was tested for any toxic substances in order to rule out drugs. The result of the consultation was that I was to be voluntarily placed in a locked psychiatric facility for several days so that I could be observed and further tests could be taken.

I had been "upstairs" before and knew the staff and facilities. In my experience, they were both kind and competent, and would not add further pressures to those that I was already under. What I was not prepared for was the medical hypothesis that came next. A series of blood tests indicated that my liver was not functioning properly and that there might be some kind of damage. Since I generally drank about two drinks a day (an amount I later learned was far too much), I didn't suspect anything serious. An ultra-sound was ordered for my liver to see if there was permanent damage. I waited two anxious days for the result and was relieved to find that there was nothing seriously wrong, but that the effects of alcohol abuse were evident.

Finally, a substance abuse clinician sat down with me and made it clear that I had a drinking problem and that unless I faced it I would not be able to deal with my manic-depressive disorder, let alone attain a healthy liver again. She strongly recommended what is called "Intensive Out Patient Treatment" for my alcohol dependency. At first I simply assumed that she was over zealous and that this kind of advice was part of her job. Yet I agreed to meet with an expert on dual diagnosis (i.e., mood disorder *and* chemical dependency) at the clinic in another part of town. What I encountered at the clinic opened my eyes more dramatically than I would have ever imagined.

On my first day there (we had to meet three hours a night, three nights a week), I took a written examination to determine if I was an alcoholic. To my astonishment, I scored in the very high percentile for the disease. I now had an objective indicator that I was addicted to something over which I might not have any control. This was the second major blow to the imperial ego. It was not enough to be manic-depressive; it now turns out that I was an alcoholic to boot. Denial set in immediately. Whenever we had the nightly ritual of introducing ourselves I always said, "Hello, my name is Robert and I am a manic-depressive who wants to stop drinking." The counselors quietly let me continue on in this way, never forcing the issue, but perhaps waiting to see how my attitude might change.

The classes consisted of a one-hour lecture or videotape followed by group sessions. The lectures were often very painful to hear, as they kept chipping away at my denial and kept showing me how deadly the disease of alcoholism is. During the entire rehabilitation process we all had to be free from *any* mind-altering chemicals, an abstinence reinforced by regular urine tests. I had no trouble stopping the drinking; I only had trouble applying the diagnosis of alcoholic to myself. After all, I had never had a DWI (in fact I doubt that I have ever driven drunk) and I certainly never drank in the quantities I was hearing about in-group sessions. I was an amateur in the drinking game.

Gradually it became clear to me that many of the personal upheavals in my life (three marriages) and much of the wild behavior (flights to Europe on the drop of a dime) were alcohol related. Yet I still connected alcohol with the romance of the genius myth, as if I wanted to be a kind of James Joyce staggering around in Zurich or Paris while writing the great works of the century. How was I to find my way clear to a deeper understanding of alcohol and its relation to the intense suffering of my disorder?

I think the moment of truth came to me during a lecture on the medical effects of drinking. In graphic detail the various pathologies caused by alcohol were related. I had known about liver damage, but was not prepared to hear about the neurological damage, much of it permanent, caused by my drug of choice. For someone who takes great pride in his mind, this fact struck me like a hammer blow. If there was any question of continuing to drink, this had resolved the issue. But how does one remain sober? Our counselors reminded us that they had heard innumerable promises over the years from people who insisted in the strongest possible terms that they would never use again, only to find many of them back in rehab.

Parallel to these psychological and medical struggles has been a religious quest to find some meaning in a world in which the parameters are shifting and divine support seems especially remote. During the state of extreme depression one is left with the feeling of Shakespeare's *Iago* that there is an evil god, or with the sensibility of Schopenhauer who affirmed that the ultimate reality of the world was a blind chaotic will to existence that could have no place for purpose or anything like human value. At the other extreme of manic inflation, one became self-divinized so that there was no need for an absolute power over and against the self. The issue has become one of finding some sense of the sacred that could be realistically affirmed while avoiding the temptations of psychic inflation.

Like most writers, I work out my basic conceptual and emotional structures through the act of writing itself, an act that results in disclosures that bring prethematic and unconscious material into the light of consciousness. In this process I have been able to develop a philosophic and theological perspective that I have named *ecstatic naturalism* that honors the dark and taciturn structures of nature and the psyche, while also affirming the meaning-granting prospects of what I term "sacred folds." These folds can be found in the self, in nature, in important historical moments, in relationship, and in great works of human contrivance. As I will argue in the third chapter, works of creativity and genius are sacred folds that have a special relevance for the life of religion and for the life of manic-depressives, especially since, as I will also argue, most geniuses have been among the small class of manic-depressives.

Looking for a particular religious community where I could work out these issues both personally and publicly, I have been especially lucky to find the once Protestant, now post-Christian movement of Unitarian Universalism. While the original impulses for Unitarianism can be traced back to Europe in the sixteenth Century, the North American form emerged in New England at the beginning of the nineteenth Century when a number of liberal theologians at Harvard decided to break away from the more conservative Congregational Church of their Puritan forebears. The movement has since gained momentum and has become one of the fastest growing denominations in recent decades. Since it has no official creed, it houses people with diverse theological (or anti-theological) viewpoints. Its primary principle is that free selves should engage in open-ended query into fundamental questions without hindrance.

While I still affirm the genius of the grand liberal tradition of Protestant thought, running from Schleiermacher to Tillich, I find myself more and more looking toward a post-monotheistic world theology that can overcome the regnant tribalisms that are creating so much damage in our social orders. It is my growing belief that there is a deep esoteric core to be found within the mystical heart of each religion and that the task of the twenty-first century is to articulate its depth-logic.

In consort with this belief, my participation in the diverse Unitarian Universalist fellowship, both as a congregant and as a lay preacher, has given me the scope and freedom I need to probe into a sense of the sacred that goes beyond the facile and patriarchal structures of the Western monotheisms. Among the lessons I have learned from my twin struggles with manic-depressive disorder and alcoholism is that the sacred must be both demonic and holy, fragmentary and unifying, indifferent to human need yet a goad to human transformation, and finally, that the human process must participate in all of this astonishing complexity if it is to gain some understanding of the depth of the world.

At the present time, I continue with my newer medication and my analysis—which is no longer Jungian and is focused on body and energy work. Denial can cover over mountains, but the repeated hammering of the disorder is bound to get through. The second danger of identifying with the disorder is harder to deal with since this strategy plays into a kind of self-pity, but I am slowly becoming persuaded that there might even be some kind of purpose behind the destructive force of manic-depressive illness that can be understood from the standpoint of individuation (the movement toward wholeness). The best evidence for this can be found in dream material, which represents a compensation for the conscious attitude.

A number of my dreams, both before and after the diagnosis, refer to the inner logic of the disorder and provide some clues as to how it can be integrated within the psyche. I must reiterate my firm conviction that without lithium (or its equivalents) there can be no integration of this disorder. With medication the psyche has a chance to find its way toward some kind of deep balance-in-tension in which the gifts of the disorder, to be discussed in more detail in later chapters, enter into the psyche in a way that promises a much richer life. In what follows, then, I will examine several of my dreams as they illuminate both the disorder and the larger psychic structure. Through the liberating power of these dreams, and many more like them, it becomes possible for me to both have the disorder and yet to be stronger than it.

B. A DREAMSCAPE

Dreams represent uncontaminated products of the unconscious. They are not forms of wish fulfillment, nor are they random bits of semiotic noise. They are accurate maps both of the state of the unconscious itself, and of the relationship between the unconscious and consciousness.[10] Generally, they compensate for a one-sided conscious attitude, giving the ego the chance to overcome its current forms of blindness. Even where known people and events appear in dreams, they are pointing to some deeper meaning that needs to be encountered by the ego. In interpreting dreams it is always important to let images and amplifications flow out of the material before any specific interpretations are chosen. If a dream is poorly interpreted, subsequent dreams will challenge the interpretation and call forth more adequate ones. Dreams are best dealt with as part of a series. No dream can be fully understood alone, but must point backward and forward to other dreams in the series.

Freud had a radically different view of dreams than the one that will be used here. My model of dream interpretation has its basis more in the thought of his erstwhile colleague Jung. In his 1899 work *The*

Interpretation of Dreams (Die Traumdeutung), actually published in 1900, Freud gave a detailed analysis of a number of his own dreams as well as those of his children and some of his patients. He developed a method that took the dream apart into discrete pieces, each of which could be related to conscious experiences undergone in the previous days before the actual dream. In this work, later condensed and popularized in his 1901 *On Dreams*, he made his famous distinction between the latent dream thought, always tied to a wish, and the manifest content, which was a disguise of the hidden and objectionable wish. The function of psychoanalysis was to work past the resistances surrounding the manifest dream content so that the latent material could be seen. The concept of the "dream work" referred to the process by which the latent wish was translated into manifest content.

Equally famous is his conception of the censorship mechanism by which the distasteful dream-wish gets displaced onto content that the waking mind can find acceptable. His argument is precise:

> The correspondence, traceable down to the last detail, between the phenomena of censorship and dream-distortion justifies us in assuming similar preconditions for both. Accordingly we would assume two psychical forces (currents, systems) to be the originators of dream-formation in the individual; one of these forms the wish uttered by the dream, while the other imposes censorship on the dream-wish and by this distorts its expression.[11]

Freud went through a variety of hermeneutic contortions to bring diverse dream material into line with his theory that dreams represent disguised wishes. He compared his method to that of decoding, although not without some qualifications, in which each specific element in a dream is to be examined as if it contributed to a hidden code to which the analyst had access. While it is easy to caricature this model, Freud at least understood that each dreamer was unique in his or her self, a point he makes several times in the text, and that any 'fit' between dream symbol and its code had to be worked out with sensitivity and care with the patient.

The dream itself is the result of a displacement of the original wish (perhaps Oedipal), and also involves condensation and revision. Freud, as noted by Robertson, placed more emphasis on linguistic play within dreams than on the visual images themselves, a ratio that was partially reversed by Jung.[12] This emphasis adds to our sense that some of the interpretations rendered in the text are arbitrary and served as show pieces for Freud's philological skills rather than exhibiting hermeneutic openness to the data of the dreams and their symbols.

In his 1901 popularization of his dream theory, Freud further stressed the issue of repression that went along with his commitment to the ideas of condensation, distortion, displacement, and pictorial translation of latent thought (read as the dream-wish). He argues:

> We cannot help concluding, then, that there is a causal connection between the obscurity of the dream content and the state of repression (inadmissibility to consciousness) of certain of the dream thoughts, and that the dream had to be obscure so as not to betray the proscribed dream thoughts. Thus we are led to the concept of a "dream distortion," which is the product of the dream work and serves the purpose of dissimulation, that is, of disguise.[13]

Consequently, the role of the analyst is privileged because he or she is in the unique position of seeing past the "dissimulation" into the heart of the latent dream-wish itself. Needless to say, the more repression there is the more resistance there will be to the hermeneutic moves of the analyst, and this will only prolong the process of dream interpretation.

Jung argued, on the contrary, that dreams emerge fully formed in an undisguised form, and that the process of dream interpretation should involve amplification of visual and symbolic material rather than reduction of dream components into latent thoughts and wishes. Put in different terms, for Jung the unconscious wants its internal material to become available to consciousness, even if it must clothe its depth-structures in nonlinguistic forms. The translation of thoughts into images is not a process of dissimulation but one of creative enrichment so that the messages of the unconscious can be more forcefully encountered.

While Freud was among the first to apply scientific thinking to the actual mechanisms of dream formation and interpretation, his own categorial system kept him from probing into the deeper rhythms of dream life. In what follows, a more capacious hermeneutic framework will be employed, one that lets the dreams encountered speak more in their own terms rather than in terms of the myth of the repressed dream-wish. Central to the analyses will be the "teleological perspective" (future oriented rather than past oriented) that assumes that dreams are pointing toward a more encompassing perspective for consciousness as it mirrors the unconscious and struggles to compensate its darker movements.

The first dream to be discussed occurred on October 14, 1993. It was during that period, mentioned above, in which my analyst and I were in the process of deciding if an analytic contract should be forged. Hence this particular dream (the "presenting" dream) deals with the onset of therapy and gives the analyst and analysand (patient or client) a first glimpse of the psychic situation:

> I am in the cockpit of a commercial jet. The pilots are flying very low over some hills and valleys. Over their radio the control tower is yelling at them to climb to a higher altitude. The pilots claim that they are high enough. A huge hill looms ahead and they climb the plane as hard as they can, but the plane crashes on the top of the hill. Interestingly, no one seems to be hurt by the crash. The plane is intact and serves as a kind of homeless shelter for the passengers.

It is always important to start with personal associations rather than rush off to some glittering archetypes, although they too will be quite present in the dream material. The first personal association has to do with my attitude toward flying. From adolescence on I have been fascinated with flying, and enjoyed the occasional flights taken by the family. Yet during the deepening of my mood swings, especially when I was teaching at Penn State, I became terrified of getting into an airplane. I will fly to England with little trepidation, but do not like domestic flights on smaller airplanes. My guess is that flying now reminds me of the dangers of my manic episodes, and of the reality of the inevitable psychic crash. Anything flying high must come to a tragic end.

In the dream the plane is actually flying too low for the surrounding terrain. It is as if the flyers are in a depressed state, not listening to the reality principle coming from the control tower. On the level of the transference, the pilots represent the analyst, whose judgment may not be trustworthy. After all, they crash the plane when they didn't have to. Yet, and here is the central piece, the plane crashes without any negative effects. The manic and depressed flight seems to end in tragedy, but the plane actually becomes a home within which the passengers can find safety.

What else is being said? All airplane passengers know the feeling of not having control. The pilots, hidden away in the cockpit, control the lives of everyone seated behind them. They are the living head of the metallic organism. When you lose your head, or when your head won't listen to the real, you are in mortal danger. For a manic-depressive, the brain is out of control, its enzymes do not function properly. Everything is behind closed doors (the skull) and there is no way to regain control. This dream is a pre-diagnosis dream, and seems to be telling me that there is an important message waiting to get through to me. I may survive this crash, but it is far more important to learn how to avoid crashes. Dreams can be proleptic, that is, they can point to possible futures that need to be actualized. They not only describe what is, but on a much deeper level, lure the psyche toward what it needs for wholeness.

In what sense is this first dream within the therapeutic relation a prediction of what is to come? It tells us that the analyst can be trusted, even if the logic of the real seems to get violated. It tells us that there will be crashes, but that they will have a positive outcome. Finally, the dream tells us that the violent oscillations of the psyche will be smoothed over and that the various aspects of the self (passengers) will be housed. But will the manic powers be missed? A subsequent dream showed just how subtle manic-depressive disorder can be, especially in the unconscious.

This second dream, and there were many others in between, took place on November 28, 1993. It announces many themes that have continued to be central to my dream work and my struggles with mood swings:

> I am in a large hall used perhaps for dining. There is a famous film director who has asked me to do a sketch and plot outline for a scene on a small island. I do not do so and am afraid that he will fire me and send me away. Other workers in the film warn me of the danger if I don't complete my assignment. The director comes up to me and asks about it. I must tell him that the work isn't done. However, I suddenly show him my magical powers. There are two

stuffed dinosaurs next to us (about six feet in length). I wave my hands over them and they come alive. One of them runs out of the room and charges around the hallways, perhaps eating an innocent worker or bystander. I tell him that with my gifts of making real dinosaurs, he can make a much better movie than Spielberg did (*Jurassic Park*). He decides that I am a very valuable asset and brings me into his confidence and his inner circle. In another room I show my ability to levitate by hovering above everyone. My wife gently but firmly tries to bring me down to earth where everyone else is. In the dream I am very happy to have these special powers and am glad to have found a place to use them.

Dreams should also be treated as plays, where a setting is established, where the protagonists encounter conflict, where there is an exposition, a plot development, a culmination, and a solution to the action. The place in this particular dream is that of an eating hall, perhaps in a church basement, while the actors are the dream ego and the director. The plot involves the transition from failure to complete a mission, to the display of a higher mission that captures the attention of the director. The play culminates in the movement of the dinosaurs and the director's affirmation of the power of the dream ego. The solution comes when the dream ego's wife tries to deflate the manic episode and bring the dream ego back to the real.

What did the dream ego fail to do? He was asked to write a plot outline for a scene on a small island. What does this mean? The island is perhaps a symbol for the conscious ego, surrounded by the waters of the unconscious. The director, a symbol of the analyst or a symbol of the guiding Self (archetype of wholeness), wants the dream ego to confine himself to this small task, the description of the ego and its little kingdom. The dream ego can't complete the task, sensing that it is not large enough for his powers. The director is dissatisfied with the dream ego until he can bring the dead to life. The dinosaur is a symbol of cold-blooded power without consciousness or human virtue. Like the great white shark, the dinosaur is a killing machine. When the dream ego becomes a kind of magician, he frees the dinosaurs. Yet he has no control over what they do, fearing that one has devoured a human being. This, however, does not seem to matter in the face of the great power the dream ego now has.

There is a very curious message contained in this dream. It is as if the director (as symbol of the whole Self) does not mind if the dream ego unleashes powers that cannot be controlled. The mania expressed by the dinosaurs is beyond good and evil. If you can unleash the great powers, then you are of value to the guiding Self. The dream ego can even levitate over those who do not have the gift of manic power. Only the dream ego's wife seems to understand the dangers in the situation. For the anima, manic illness must be overcome by a good dose of the real.

This analysis does not have the last word however. For dreams also function as compensations, giving the much-abused ego a larger sense of its scope and power. During highly depressed states, dreams may provide a vision of the manic possibilities currently lying dormant within the psyche. In the solution to the play, the anima provides the corrective that holds the manic and depressive moments together. Yet even with this culminating structure, the role of the director remains fascinating. If the psyche is rooted in nature, and nature is beyond good and evil, is there a sense in which the guiding Self is telling the dreamer that his illness is neither good nor evil but a sheer natural force? Is manic-depressive illness good for the species, even if it is hell for its individual host (as Kay Redfield Jamison has argued)?

This issue goes back for me to the period of the divestment campaign. As noted, one colleague was convinced that I had a death wish that pushed me into the public limelight in such a way that I would be slapped down by the system. I reject this view, but want to radicalize another possibility that is rarely dealt with in the literature on manic-depression, though Jamison hints at it. My thesis goes something like this: nature does not care either way about the carrier of the manic-depression gene. There is cunning within nature, especially as manifest in the archetypes (the ancient universal forms within each human psyche), which wants some kind of expression to manifest itself. The individual is a host, carrying something analogous to a virus. The virus, in this case, the mania, must express itself and even evolve by using the host, perhaps using the host up. The mania will out, and it will carry with it both wisdom and madness. The mania moves the self beyond its current configuration so that it can engage in some work, public or private. Once the expression has occurred, the mania withdraws. Now it is important to stress that this is not a conscious or intentional process, i.e., nature does not "consciously" use human beings for predetermined ends. Rather, the defects in the psyche produced by the gene are places where larger forces can become operative.

Mythically this is the image of the wounded king who guards the Holy Grail. His wound is deep and points toward his death, yet he keeps watch over the Grail so that the redeemer figure of Parsifal may appear and fulfill the hoped-for transfiguration. This makes the Grail the central piece in world-transformation. In the present context this means that the wounded self, the self of manic-depression, must await the redeemer figure who will heal the wound and make a life of individuation possible. The redeemer figure is the guiding Self that is most often present in dream material. For reasons buried in the cunning of nature, only a wounded king can preserve the wisdom of the Grail. None of this is meant to be taken literally, but should be seen symbolically as a form of the numinous (emotionally charged and religious) transformation of the commonplace.

It does not follow that mania is somehow a benevolent force. Such a view would be an insult to all sufferers of manic-depressive disorder. What does follow is that mania is beyond good and evil and that it represents one of the ways in which nature manifests both demonic and divine powers. The connection between manic-depression and religious ecstasy is well known. In a later chapter we will discuss the debated connection between manic-depression, creativity, and genius. In the present context the connection is between the woundedness of the psyche and its openness to the numinous.

I want to ask a specific question: is there something like an archetype of justice, a universal form of equality, that is so overarching in its demands that it shatters our feeble cost benefit analyses? Does this archetype need to pull us beyond our ego configurations so that we do things that are not in our own best interests? My sense is that there is such an archetype and that it will burst into our awareness with a force that cannot be denied. Mania, or at least hypomania, may be the vessel that carries this archetype forward into the world. The death wish that we experience will not be for our own being but for our narrow persona or ego that refuses to become a locus for the archetype of justice. Nature, as concresced into the archetypes, "uses" the manic-depressive for ends that are not personal. This argument has been applied to the reality of the genius. I wish to extend it to the reality of the social and religious prophet, as well as, of course, the writer, artist, playwright, etc.

In the third dream to be examined, the issue of the danger within the psyche returns with some force. The previous dream showed the ambiguities of manic and magical power as they relate to forms of creativity, in that case film making. In this dream there is the issue of sheer survival against some of these same energies. The dream took place on December 31, 1993:

> I am running away from a large herd of dangerous and stampeding African animals. Among them are elephants, rhinos, etc. Several men and I go into a small wooden shack on the path where the animals will rampage. The setting is not Africa, but is more like a North American forest with a dirt road (perhaps a fire break). We huddle in the shack, which is right in the middle of the road the animals will charge down. I notice that I have a small 25-caliber pistol, the kind issued to James Bond (a Walther PPK). I know that it will not stop any of the animals, but I keep it ready nonetheless. The animals charge past the house (there must be hundreds of them), but the little shack is not harmed. We are able to walk out alive.

The obvious contrast in the establishing of the scene is between the small and extremely vulnerable shack and the almost infinite power of these wild animals. There are four protagonists in the scene, the dream ego and his colleagues, the pistol, and the animals. The road upon which this little hut sits may be a firebreak, a form of protection against the fires within, while the animals may represent manic energy that is unleashed against the fragile hut and its occupants.

Of special interest is the role of the pistol. It is directly connected with James Bond, and thus with the male hero myth. There is nothing on earth that can conquer James Bond, and he only needs a small pistol for protection. Yet here we have a situation in which such a small caliber weapon has no value. Its bullets could not even penetrate the tough hides of the charging animals. The dream ego represents the conscious ego standpoint, and justly fears the power of the animals that by all rights should crush the ego. They pass by without harming a hair on anyone's head. In a sense this shows the dream ego how hollow the hero myth is. No pistol can withstand the force of nature, the forces surging within the psyche. Yet those forces themselves save consciousness.

My reading of this dream, which is still a pre-diagnosis dream, is that it points to the recognition that the ego is powerless to deal with the disorder that is dimly sensed within. Pistol-packing heroes may be sufficient to deal with a neurotic compulsion or complex, but they can do nothing against a disease of this power. I am persuaded that the death of the hero myth, whether it be exclusively patriarchal or not, is essential before the self is ready to confront something like manic-depressive disorder. The wounded king who guards the Grail is already moving beyond the hero myth by exposing his wound to the world.

I want to move forward to the dream that occurred on the night of my diagnosis. Two days after this dream I started taking lithium. The scene portrayed in the dream is a powerful evocation of some of the issues connected with both the disorder and lithium. It took place on February 7, 1994:

> I am somehow standing or sitting underwater, but can survive. A few feet to my right is a naked man strapped to a simple wooden chair. He seems to be in his 20s or 30s. He is struggling to hold his breath. There is another person underwater with us on my left whom I do not see, and we seem to know that the person in the chair will die if he breathes the water. He gasps and starts to suck in the water. Small fish hover around him, waiting to devour him the second he expires. He seems to die and the fish start nibbling. I have a horrible bodily feeling as the fish rush past me for their meal. I wake up in terror.

The sensation of being under water is well known to lithium takers, at least in the early part of treatment. It is as if you are taken from the air, where manic energy lives, and pulled down to the opposite element. Living underwater makes you vulnerable in a different way. The fear is that in this diminished capacity the small creatures, just the opposite of the African plains animals, will nibble away, one small bite at a time. The man in the chair represents the shaming that comes with the disorder. It harks back to the medieval practice of establishing guilt or innocence by dunking. This is, of course, a no win situation, and death is the only possible outcome. The scene does not conclude like a normal stage play, but is abruptly cut off as the dream ego faces his own imminent death. There seems to be no protection against the onslaught of the small forces in the community, the devouring fish.

As noted above, manic-depressives fear being "found out" by the normal people of the world. One's colleagues can easily put one into the chair of shame from which there is no escape. The dream reignites this fear, while also accurately portraying the effects of lithium yet to come. For at least a month after starting lithium I did feel very much under water. It was difficult to give lectures or to conduct the normal business of being a professor. I also feared that there would be some who would misunderstand my diagnosis and dismiss both me and my work as being somehow deeply tainted. In short, I felt as if the dunking chair was being prepared for me behind the scenes.

I want to conclude with a fifth dream that shows how the psyche moves forward in spite of what might seem like overwhelming odds. It involves the power of the sisters, in this case, of the anima, and has a four-part structure. It took place on November 15, 1994:

> I am with some friends at a play. We are sitting on the right side of the stage watching some preliminary part of the play take place. Suddenly an actress appears and my male friends and I shout "the anima!" We are completely transfixed and cannot take our eyes off of her. She quickly dominates the stage. She is tall and muscular, regal in bearing, with pulled-back dark hair. She has some kind of crown.
>
> In the second scene, I am sitting next to another stage set that is filled with round tables. I start talking to one of the male actors during the scene itself. He hands me some coins (the scene is part of a dinner). I accept the money and other audience members seem envious of my intimate relation to the play.
>
> In the third scene I am walking with a male friend along a pier. Suddenly we see the anima/actress dive gracefully into the bay.
>
> In the fourth scene I am in a Chinese restaurant where we are finishing a meal. We have small plates of cashews that we pass around. A woman who describes herself as having

had many sexual experiences is also interested in eating a cashew from the plate.

About six months before this dream occurred, my mother died and was buried in a pauper's grave. The biological "death mother" was no longer part of the world of consciousness and the living. Her presence, needless to say, remains within the psyche, especially during acute and suicidal depression. The anima provides protection against the machinations of the death mother, and has a kind of semi-divine status within my psyche. My mother was a stage actress and the transformation of the mother into the stage anima in this dream is deeply significant. It is as if some of her destructive energies have now become transfigured into healing energies.

When this dream occurred, I had been on lithium for about ten months. The dream signals that the stabilization process, never fully complete, had begun, even though many storms were to follow. Consequently, my psyche was in a position to move slowly toward individuation and to find some sense of a secure horizon of meaning. The quadratic structure of the dream indicates that an almost holy atmosphere surrounded the action within the dream. Let us examine each scene of the drama to see how the anima presence became transformed.

In the first scene the dream ego is watching a play with some of his male friends. The scene is quickened when a magical being appears. She is clearly of royal lineage and has a numinous crown to prove her ancient and sacred status. The dream ego has no difficulty realizing that she is the anima, and his friends, acting like a Greek chorus, make it clear even if he should fail to see. She is the center of the small universe marked by the boundaries of the stage.

In the second scene the dream ego actually enters into the inner heart of the drama by accepting some money from the stage, thus showing that the actors are aware of him by breaking through what is called the "fourth wall" which usually separates the drama from the audience. His close relation to the drama provokes envy. Money can symbolize many things, but in this context it seems to represent part of a meal that can be expressed in the form of round coins. Are these coins a form of communion wafer? Are they a symbol showing that the dream ego and the actor are deeply joined, that there is some common currency between them? On the stage the other actors are eating a meal. This theme is picked up in the final scene of the drama.

The third scene shifts to the larger world outside of the theater. The dream ego and a friend are walking along a pier when the actress of the first scene dives into the bay. The magical anima goes from the stage, to the air outside, to the water. Perhaps her element really is the water, and she returns to it when she is not on stage. Within the fourth scene there is a shift as the dream ego and his friends enter a Chinese restaurant. A meal is consumed and a plate of cashews is passed around. This second meal links with the staged meal, and also involves a symbol of connection and wholeness. The cashews are an analogue to the coins of the stage dinner. The sexually experienced anima also wants to partake of the liturgical completion of the meal by eating a cashew. Her sexual prowess is in marked contrast to the stage anima who remains distant from the dream ego and his male friends.

What is this four-fold dream saying to the dream ego? The fact that it has four parts points to the quaternity, the figure of wholeness that brings the missing fourth element to the trinity. The anima is the missing fourth that has been denied by the death mother. It seems clear that there has been some progress from the terrifying dream of February 7, 1994, where the issue was that of coping with the psychic dunking that had just come from the psychiatrist's diagnosis. By November the psyche had made some striking moves to integrate the power of the anima with the somewhat more stable ego. The anima comes to occupy the professional place of the mother, namely, on stage for all to see. She is not yet the healing sister, but is no longer the devouring black hole of the death mother. The sexually active anima at the second meal is much closer to the saving sister, as she has tasted the fruits of the world while still desiring wholeness.

In amplifying dream material, personal associations are always important. One of the very few memories I have of my mother is of her rehearsing her part in a play. I was around five at the time. I do not remember the part or the play, if I ever knew them, but was impressed with her entrance out of the darkness onto the light of the stage. The director was correcting her interpretation and she struggled to get her part right. I was left in the darkness in the back of the theater, feeling rather alone. Whenever I go to the theater today, which is quite often, my senses and mind become electric with hypo-manic energy. For me, the theater is the most sacred place on earth, the locus for both secular and divine liturgies of the word and gesture. Whenever my budget allows, I fly alone to London to see plays at the National, the Barbican, and the West End. I know most of the theaters there by heart and treat them as old friends, especially the Haymarket and the Old Vic. When I am at a play I see the anima and not the death mother. And I remember almost all of the great actresses and actors whom I have seen.

The evolution of the five dreams discussed is fairly clear and presents a trajectory that is somewhat hopeful. From the initial fear of crashing, to the resurgence of manic energy in an artistic context, to the apparent ferocity of nature's most dangerous land animals, to the horrors of the dunking chair and the sea creatures, to the appearance of the healing anima, the psyche moved through many of the crucial aspects of manic-depressive disorder and compelled the ego to take them seriously. Denial can exist in consciousness, and even within the unconscious when the ego is not yet ready for the cold hard truth of the situation. Yet a much higher logic is also operative here, in which the unconscious will bring to consciousness what it is ready to assimilate. The importance of having another witness to this inner drama, in my case the analyst, is clear. The third person, since dreams can always be seen in personal or personified terms, helps with the hermeneutic task of bringing the "person" of the dreams together with the person of the analysand (the patient or client). Dreams can often seem to come from an alien kingdom, to have a deep otherness that renders them opaque. In having a knowing hermeneute (analyst) present when the dreams unfold, it is possible to go from a sense of otherness to one of ownership. I have no doubt that the psyche responds to such a presence and intensifies its efforts at helping the ego individuate.

For those who cannot be in an intense analytic environment, for financial or other reasons, I strongly recommend a dream group as a vessel for dealing with this precious material. Any such group should try to meet at the same time and place each week, and all presented material should remain within the group. The unconscious always seems to know the quality of the vessel within which its work is amplified. If the vessel is appropriate, the psyche will respond. A dream group composed of manic-depressives, perhaps with a knowledgeable leader, can intensify the healing process in ways that would be impossible for the isolated individual. Heretofore, my life has been one of intense extremes, from manic attacks where I tried to heal the homeless, to suicidal ideation during which I experience the death mother and her uncanny logic. Now I am ready to enter a much more integrated phase of life. I will miss the manic and hypo-manic highs, sometimes desperately, and be tempted to invoke them by means fair or foul. Yet I will also know that the death mother may finally start to withdraw and be replaced by the anima and the guiding Self. This is my hope.

In the following chapters I will present the medical aspects connected with this hope as well as probe more fully into the intimate correlations among creativity, genius and manic-depressive disorder. Like Jamison, Hershman, Lieb and others I am persuaded that there is a deep connection between extreme mood swings and creative genius and that it too represents part of the cunning of the unconscious. Finally, I will say much more about the survival strategies that we all need, whether we are on lithium or not. These strategies are themselves in the service of individuation, for we are not on this earth merely to cope, but to become whole. For those of us with this disorder the journey is more complex, but it also contains its unique riches.

CHAPTER TWO: BODY AND SOUL
— MEDICAL AND PSYCHOLOGICAL VISTAS

Humankind has long been aware of the existence of mood disorders and has struggled to define them as they relate to so-called ordinary forms of experience. Mania, more than depression, often had a religious status, as it seemed to connect its carrier with the divine powers. Even as sober a thinker as Plato, writing in the fourth century before the Common Era, found a small place in his rich philosophy for mania. In his rarely read dialogue *Ion* he augments his understanding of the route we take to the eternal forms, via reason and recollection, with an evocation of the inspiration or mania of the poet who can ascend to these eternal structures by a depth transformation of mood. The inspired and possessed poet can get to the forms more quickly than the dialectically driven philosopher who must use reason (the Logos) to get out of the cave of ignorance. In some senses, mania transcends reason's gifts. Referring specifically to the lyric poets, Plato has Socrates say:

> ... as the Corybantes are not in their senses when they dance, so the lyric poets are not in their senses when they make these lovely lyric poems. No, when once they launch into harmony and rhythm, they are seized with the Bacchic transport, and are possessed—as the bacchants, when possessed, draw milk and honey from the rivers, but not when in their senses. So the spirit of the lyric poet works, according to his or her own report. For the poets tell us, don't they, that the melodies they bring us are gathered from rills that run with honey, out of glens and gardens of the Muses, and they bring them as the bees do honey, flying like the bees? And what they say is true, for a poet is a light and winged thing, and holy, and never able to compose until he has been inspired, and is beside himself, and reason is no longer in him.[1]

We are led to conclude, in spite of the layer of Socratic irony, that the poet has access to some dimension of the world that is not available to those of more sober temperaments. Plato's student Aristotle will find himself less inclined to favor such divine transports in his depiction of the ideal Athenian life, perhaps because of that perennial fear that with the death of the gods, some sense of measure and harmony needs to be preserved. Yet for Plato, when inspiration is kept in bounds it can form an important part of the life of the community (polis).

Readers of Homer will also recognize the presence of mania in the *Iliad* where the author describes the endless battles around the besieged city of Troy. There is a connection in the archaic and classical mind between the loss of self-experienced in mania and the wisdom of the heavens as embodied in the shining ones on Mt. Olympus. If a great hero such as Hector or Achilles can experience mania, than surely they have a connection to the gods who govern the lower orders, e.g., Poseidon or Orpheus. From the beginning, humans have connected mania with religious insight, or with a momentary infusion of the god or goddess into the self.

From our contemporary perspective, deeply attuned to psychopathology, mania and depression have assumed a new cloak, one that strips them of divinity and moves them into the domain of the genetic and biochemical. Only the most misanthropic antiquarian would consider this to be a regressive move, especially when one considers the sheer damage that could come from unchecked mania, a carnage that Homer details in exceedingly gory fashion. Manic rage can transform a warrior into a slaughtering machine, but even here the mania usually ends in a tragic reversal with the so-called hero ending either in disgrace (by being dragged around the battlefield by his heels) or in personal and political ruin. Mania may have some short-term benefits to the self and community, but it must always come crashing down into its opposite. Plato, of course, was deeply disturbed by these Homeric tales and, as we have seen, only gave the most circumscribed role to mania in his perspective. After all, he wanted to banish most poets from his ideal city. He allowed only those who would sing the praises of the gods without telling stories about the licentious doings on Mt. Olympus. In the Greek world, mania was both admired and feared.

In the ancient religious order there was a tension between the followers of Apollo, who celebrated balance and reason, and the followers of Dionysus, many of them women, who celebrated the shattering of form and boundary. At the most holy religious site of Delphi a large temple served both religious communities by turns. Many, because of their practice of moving into the hills for several days of wild celebration in which live animals, as incarnations of Dionysus, were torn apart feared the followers of Dionysus. The historian of religion, Mircea Eliade, describes the psychic inflation that came with closeness to Dionysus, a god whose history straddled the archaic and classical periods:

> At the center of the Dionysiac ritual, we always find, in one form or another, an ecstatic experience of a more or less violent frenzy: *mania*. This "madness" was in a way the proof that the initiate was *entheos*, "filled with the god." The experience was certainly unforgettable, for there was a sharing in the creative spontaneity and intoxicating freedom, in the superhuman force and invulnerability of Dionysus.[2]

Here we see an example of a liturgically controlled mania that only took place under certain conditions, during a specified time of year. Self-divinization, however controlled or short-lived, is an experience central to manic-depressive disorder. The Greeks were deathly afraid of their own tendencies toward mania and struggled to confine them within the powers of religion.

The oracle at Delphi is thought to have chewed on special leaves, thus moving her into a hypo-manic state in which she could give direct, if rather cryptic, utterances from the gods. Socrates describes his real or fictitious journey to one such oracle, Diotima, as he sought the meaning of his own vocation as an Athenian citizen. She helped him to see his unique role as a midwife-philosopher who would goad others into seeing the higher truths. It is interesting that even the philosopher, perhaps the ultimate symbol of autonomy in the ancient and modern world, has to go to the manic seer who alone could speak for the gods. Even with the thick layer of irony present in his account, which Plato constructs in his dialogue the *Symposium*, it is clear that Socrates honors the powers that eclipse his own. He knew that he needed help in moving from the finite to the infinite. Ultimately he invokes the spirit of *Eros* who is neither god nor mortal to ply the path between the two worlds. One can certainly read the *Symposium* as a celebration of hypomania as a means toward love, sexuality, and wisdom.

As we will see in the next chapter, there is also an ancient connection between mania and creativity, especially as manifest in its highest form, the genius. The religious energy around this issue gets transformed, certainly by the nineteenth century, into the romantic myth of the genius who transforms our meaning horizons. The creative artist, thinker, scientist, and cultural hero, embody manic or hypo-manic energy to build their great works. There is clearly a quasi-religious mythology at work in the genius myth, even if the metaphysical underpinnings of the myth have shifted. The sea change is quite interesting. From the uncontrolled mania of the Greek and Greco-Roman world we move to the controlled and highly personal mania of the modern period. The hero myth, deeply patriarchal, moves from the warrior to the creative artist, with the connecting link being the religious or quasi-religious notion of manic possession. The warrior is the most clearly patriarchal because he attains his glory by beating other men and by utterly suppressing the maternal origin. The creative artist has partially integrated the rage of the warrior and has also moved toward some rapprochement with the maternal ground. The linking reality of religious mania points toward the warrior past and toward the aesthetic transformation of the powers in the future.

In the second half of the twentieth century our understanding of mania and depression has shifted yet again. We are more inclined to see the human toll of manic-depressive disorder or behavior and to be less inclined to romanticize this illness. However, there is the equal danger that we have gone too far and have reduced this cunning disease to something that is *only* pathological. In what follows I want to review the medical and psychological thinking about manic-depressive disorder and see if there is any way past the either/or of Greco-Roman religious awe on the one hand and sheer psychopathology on the other. In finding this possible third ground it is always necessary to face the stark reality of manic-depressive disorder, which can surely be destructive of its host, while considering the prospects for healing that come from lithium or other drug treatments. However, the ambiguities of lithium must also be dealt with. As noted in the previous chapter, lithium non-compliance is a very serious issue, with almost half of all patients electing to ride the Windhorse without benefit of this simple salt.

A. MEDICAL VISTAS

One obvious place to start in reviewing the medical thinking on manic-depression is with designating the major tool of diagnosis that enables physicians and therapists to reach an accurate picture of the illness and its course in a given case. The tool that has become normative for the entire medical and psychological community is the *Diagnostic and Statistical Manual of Mental Disorders, Fourth Edition*, usually referred to as *DSM-IV*. The publication of this 886-page manual in 1994 by the American Psychiatric Association was not without its controversy. Yet the authors worked hard to include gender and race issues, as well as cross-cultural dimensions of diagnosis. It is a highly detailed and careful study of the forms of pathology that can often be brought under some form of treatment. Reading it can be depressing, especially if one is perusing one's own category. Yet it also contains a wealth of information that is difficult to find in another single-volume source.

The authors rightly caution the reader that their classificatory scheme is not absolute, and that each person is unique in the way in which he or she will manifest symptoms. There is also an effort to remind psychiatrists that there may be underlying physical conditions that could complicate diagnosis. In the case of manic-depression, for example, one has to rule out certain thyroid, heart, neurological (e.g., multiple sclerosis, brain tumor), and metabolic conditions before prescribing medication. At the same time, care is taken to show how several interlocking conditions can be present, such as substance abuse. Manic-depression could be primary with substance abuse secondary, or vice versa. This makes diagnosis an art involving sensitivity to many variables.

The logical structure of DSM-IV is its numerical system, which gives a very precise code for each diagnosis. The system involves a three number prefix, stating the disorder, with a two-digit code that describes the status of the disorder. Your physician and or therapist will assign you a code that is in turn passed on to the insurance company. There are strong economic incentives for doctors to use DSM-IV, and this fact has distressed some critics. There are also some more neutral categories that can be used when a too-specific diagnosis would be premature or inappropriate.

Let me give an example of how the numbers work. My own assigned diagnostic code is 296.66. By going to the back of the manual I find that this translates as: Bipolar I Disorder, Most Recent Episode Mixed (the 296 part of the code), In Full Remission (the .66 part of the code). The rather optimistic suffix of .66 (In Full Remission) means that

I have not had a major episode in at least two months. The prefix 296 means that I have the more severe form of the disorder. Bipolar II is less likely to have the full-blown mania associated with Bipolar I forms of the disorder.

Needless to say, seeing such a number can have a chilling or even numbing effect on the psyche. For the philosopher this opens up the problem of class-inclusion, namely, the issue of how one determines membership in a genus or specific group. Philosophers are inclined to talk of things like "necessary and sufficient conditions for class-inclusion." With something as personal and intimate as a major disorder, the concept of class membership becomes a vexing one. In the previous chapter, I described my struggles with identification with the disorder. For a period I *became* manic-depressive disorder, and there was nothing of the self left over. In being assigned the 296.66 code, I had to confront a stark, almost naked, reality that would not let me maneuver in and out of my class designation. There are necessary conditions for membership in this class: manic episodes of such and such a type, depressive episodes of such and such duration, suicidal thoughts and acts, etc. Are there sufficient conditions (a much stronger category)? This issue is for me more complex. I am less inclined to find a list of sufficient conditions, preferring to think that there are clusters of necessary conditions that add up in a somewhat ambiguous way to the disorder itself. And these necessary conditions can shift and alter their contour over time. This makes diagnosis even more difficult.

The authors of *DSM-IV* point out that manic-depressive illness is self-cloaking. That is, the individual sufferer has a kind of amnesia concerning his or her episodes. Self-reporting can be notoriously tricky. That is why they recommend that family members and friends be consulted about specific events. Recently my wife has reminded me of an intense manic episode that I had forgotten about. It came after a one-week non-political fast, another curious form of behavior well known in manic-depressives. I know that she tells the truth, so I am forced to recognize that this illness has an uncanny ability to mask itself. This is why, I suspect, that one or two out of three manic-depressives never go to a psychiatrist or therapist for a diagnosis. After all, what is to diagnose? If I had not had a serious suicide scare, forcing me to become aware of the utter severity of my situation, I might still be struggling without medication and without a proper self-understanding.

What, then, are the necessary conditions that must be present before there is a reasonable likelihood that manic-depressive disorder is indicated? *DSM-IV* has convenient charts and tables that come at the conclusion of the description of the symptoms found in any given illness. I will abbreviate the list and description to focus on the most essential and pertinent traits. Among the criteria for a manic episode are: a prolonged expansive, elevated or irritable mood, inflated self-esteem or grandiosity, less need for sleep, increased talking, flight of ideas, distractibility, increase in goal directed activity, excessive involvement in pleasurable activity (sex, buying sprees, etc), and possible impairment of occupational functioning.[3] Whenever three or more of these traits are present (excluding the first which must be present), then it is appropriate to assert that a manic episode has taken place. Of course, there are degrees of severity, with the more intense manifestation pertinent to a Bipolar I diagnosis.

The criteria for depression form a similar list. They are: depressed mood most of the day (nearly every day), diminished interest in pleasurable activities, significant weight loss, insomnia, psychomotor agitation, fatigue, feelings of worthlessness or inappropriate guilt, indecisiveness, and recurrent thoughts of death.[4] The diagnostician seeks five or more symptoms before making the assessment that a major depressive episode has taken place. Specific triggers such as the death of a loved one must also be ruled out, along with any underlying substance abuse.

The above lists are daunting in their implications, yet they represent the necessary conditions for the existence of manic-depressive disorder, whether in its more intense form of Bipolar I or in its less intense form of Bipolar II, which can, under certain conditions, evolve into Bipolar I disorder. There is a gender-specific variable connected with the emergence or intensification of manic-depressive disorder that needs to be mentioned. In the previous chapter I pointed out how my mother quickly sank into postpartum depression, which irrupted into full-blown manic-depressive disorder. Here is the description of this situation.

> When delusions are present, they often concern the newborn infant (e.g., the newborn is possessed by the devil, has special powers, or is destined for a terrible fate). In both the psychotic and nonpsychotic presentations, there may be

suicidal ideation, obsessional thoughts regarding violence to the child, lack of concentration, and psychomotor agitation. . . Infanticide is most often associated with postpartum psychotic episodes that are characterized by command hallucinations to kill the infant or delusions that the infant is possessed, but it can also occur in severe postpartum mood episodes without such specific delusions or hallucinations.[5]

My mother experienced extreme "psychomotor agitation," that is, uncontrolled pacing and shouting, throughout her struggles with manic-depression. Sometimes she had to be restrained and on some occasions was placed in solitary confinement without any clothing. I have no knowledge of her ideational processes at the time, but as a child was deeply aware of the infanticidal rages that would erupt without warning. The sad irony of such situations is that the child may not only receive the manic-depressive gene, but may also get a heavy dose of disturbed manic "parenting" which is almost guaranteed to intensify the later appearance of the disorder in his or her late teens or early twenties — the classic "double-whammy."

While incidents of manic-depressive disorder within the general population are equally divided by gender, women have an extra burden if they are of childbearing age and wish to have children. Lithium is not recommended for pregnant women, as it may have an adverse effect on the fetus.[6] Also, manic-depressive women who give birth experience the loss of natural lithium for almost nine months. This chemical imbalance is compounded with the danger of a postpartum episode, which, if is going to happen, occurs within four weeks after giving birth. Interestingly, unipolar depression is much less democratic than bi-polar disorder, being much more common in women than in men by a ratio of almost two to one.

The disease has fairly clear onset and developmental patterns. As noted, it often appears in late adolescence with a specific manic or depressive episode. Then the individual can go into remission for years, while the disorder goes underground. However, this is a progressive disorder and grows in intensity over time. Each untreated episode seems to leave its own trace within the system, much like water wearing away at a soft rock over time. Each manic episode is paid for by an equally strong, if more enduring, depressed episode. Even a milder hypo-manic episode must be paid for, in a kind of psychic version of Newton's Third Law of Motion: for every action there is an equal and opposite reaction. Yet this law must be modified in the case of manic-depressive disorder, because the reaction is actually stronger than the original action. Psychiatrists are constantly trying to keep their patients from their beloved hypo-manic states, even when they seem harmless at the time. Unfortunately, there are no harmless hypo-manic states, and no harmless mild depressions. Each episode leaves its traces, the rock is worn away that much more, making the next episode more likely to manifest an increase in intensity.

This is one reason why early diagnosis is so crucial. While my mother was beyond help for most, if not all, of her life, I would have been dramatically helped if I had started lithium treatment when my symptoms began to emerge. Lithium finally became available for medical purposes in the United States by 1971, largely through the efforts of its early and continuing champion Dr. Ronald R. Fieve.[7] The onset of my illness was slightly before this time, but thirty years of lithium treatment would have prevented most of my manias, depressions, and suicide attempts.

While *DSM-IV* is crucial as a means of establishing whether or not one has manic-depressive disorder, it gives us little insight into the real mechanisms of the illness, any more than it gives us a hermeneutic guide to its possible meanings. Many manic-depressives have had the experience of talking to their prescribing physician about the larger issues connected with the disorder, only to find that their doctor's training and inclination does not lend itself to such ruminations. A good analyst, who may be either a medical doctor or someone having an advanced degree in a non-medical specialty, on the other hand, is deeply concerned with the existential and psychological dimensions of something that usually seems like the beast within. In my view, this is one of the reasons why it is important to separate the healing functions, with the analyst working through the transference, and the psychiatrist, who is, of course, a medical doctor, monitoring medical compliance and success. Sometimes I experience a real psychic dissonance when I talk to each healer in turn, and it is my job to reconcile both horizons. In the fourth chapter, I will deal more explicitly with this issue, which often expresses itself as the tension between a survival and tactical mode on the one side and a much deeper hunger for meaning and individuation on the other.

For the hardy soul, the most valuable work for studying many of the basic aspects of the disorder is the standard reference and textbook, *Manic-Depressive Illness*, co-authored by Frederick K. Goodwin and Kay Redfield Jamison.[8] There simply is no other text of its scope and caliber, although its original authors are currently revising it. Goodwin is connected with the National Institute of Mental Health, while Jamison is on the faculty of Johns Hopkins University. It is highly significant that Jamison is herself a manic-depressive and thus has both an insider and outsider's view of this disorder.[9] The text covers everything from diagnosis, to the history of the concept of the disorder, to substance abuse, to suicide, to personality issues, to perceptual and cognitive aspects, to genetic foundations, to treatment, to issues in creativity, to leadership issues, and to compliance problems. One can dip into it an any number of ways, and always come away enlightened. I will highlight some of the ideas and insights in the work to show just how sophisticated thinking has become on manic-depressive disorder and its relation to larger evolutionary dimensions of the social order.

One especially valuable feature of the book is that it weaves anecdotal and clinical material into the formal analyses. The authors are very concerned that the human side of the disorder comes to the fore so that the general principles are embodied in a way that compels the clinician to understand the immense sorrow and joy connected with this curious malady. Thus the book is both scholarly and deeply humane at the same time. I can only refer to a few of the riches contained here, but will focus on those that help to move us toward the eventual goal of understanding the possibilities of wholeness slumbering within the disorder.

One such key issue is that of personality transformations under the influence of manic-depression. It is one thing to describe behavioral changes; it is another to look into the psyche and to gauge what it is experiencing as its illness takes over. The first thing to note is that moods are also social, and that any severe mood change will have ripple effects within the immediate social environment of the sufferer:

> Moods are by nature compelling, contagious, and profoundly interpersonal. Mood disorders alter the perceptions and behaviors not only of those who have them but also of those who are related or closely associated. Manic-depressive illness — marked as it is by extraordinary and confusing

behavior — inevitably has powerful and often painful effects on relationships. Violence, poor judgment, and indiscreet financial and sexual behavior are almost always destructive and embarrassing to spouses, children, family members, and friends.[10]

This extreme acting-out forces the psyche into a dual mode. There is the self of manic excess, and then there is the depressed self of shame and guilt that struggles to make some sense of the just concluded manic episode. There is the real issue of damage actually done, and the internal issue of the strong super-ego that haunts and harasses the self, convincing it that its crimes are of truly monumental proportion. How does the personality sort out all of these prospects so that some sense of the world outside of the self can become stabilized?

Sexual acting-out is quite common in the manic phase. Goodwin and Jamison estimate that 57% of manic-depressives experience hyper sexuality, and up to 78% of manic-depressives in their manic phase experience an increase in the frequency of sexual intercourse.[11] The sexual issue is connected with the general heightening of perception and sensation that occurs during a manic episode. Everything and everyone take on an almost magical hue that seems to beckon the self forward. Conversations become eroticized and all the signs seem to point to the unfolding of a deep erotic drama. Each person encountered is an infinite well of fascinating and seductive power. The signs are exploding off of every object of perception, and the human signs are the richest of all. Add to this heightened perceptual and sexual tension the inner sense that one's own self is grand and omniscient, and it is easy to see a situation ripe for uncontrolled forms of acting-out, whether sexual or not. It is almost as if the universe is an undulating presence that promises an ecstatic transformation to the special devotees of this peculiar illness.

The vexing issue is that the manic state often is capable of insights that are not found in either depression or the normal and stable state.[12] There is an uncanny ability to look into the unconscious background of another self, even though these perceptions quickly become tangled with others that seem to float in from elsewhere. The vision is soon lost, and the extraneous aterial may float around for some time, while the self struggles to regain its perceptual and existential balance within the firestorm of the disorder. But some personal and cosmic door has been opened, only to slam shut as the self crashes into the depression that seems to dampen all hermeneutic horizons. The depressive sees almost nothing of the background of the world, and objects seem to recede and become dull and listless. What was once a world filled with signs is now hardly a world at all. It has been reduced to gray surfaces that hug their treasures like some miserly Scrooge.

I have been using the term "hermeneutics" whenever issues of interpretation come to the fore. In addition to this key term is a linking term that shows us where hermeneutics is operating, namely, the term "horizon." All interpretive acts take place within a total horizon of meaning that locates each act. The horizon is the full field of experience in which we live and move. For example, as a white male using the English language I have a particular horizon that cannot be directly or fully shared by non-whites, women, or persons of another language. The horizon surrounds me like an extended body and it grants me both possibilities and actualities. It also removes innumerable others. I will never experience giving birth or menstruation. Nor will I experience another language as my primary home. We all live in such horizons, but they are rarely self-conscious. In fact, it often takes a crisis to understand not only *that* one has a horizon but also that it has very specific features not shared by others.

The point of this technical terminology is to help us see more clearly what happens when we go from a manic to a depressed state. In the manic state, objects and persons have a very specific look, and in the state we assume that this is the true horizon while the others are all false, if not simply forgotten. The manic horizon described above, deeply erotic, intuitive, expansive, and boundary-less, has a profile that can be philosophically described. It is a slightly domesticated version of the horizon of Dionysus with which we opened this chapter.

By the same logic, the cold, flat, gray, and energy-less horizon of depression can be described philosophically. All meanings seem to pull back into the objects from which they came. It is as if the world becomes like a giant black hole from which no light can escape. Philosophically it is important to stress that these moods are not only about the self and its internal states, but are also about the projective fields that enter into all aspects of the world that surrounds the self. These unconscious projective fields reach out and color all aspects of external interaction but are rarely seen *as* projections.

Hence, we all know the simple truism that for a sad person the world is sad. We can take this piece of critical common sense and radicalize it to deal with manic-depressive disorder. In mania all relations and all objects explode with meaning. In fact, with the racing of thought and general distractibility that goes with this illness, the world suddenly contains far more meaning than it can sustain. It is as if the radiance of the world hurts the eyes and mind. The fervid mind spins too many webs too quickly and the meaning horizon fills up and becomes tangled beyond hope. So too with the depressive meaning horizon, signs start their uncanny journey back inside the now opaque objects and selves from which they came. Again, the problematic issue is that these extreme horizons often contain some truth. I think that a good analogy here is between manic-depressive horizons and alchemy. In each case the important thing is to transform something base and chaotic into something containing wisdom and the waters of life. It is extremely tempting, when in the throws of a recovery depression, to completely deny the insights that came out of the manic phase. This is especially the case when excessive shame and persecution anxiety color the depression. Yet even in this state it remains important to remember those insights, which can transcend the mania and redeem a situation that often seems outside of any healing powers.

Returning to specifically medical issues, we need to take a more thorough look at the course of this illness, from its onset to its various possible outcomes. And we need to look at the genetic component, and at the issues surrounding treatment. The issues involved are highly complex, with competing research results that often tilt the analysis in different directions. Goodwin and Jamison are nothing if not thorough in listing the various studies and making their painstaking way through them so that some reliable profiles emerge. Thus, in what follows, I will be distilling their distinctions on this material, looking for some generally reliable parameters within which to frame the medical and psychological issues.

The first thing the authors note is that manic-depressive illness has a much more optimistic trajectory than schizophrenia. They cite the 1921 work of one of the great pioneers of psychopathology, Emil Kraepelin:

> He observed that whereas dementia praecox (schizophrenia) tends to be chronic and follow a deteriorating course,

manic-depressive illness is episodic and ultimately exacts a less devastating toll from those affected.[13]

The authors note that any study of the progress of the disorder is complicated by the appearance of lithium and other drugs after many of the early studies were written. It is difficult to fully understand the figures and statistics surrounding manic-depression until all treatment variables are accounted for. The issue is further complicated because many studies use hospital admission as a criterion for the occurrence of an episode. Many manic-depressives, of course, "tough it out" without seeking hospitalization for their affliction. Even those in the hospital may be manifesting a variety of other underlying conditions, etc.

With these provisos in mind, some insight can indeed be gained about how this disease unfolds in time. I have already mentioned some aspects of the onset patterns. Compiling around ten such studies, the authors indicate that the highest number of patients experience their first major manic or depressive attack in their twenties. The second highest group will experience onset between the ages of ten and nineteen. The scale descends as patient's age. There is a sharp drop after age twenty-nine, with a dramatic drop by the sixth decade.[14]

The first episode is followed by a latency period that soon gives way to a pattern of mood swings that are unique for each individual. Some patients can go years without an episode, while rapid-cyclers often have four or more a year. More rapid-cyclers are female than male, and their illness is more likely to begin with a depression.[15] Unfortunately, the prognosis for rapid-cyclers is less optimistic than for those whose cycles are more spread out in time, particularly because they are less responsive to lithium. For most manic-depressives, the depressed periods are of longer duration than the manic episodes.[16] This seems unfair, especially since the manic or hypo-manic episode is so prized in retrospect. Yet there may be an evolutionary advantage to this rhythm, in that the depressed state allows us to sort through the debris and the productivity of the manic phase and to cull out the extreme material.[17] Each aspect of the disorder contributes something, almost in spite of itself, to the growth of a horizon of meaning that can shape the texture of fragmented experience.

I have also noted that the onset and unfolding of manic-depressive disorder is related to trigger situations in the environment. Many physicians tend to privilege the role of internal biochemical and genetic variables in determining how and when an episode will take place. My own tendency is to err a little on the side of psychological stressors, because they have such a clear causal trajectory in pushing the self toward the extremes. Here is how Goodwin and Jamison define this issue:

> Early precipitating events, rather than merely influencing the timing of an episode, may actually activate the preexisting vulnerability, thereby making the individual more vulnerable to the next episode. . . . Knowing that certain experiences do trigger episodes of mania or depression or that certain times of the year are associated with increased vulnerability, the clinician can help patients avoid or learn to cope better with high-risk situations.[18]

In recent years some doctors and psychologists have argued that stressors in the environment can shape the growth of the infant's brain. Prozac is held to be effective because it responds to some hard-wire changes in the brains of individuals who underwent some acute or sustained trauma in their early years.[19] The future of such arguments is, of course, uncertain, yet many of us have an educated intuition that internal states are what they are because of the still dimly understood correlation among genetic inheritance, biochemical activity within the brain, and strong environmental traumas.

Perhaps the most judicious perspective is one that accepts the notion that an intrinsic vulnerability can be exacerbated by trigger situations, combined with the idea that triggers can actually have their own causal force in precipitating an episode. The healer comes to recognize what these triggers are and keeps an eye out for them as a part of treatment. Lithium can soften the blow, but it cannot erase the psychological vulnerability that has an almost predictive force. I now know, for example, that if I participate in certain public or political events that I will have to pay for it by a depression. I am prepared to call this a causal relation, particularly since it has an almost 100% predictability. In philosophical terms we can say: if A then B, where A is the trigger event, and B is the resulting depression. There is a parallel here between the force of logical entailment and the causal sequence that results in the mood change. Goodwin and Jamison acknowledge something akin to this when they list specific and highly predictable events, such as bereavement (which is not, of course, avoidable), sleep deprivation (such as flying long-distance over several time zones), and malnutrition (perhaps caused by fasting).[20]

What is the trajectory of the illness for those who are untreated? As noted, the time between the first and second episode may vary considerably. For some, there is as much as a five-year gap between the onset of the illness and the second of what is likely to be a series of cycles. Many patients may have ten or more extreme episodes in a lifetime, with some narrowing of the timing between them likely, although not necessary.[21] The effect of manic-depressive disorder on personal life can be devastating: increased divorce rate, substance abuse that can shorten life, loss of jobs, disaffection of family and friends, and the ever-present risk of suicide which can take place during depression or mixed states.[22] Without treatment the prognosis is not good, even though mood disorders, as I have mentioned, are less severe than thought disorders like schizophrenia.

The trajectory of manic-depressive disorder has an unrelenting logic that can in no way be reduced to psychological choice. Of all of the major psychiatric disorders, manic-depression has the clearest genetic link. If one or more parent has this illness, it follows that a child will be far more likely to get it than otherwise. In his guest essay appearing in *Manic-Depressive Illness*, Elliot S. Gershon summarizes the results of various studies of genetic inheritance:

> In 300 adult offspring of one bipolar parent (other parent not ill), the risk [of inheriting manic-depressive disorder] was 29.5 percent.... When two parents had affective illness, with one of them bipolar, the risk of major affective disorder was 74 percent among our 28 offspring.[23]

So if you are a child of a parent with the disorder, you have a one in three chance of coming down with it in your teens or later. If both parents have affective disorder, one of them being manic-depressive, then your chance is three in four of inheriting the disease. Needless to say, these are striking statistics, since the occurrence of the disorder in the general population is around 0.8% (for bipolar I) and 0.5% (for bipolar II).[24] From these statistics, it does not seem that the disorder can be purely psychological in origin. Efforts continue to isolate the gene or genes responsible for manic-depression, although the practical issues remain daunting. And there is an abyss standing between any such discovery and a medical way of affecting a cure through genetic manipulation.

Even ore recent research on identical twins has lent further credence to the claim that manic-depressive disorder is a genetically transmitted disease.[25] From the moment that the embryo starts to develop, the gene(s) lies ready to manifest itself in around two decades or so. The individual is helpless against its onslaught, which reminds us once again of the urgency of early detection and treatment. Like many cancers, manic-depression clusters around certain families. It represents a kind of scarlet thread that weaves in and out of the family saga, providing a stark reminder of the ubiquity of genetics in shaping our inner and outer lives. Every family should undertake to do a mood disorder profile of present and preceding generations, thus giving the clinician a much-needed tool in diagnosis. Unfortunately, while we are often on the alert for manifestations of thought disorder, we rarely think of mood disorders in clinical or pathological terms. A moody uncle or a manic grandmother is rarely seen to have a psychosis requiring treatment. Yet their genetic material is in the current mix, perhaps waiting to strike again.

The most recent research indicates that manic-depressive illness has a complex genetic origin. Unlike single gene disorders such as Huntington's disease, the causes of manic-depression are much harder to trace. In a detailed analysis of the history of generic research leading up to current thought on manic-depression, Samuel H. Barondes concludes:

> But manic-depression illness is not a simple Mendelian disorder. Instead, like many other prevalent diseases such as diabetes, it is a complex disorder that appears only through the combined effects of alleles of susceptibility genes and environmental factors. . . . We already know that if two people have *exactly the same* combination of mood-gene alleles — as in the case with identical twins — this doesn't guarantee that if one develops manic-depression the other will as well.[26]

This means that the causes for manic-depression are polygenic on the one side, and environmental on the other. The term "allele" refers to variations within a given gene itself. When all of these variables are brought into consideration it becomes clearer why it is difficult to isolate absolute and precise variables for manic-depressive disorder. And the vexing question remains: what is the relationship between environmental stressors and the activation of susceptible alleles? Answers may indeed be forthcoming but not without elaborate conceptual and empirical models that can handle the variables involved.

We have described the symptoms connected with the illness (via *DSM-IV*), and have looked at the onset and history of manic-depression, as well as at the strong genetic foundation that pulls certain families into its uncanny circle. It is now important to look at the pharmacological aspects of treatment and their bearing on the psychological aspects of psychic growth and well being. As noted, the primary medicine given in treatment programs is lithium. In addition are the more recent anti-convulsants that have been approved for the treatment of manic-depression: e.g., valproate, and carbamazepine.[27] Other drugs continue to be developed or be approved, but for the foreseeable future, lithium seems do be the drug of choice.

Lithium is a fascinating drug for many reasons. For one thing, unlike so many of the exotic designer drugs like Prosac, lithium is a simple salt, one of the most basic elements in the universe. It has been detected in stellar material and was an early product of the Big Bang.[28] It comes from rocks that can be easily mined and crushed, thus making lithium one of the least expensive of medicines. It has a dramatic calming effect on the psyche and the body, although it does not have the kind of "druggy" effect that one would get with something like Valium or other tranquilizers. In fact, at one time, lithium was so widely used as a table salt that it had to be banned because of the kidney damage that can result from toxic doses.[29] It is even found in some mineral waters used at Spas. When one may be required to take this salt for over a lifetime, it begins to assume mythical proportions. Its very chemical simplicity stands in marked contrast to the complex swirling currents of mania and depression.

Its original medical use was discovered by accident by the Australian physician John F. Cade. In 1949 he found out that lithium had a calming effect on some of his agitated guinea pigs. From this he inferred it might have the same effect on his manic-depressive patients while they were in their manic state. The effects turned out to be the same, and he was able to publish his findings and bring the amazing cure to the world.[30] The world, of course, has its own rate of assimilation for new cures, and it took over twenty years before lithium was put into general use in the United States. It had been used in clinical trials in hospitals before that time, thus helping to prepare the way for its acceptance by the Food and Drug Administration.

However, lithium toxicity can be a real problem for manic-depressives. A large enough dose can kill the patient, but a suicide attempt with lithium can be a profoundly unpleasant experience.[31] Short of such desperate measures a toxic amount of lithium can produce a list of mild to severe debilitating symptoms: diarrhea, vomiting, fever, unsteady walking, fainting, confusion, slurred speech, rapid heart rate, or severe hand tremors.[32] In more extreme cases toxic levels can result in coma or death. I have experienced several of these toxic symptoms on occasion. For a while I had to hold on to the handrail when going up or down stairs, and diarrhea would come and go for reasons that probably have to do with fluid levels. Dizziness during those times was my constant companion, compelling me to get up very slowly from a seated position. Also, as every manic-depressive on lithium comes to know, increased frequency of urination makes it necessary to plan one's day more carefully.[33]

Lithium non-compliance is, as we have repeated, close to 50%. The side effects alone cannot explain this fact, but they are clearly a contributing factor. For those of us in academic or intellectual work, where the ability to concentrate and speak clearly is essential, and the side effects might weight more heavily. Jamison recounts how her lithium dose made it impossible for her to read a serious book from cover to cover for more than a decade.[34] The temptations to give up lithium and recover one's mind could become overwhelming in such a situation. After all, there is the well-known amnesia, especially about one's depressions, and there is always the possibility that one will stay in remission without lithium. This latter claim reminds me of the Atlantic City gambler betting everything against the house. We all know who will win that bet. But, of course, manic-depressive illness does not operate through a sober cost-benefit analysis.

But what are the predictable effects of lithium for those who choose to stay with it for the long haul? Are there statistical studies that show just how valuable this medication can be to the sufferer who is so tempted to say good-bye to this simple salt? The good news is that lithium is highly effective as a treatment and that its effects have been measured with great care for well over two decades. Goodwin and Jamison present the current accepted opinion:

> . . . research demonstrates that 80 to 90 percent of bipolar patients show some prophylactic response to lithium. . . . The most consistent finding in the literature is a decrease in intensity of subsequent episodes. This is probably the fundamental effect of lithium on the illness, and it is fair to say that most patients with typical bipolar illness experience some attenuation of episodes on lithium. . . . By lessening the intensity of episodes, lithium also decreases their frequency, since most, if not all, expressions of the cycle are brought below a threshold necessary to be considered an episode.[35]

This is why so many physicians consider lithium to be a wonder drug. In spite of its side effects it has an astonishing success rate with an illness that is so intense in its manifestations. Of course, no patient will become free of all symptoms, and our authors acknowledge that some manias and depressions can break through the lithium barrier. In such cases they recommend that the physician look for other factors, such as hypothyroidism (an occasional effect of lithium). One piece of further good news is that, ". . . the overall quality of the prophylactic response to lithium does appear to improve with time."[36]

Here we have the internal contradiction that puzzles the medical community more than it puzzles patients. We have a devastating disease that no "sane" person would want to live with, combined with a near total cure provided by an inexpensive salt with few side effects. These side effects, in fact, are dwarfed by the immensity of the disorder itself. Yet half of all patients jump ship. Jamison struggled with compliance for years before she finally accepted the necessity of her treatment program — and this behavior from someone who had spent years writing and lecturing on the subject! Philosophers and theologians have written brilliantly for centuries on the self-contradictions built into human nature, and here we see a perfect example of what they have been describing. It is as if one piece of the psyche is at war with another. From Augustine's *Confessions* to Sartre's *Being and Nothingness*, we see how the movement toward authenticity must struggle against deep antagonistic currents within the self.

For me, the issue remains a hermeneutic one, namely, how the self must piece through a swirling cloud of contradictory signs and symbols to find some stable and reliable horizon of meaning. For the manic-depressive, lithium can feel like an alien invader, reminding one of those B movies of the 1950s in which one's soul is be taken over by the pod people. The act of taking one's medicine is fraught with emotional complexities, for I must allow this primal element (or others like it) into my body and have absolutely no control over what it does or how it does it. I live on trust that the medical community knows what this alien presence will do. I also know that I am now a different person than before. Is the post-lithium person truer to my essence than the pre-lithium one? The people around me seem to think so, and I have decided to take their word for it.

In addition to an anti-mania medication such as lithium or Depakote (which I personally prefer), patients are often given an anti-depressant to shore up the "bottom" of their illness so that stability is felt at both ends of the mood swing cycle. This is a tricky process because too much of an anti-depressant can produce a hypomania. There is an even greater danger when a manic-depressive is misdiagnosed as suffering from unipolar depression and an anti-depressant alone is prescribed. This can produce a full-blown and even psychotic mania until the anti-depressant is stopped. Samuel H. Barondes describes what happened in just such a case of misdiagnosis:

> Six weeks later I received an urgent call from Marcia. She was having some trouble with Michael. She had begun to worry after Michael had taken the first few doses of the drug [Prozac], which seemed to make him unusually restless. But she didn't become really concerned until he had been taking it for about a month, when major changes became apparent. The first one she noticed was that Michael, normally a sound sleeper, was up most of the night. Then she learned that he had been having shouting arguments with several colleagues at work and that he had been liquidating his retirement fund in order to raise cash for a very speculative investment. When a neighbor mentioned that she had seen Michael having dinner at a restaurant with a young woman who lived down the street, Marcia called to ask if I might be able to help.[37]

Thus within a few weeks Michael had gone from a mild depression into a full blown mania in which he was starting to act out sexually and financially as well as exhibit the typical patterns of irritable and combative behavior. The changes in his brain chemistry caused by altering his Serotonin level had a dramatic effect. Once the Prozac was discontinued his behavior returned to normal. I can strongly relate to this experience because I was first misdiagnosed in the same way and went into wild mood gyrations under the influence of Prozac. This in itself is a good indicator of an underlying manic-depressive disorder.

Before moving on to specifically psychological issues, I want to probe more fully into the issue of suicide. In the previous chapter I gave a brief account of the internal psychological dynamics of the desire for suicide. Here I want to look into the medical and statistical dimensions of this most dreaded outcome of manic-depressive disorder. The first thing to acknowledge is that manic-depressives have a much higher rate of suicide than the general population. The statistics are still somewhat tentative, especially as we are still about a decade away from knowing about the statistical effects of lithium on the suicide rate among manic-depressives.

For many people, mood disorders are still seen as a matter of the will, and suicide is seen as a failure to stand up to internal and external pressures. However, the biological and chemical aspects of suicide, which are now being studied more thoroughly, point to a deeply disturbing fact, namely, that a tendency to suicidal thoughts and to the act itself may be genetically programmed into some individuals. Goodwin and Jamison remind us of how serious the situation is for this disorder:

> Patients with depressive and manic-depressive illnesses are far more likely to commit suicide than individuals in any other psychiatric or medical risk group. The mortality rate for untreated manic-depressive patients is higher than it is for most types of heart disease and many types of cancer. Yet this lethality often is underemphasized, a tendency that may be traceable to the erroneous but widespread belief that suicide is volitional.[38]

For the general population, the suicide rate is around 1%, while for manic-depressives it is closer to 20%. That is, if you are an untreated manic-depressive, you are twenty times more likely to commit suicide than an individual without this affective disorder. Even on lithium there may be close to a 10% possibility that you will end your own life. If you are manic-depressive and also abuse some substance, your chances of committing suicide go up yet again, to perhaps as high as 50%.

For the clinician, this high rate of suicide presents many problems. Suicides can take place even among those who regularly visit psychiatrists, thus complicating the hermeneutic picture. Potential suicides do communicate their intent before the fact, but it is usually to spouses or close friends, more rarely to their physicians or therapists. The various studies indicate that suicide is not an impulsive event of the moment, but something that has its own complex ideational patterns that need to unfold through time. Suicide attempts in the manic state seem to be extremely rare.

The most dangerous state seems to be the mixed state, rather than a depressed one. In a mixed state there is the combination of extreme melancholy, the feeling of being locked out of the normal world, and an agitation and irritation that can bring the deed to fruition. In my own suicide there was this precise correlation of the melancholic sense of utter failure and total isolation, combined with a kind of agitated rage that wanted to damage and ultimately destroy the self that was such an open wound.

What about suicide in the general population, that is, including those who were not manic-depressive? Here the statistics are even more intimidating. Jamison puts the contrast between the two sets of statistics this way:

> A recent review of thirty studies found that, on the average, one-fifth of manic-depressive patients die by suicide. From a slightly different perspective, at least two-thirds of those people who commit suicide have been found to suffer from depressive or manic-depressive illness.[39]

I doubt that you will find a more sobering statistic in this book. Jamison brings home the point that suicide will continue to harvest from among those with affective disorder, and that this harvest is related to underlying biological and genetic conditions.[40] Perhaps the most deadly combination is that of manic-depressive disorder and alcohol. Studies have revealed that alcoholics have different levels of one of the chief Serotonin metabolites, and that these different lower levels are also found in patients who make more violent suicide attempts.[41]

As there are complex genetic variables at play in manic-depressive order itself, so too there are some subtle changes in brain anatomy (and its genetic antecedents) in those with a tendency toward suicide. In her most recent book, Kay Redfield Jamison talks about Serotonin levels in the brain:

> The association between Serotonin and suicide is further supported by postmortem studies of the brains of individuals who have killed themselves. The evidence is strong that there are Serotonin abnormalities in the prefrontal cortex of the brain, an area strongly implicated in the inhibition of behavior. Reduced serotonergic functioning in this part of the brain may cause disinhibition, which may in turn result in acting precipitously on suicidal thoughts and feelings.[42]

She further argues that there is some evidence, still a bit inconclusive, that these abnormalities may have genetic origins. In studies of other primates, Serotonin levels are clearly related to levels of aggression and high-risk behavior. For those primate individuals in a group with low levels, there is an increased risk of a shortened life span due to conflicts with other members of the group, as well as the risks that come from failure to take the normal precautions in such activities as in the case of chimpanzees swinging from branches high above the ground. The corollary to human behavior might be the conscious decision not to fasten a seat belt or in severely reduced Serotonin levels, risky maneuvers in high speed vehicles.

Further, there are apparently other brain differences between those humans who are at higher risk for suicide than for those who are at normal risk. As discussed above, the correlation between (poly) genetic factors and environmental triggers or stressors is a complex one, but the result of this correlation can be more accurately measured on the brain than before. Again Jamison tells the tale of what happens to the human brain for those in the high-risk category for suicide:

> Scientists have repeatedly found significant brain pathology when conducting imaging studies (pictures taken of the brain such as positron-emission tomography, or PET, scans) of the anatomy and functioning of the brains of patients with depression, schizophrenia, or manic-depression

— showing, for example, in bipolar patients that there is an enlargement of the amygdales, which is involved in generating emotions and regulating mood; an increase in white-matter lesions, known as hyperintensities, which are associated with the water content of brain tissue; and severe depletions in the number of glial cells, which are involved in the development of the brain and also provide growth factors and nutrients to the nerve cells — and it is possible that repeated psychosis or depression may exacerbate the already fragile chemistry of the vulnerable brain.[43]

Given the number of cells involved and the gross and subtle anatomical changes in the brain, it is small wonder that there are deep physical and chemical determinants in making some persons more vulnerable to impulsive suicidal acts. If a disinhibiting chemical like alcohol is added to this already "fragile chemistry," then the odds of a suicidal act taking place climb dramatically.

I cannot resist one final quote from Jamison's masterful study of suicide because it perfectly describes the intense self-reinforcing feed back loop among the various known determinants leading to suicidal ideation or behavior:

A man who is born with a genetic predisposition to manic-depressive illness, has impaired serotonergic functioning, and comes from a family with a history of suicide is at high risk to kill himself. But his risk may increase even further if he drinks when he is depressed or manic, because this will increase the likelihood that he will have problems with his relationships and his work. It will also make it more likely that his illness will get worse, that his treatment will be less effective, and that his Serotonin functioning will be compromised even further.[44]

Consequently, it is imperative that we continue to learn as much as possible about the role of neurotransmitters (such as Serotonin, norepinephrine, dopamine, and dozens of others) and their relation to both alcohol and anti-depressants. We have an infinitely complex stew in which brain anatomy and chemistry is blended with external medications and drugs, genetic heritage, environmental triggers, and current social and professional variables. Any serious treatment plan for manic-depressive disorder must function on all levels simultaneously so that there is some hope of balancing these deeply embedded structures.

For the relative or friend of a manic-depressive, there is one very important clue that the possibility of a suicide attempt is in the offing. Manic-depressives, and I can attest to this, often have disturbed sleep patterns. We fall asleep slowly, and sleep more lightly than many people. When insomnia becomes more acute, with constant waking and agitation, then a manic episode may be around forty-eight hours away.[45] The manic episode can give way to a mixed state in which suicidal ideation resurfaces. I well remember being asked about my sleep patterns on the day I was finally diagnosed, wondering what on earth they had to do with my recent suicide. Sleep deprivation obviously produces a physiological vulnerability that the disease can exploit, especially when the disorder caused the sleeplessness in the first place.

We have all heard *ad nauseam* that people who talk about suicide are really contemplating it. This truism is itself fascinating because it is almost as if the potential suicide is working through a kind of dress rehearsal to test his or her lines and character before opening night. I think that this analogy with acting makes strong sense. When you are assigned a part in a scene you must not only learn the lines, but also usually work closely with a partner who will be feeding you the framing lines. In acting this process is known as the "pinch and ouch" technique, a term from the brilliant teacher Sanford Meisner. Your partner will pinch you with a line and your response will be the ouch, or vice versa. The responses to each other must be natural, intimate, and deeply connected. Learning from this process is far more important than simply memorizing the lines, as your lines will emerge from the pinch rather than from the script. You learn to read your partner's face and gestures as if they were inside of your own head. Everything becomes electric with the almost erotic dance of reading off of each other. As my acting teacher used to say, "Your partner is your life-line on stage."

I think that this translates into suicide rehearsals in a direct way. Usually you are very selective as to whom you will reveal your suicidal ideation. You pick a partner who will hear you as you frame lines that have an objective. For any actor, discovering the objective of his or her character is crucial. For example, my character may want to seduce his partner on stage, and everything must lead up to this moment. One also needs the so-called "preparation" in which you rekindle a strong emotion from your own life, or an imagined one where necessary, that can enter into your characterization. So, for example, if you have to play someone who is deeply wounded (e.g., Willy Loman in Death of a Salesman), you resurrect your most humiliating experience and allow it to course through you as you prepare for that scene. This fulfills your preparation, which is a form of self-stimulation, and ties it to the objective. Meisner has defined acting as "living truthfully under imaginary circumstances."[46]

Now, my claim is that my suicide rehearsal has the objective of informing my partner of the utter urgency of my situation. At the same time it has its own preparation in that it brings with it intense earlier or current psychic material that surrounds the imagined character like a leaden horizon. It can also be put this way: when I am caught in a mixed state in which suicidal ideation is almost inevitable, I imagine a future self (character) that has fulfilled his or her objective (death). Yet there is also a buried sign that this death is a kind of resurrection. Suicide is deeply ambiguous because it involves what religious consciousness would call "eschatology," that is, a drama about a fulfilled ending to a personal history. I know from my own experience that when the death mother has called me toward my death, I go through an elaborate ideational process that is really an extended stage play. There is the opening, the development, the reversal, and the final curtain (solution). In talking to my partner I really am entering into a heightened form of the "pinch and ouch" process. He or she is asked to appear on my stage and to feel my pinch in an almost violent way. The response, given that I have chosen the right partner, will be an equally strong ouch. This gives me permission to move forward with the next line, to live truthfully under imaginary circumstances.

It is extremely interesting to me that when I was actually in rehearsal I had absolutely no sense of the death mother or of suicide. I experienced life in its fullness, and found a way to outsmart the suicidal ideation that puts on a rather inferior drama to the one I am currently working on. Many have said, including Shakespeare, of course, that we are all actors, but few understand the implications of that statement. The craft of acting is as complex as any other in our world, and it reaches down into the depths of our psyches. The ersatz drama enacted by the potential suicide is but a pale shadow of the real thing. The ultimate point of my comparison is that the suicide rehearsal remains too tightly bound within its own self-validating parameters. There is little of the rich and breathtaking permeability that comes from working with another person on stage. The analogy, however fruitful, breaks down at this point, and the potential suicide must climb out of his or her dense circle and allow the power of the inner and outer worlds to speak. There is thus an abyss of difference between the many resurrections on stage and the illusory resurrection waiting at the end of self-inflicted death.

This is the second time that the stage analogy has appeared in this book. In the previous chapter I analyzed five of my dreams from the pre- and post-diagnosis periods. The hermeneutic horizon used there derived directly from Jung's understanding of dreams as miniature stage plays. For some reason there seems to be a depth structure in the unconscious that is richly attuned to the dramatic presentations of our conscious world. Looked at from the other direction, our stage plays represent one of the most intense places where the unconscious can work out its own special logic. Yet we must be careful of overdoing the analogy of play here. Many contemporary perspectives assume that all mental and cultural products result from a kind of free semiotic play in which there are no constraints from either the origin or objective. This corrosive view actually strips play of all its healing power and renders it a kind of elite manipulation of structures and signs with no depth. The view that I will unfold in what follows sharply diverges from postmodern views of play and insists that all stage plays, as one of the most intense forms of play, are either rehearsals of profound transformation, or embody that transformation itself.

B. PSYCHOLOGICAL VISTAS

In my analysis of the psychological aspects of manic-depressive disorder I want to work through the complex correlation between consciousness and the unconscious. The genetic foundations of this disorder need a place or sphere within which to operate. The analogy I will use is as follows: the manic-depressive gene, or genes, represents an underlying code that manifests itself through an encoding process that is transmitted and then received by the distressed organism. Hence we have a simple structure: code as encoding, transmission, and decoding. The code is always in place, while the transmission will be sporadic, with the reception dependent upon that transmission, and on the state of the receiving system, be it organic or inorganic. This is the basic semiotic model of codes that has been most fully developed by Umberto Eco.[47] For intra-psychic reality, we can say that we are born with the code that has appeared here and there in our family history. It has its dormancy period, battered on by external traumatic events, which pass over into its first intense manifestation. A process of translation in which the brain decodes the encoded message and the rest of the system make the manifestation, in either a manic or depressive episode, possible. We can even say that the episode is the decoding process itself. This encoding/decoding link is non arbitrary, that is, there is little or no room for choice in either end of the code. The encoding comes from genetic material that is at least as old as the species itself (currently held to be around 4.5 million years), and the decoding is highly compulsive and directional. When insomnia, for example, drives you toward a manic attack, there is little hermeneutic maneuvering room allowed. You are going to manifest the decoded material whether you like it or not. More strongly put, you will *be* the decoding.

For some reason, I find this semiotic model comforting. I am reminded of an experience that many of us have had of witnessing a full-blown epileptic seizure, perhaps from a stranger on the street. After the seizure abates one rushes to the victim and piously explains to them: well, you had an epileptic seizure, and I since I understand something about the disease I can help you. We are often astonished to find out that they deny having undergone any such thing. I have a clear picture of one such soul on a street in Philadelphia. The dazed and confused look on his face was haunting, and strongly reminds me of how we manic-depressives often look at our own behavior. For me, the value of semiotics is that it can take away some of that astonishment and bring us toward a deeper understanding of the inevitable trajectory of the genetic material in our own body. In particular, I want to concentrate on the idea that our attacks are the decoding process.

I need to introduce one piece of technical terminology, but once learned it will quickly show its usefulness. It comes from the manic-depressive philosopher Charles Sanders Peirce, briefly discussed in the previous chapter. Peirce was one of the chief founders and architects of the philosophical movement known then and now as pragmatism, although he called it pragmaticism. In addition, he also created the modern field of semiotics, or study of signs, and has had a truly astonishing influence on semiotic thinking around the world. In looking at signs he decided that they were of almost infinite complexity in form and function but he wanted to distill some of these swirling waters down into a clear essence. He asked himself the classical philosophical question: just what is the world made of? He answered by saying that it was made of objects, which were partially hidden, signs, which can point to these partially hidden objects, and interpretants, which are new signs. It goes something like this. I look at a strange object out in a field. It could be very ancient but I don't yet know what it is. As I peer down at it, afraid to touch it, I begin to see some strange lines and ridges on it. As my vision clarifies, it becomes obvious that the lines are of some ancient sea creature. I have already made an important move: the object is some kind of rock containing a fossil. The rock is the object, while my use of the word and concept "fossil" gives me the first sign. But I don't stop there. I want to enrich my sign by probing more deeply into the object, so I run home and get a fossil book that will tell more specifically what I am looking at. Upon my return I notice that it is such and such a fish from such and such an era. This gives me new signs to augment and enrich the first. These new signs are the interpretants that point both to the first sign and to the object.

Through the series of interpretants, the object is becoming clearer and clearer. The process deepens yet another step if I bring in friends and experts who can add their own signs and interpretants to the original object. For Peirce, this process can continue indefinitely, and this is precisely how science works. The triad of sign/object/interpretant really functions to unveil the features of what is, and I will use it to illuminate the psychological features of manic-depressive disorder. Already we have a key ingredient, namely, that of the genetic code that unleashes the disease on the psyche. I will call this code the object part of our triad. We know it only through signs and interpretants. Earlier I argued that manic-depressives couldn't read the signs. One fundamental reason for this is that the genetic code responsible for the illness works precisely by scrambling the signs so that they cannot be easily read. This makes it far more difficult for us to find out which signs point to the object and which point only to other free-floating signs. Put in another way, what we are seeking are signs that are rooted in objects and which generate reliable interpretants.

Let me give one more example to help this framework gel in the mind. Suppose I wake up one morning and notice that there is a strange circular rash on my arm. For some reason there is a small bump right in the middle, like a bulls-eye. I also have a fever and experienced violent muscle spasms during the night. What we have are a series of signs awaiting an interpretant. The object behind the signs is unknown to me, but has clearly caused the symptoms. What do I do? If I am smart, I go to a doctor who can provide the interpretant and tell me the true origin of the symptoms. Upon showing her the rash, and describing to her the other symptoms, she makes the almost instant diagnosis, Lyme disease. Thus the object, Lyme disease that comes from a very small tic, caused the signs, which called forth an interpretant from the one person qualified to give it, the doctor. Since this happened to me in exactly this way, it remains a strong example of the power of Peirce's sign/object/interpretant triad. As I live in a Lyme disease zone, I had already made my tentative diagnosis, that is, generated the interpretant, but needed corroboration, not to mention, medicine.

The semiotic model actually came out of medical diagnostics, and, in a very different way, mystery stories. Doctors and detectives make excellent semioticians, and their tactics can be put to good use by manic-depressives. For we have a life-long illness that is always ready to erupt in major or minor ways, and we need to learn the signs so that we can also generate the proper interpretants. Our psyche is often showered in ersatz signs and these can do harm unless they are brought under the discipline of more public interpretants.

If the genetic code, only recently understood, and only in an incomplete way, is the object in our semiotic triad, then what of the symptoms that erupt because of the operation of the code/object? Here we need to be a little subtler in our analysis. If I am suddenly visited by a manic episode, say my first at age ten or so, do I have a series of interpretants given with the symptoms? The answer is: yes and no. I do not have an interpretant insofar as I dumbly suffer something that actually makes no sense at the time. I have symptoms, that is, I act-out a decoding process in which there is no conscious decoder. The decoding happens to me as the symptoms themselves. This process often leaves the sufferer astonished and rather mute as to the meaning of the events. Yet I am also struggling, sometimes with all of my conscious resources, to find a meaning, an interpretant, for what has pushed its way through me from the recesses of the unconscious. The most accurate way to understand the situation is that the self is drowned in signs that are internally pushing toward their rebirth into interpretants.

The plot thickens because many manic-depressives don't even know that something is wrong. Psychiatrists and therapists often wait that moment when a patient will suddenly find the right interpretant and say, for example: no more self-medication! This is a genuine breakthrough because it signals that the sufferer has connected the mute but violent signs, with a trajectory of healing that comes from the string of interpretants embodied in consciousness. Interpretants point in (at least) two directions. They point forward to further prospects of interpretation and healing, and they point backward to the original signs that suddenly appeared in and as the symptoms of the disorder. What happens in the latter dimension is that the original signs are reborn as interpretants, which means that the disease begins to have a shape and meaning that can be assimilated by consciousness.

Our semiotic triad, then, can be summarized in a clear way. The manic-depressive genetic code unleashes itself on the individual (for reasons that are still partially veiled in mystery). The code is transmitted from the brain to the psyche so that outward and inward forms of extreme mood and behavior are manifest. These manifestations are unconscious forms of decoding, direct one-on-one responses to the encoded signs of the disease. The analogy between this process and that of Lyme disease is precise. The symptoms, which leave the individual dazed, cry out for their interpretants. Sometimes these interpretants never come, as in the case of the untreated and undiagnosed manic-depressive who commits suicide. Sometimes the right interpretants come only after strenuous denial and resistance. Sometimes the wrong interpretants remain in force for decades. In the case of manic-depressive disorder, the right interpretants arrive when we have the possibility of remission. If medical treatment is applied, and if it is successful, then, baring a simple short-term natural remission, we have interpreted the situation correctly. Here we see the pragmatic dimension of semiotics. If a therapy regimen works, then we have the right interpretants. This part of the puzzle is actually quite simple.

We see here a genuine dialectic. The term "dialectic" [*die Dialektik*] comes from the nineteenth-century philosopher Hegel and is unnecessarily shrouded in mystery. In its most basic sense, the term refers to both energy and movement. The energy comes from the psyche, which has a rich store of energy that is both conscious and unconscious. The movement comes from what this energy does. Psychic energy moves back and forth between consciousness and the unconscious, sometimes changing the direction of its flow for no apparent reason, sometimes following a pattern that we can discern. If the dialectic brings energy into consciousness, then there is a heightening of mood, while if the energy moves in the opposite direction and disappears into the unconscious; there is a depressing of mood. Most of the time this dialectic is gentle and follows a course that is responsive to external stimuli, such as the change of light intensity. Yet for manic-depressives, there can be a precipitous energy change that can propel consciousness in one direction or another almost without warning.

For years I had dreams of standing on a beach while a gigantic wave, perhaps one hundred feet high, came crashing down upon me. I always survived this process, but woke up in great distress. One day I was casually looking through pictures in a print shop and noticed one that was absolutely captivating and could have been from one of my dreams. The photograph is taken from a helicopter and frames a lighthouse on the end of a sliver of land. Standing in the doorway at the base of the lighthouse is the figure of a man who has casually stuck his hand in his pant's pocket as he looks up at the photographer (the Frenchman Jean Guichard). The lighthouse is made of dark gray stones and is not painted. Behind him, however, a massive wave, a beautiful shade of light green, is crashing around the lighthouse. The wave appears to be fifty feet above him. Needless to say, I immediately purchased the print and had it framed so that it now hangs in the bedroom. The salesperson assured me that the man standing in the door drowned after this picture was taken. There are few iconic signs that speak so clearly to this uncanny disease.

In my semiotic analysis of the print I would say that the man is a symbol of the ego and its utter fragility when confronted with the energy surges of the unconscious. His nonchalant attitude is a warning that we had better look behind us to see if the Windhorse is once again stirring. There is even a Freudian reading possible here, namely, that the lighthouse represents great phallic power that comes into its own amid the crashing forces of the disorder. This argument, of course, only works for males, yet it can be translated into female reality if the lighthouse is deliteralized. That is, hyper-sexuality is manifest when the waves of mania surround the ego and carry it into foreign waters.

Iconic signs are extremely important to the ego. The unconscious is deeply alien to us and seems to speak an utterly foreign language. However, the unconscious very much wants its semiotic codes to become manifest and decoded by consciousness. One of the most direct ways in which this can happen is for the unconscious to send us a visual image that contains strong conceptual content. It is as if the unconscious needs to be personified in some content that can reach us outside of conscious forms of ideation. I think that one of the best iconic signs for manic-depressive disorder is that of a storm at sea. Because a storm at sea does not seem to rest on anything, there is no place for escape. Thus the crashing of the waves is something from which our fragile vessel cannot flee. And when a monstrous wave makes its way to land and crashes on the inhabitants there, we have an even clearer symbol of psychic devastation.

Volcanoes are also excellent iconic signs of the manic phase of the disorder. Desert landscapes may be among the best signs or symbols of the depressed phase. In Jungian therapy it is important that symbols, visual, tactile, acoustic, etc., emerge to help give some shape to self-understanding. Personification of unknown and feared forces can actually begin the process of depriving them of some of their uncanny power. Naming is an act that gives shape to an elusive infinity. From the standpoint of consciousness, manic-depressive disorder seems to be what Hegel called a "bad infinite," [*schlechtes Unendliche*] that is, an infinite that cannot be tamed and brought under the governance of consciousness. By fixing this bad infinite in images, like that of the tidal wave, consciousness has given shape and immediacy to something that has eluded all shape. When the manic energy soars again, we at least have an image through which to understand and perhaps channel its energy. Jung did not write much about manic-depressive illness. In his eighteen volume collected works, he mentions this disease by name only a handful of times. He does, however, say far more about mania as both a religious and a psychic state. It must be remembered that until the 1950's, medical diagnosticians were more interested in schizophrenia than in the mood disorders. And, as noted in the previous chapter, many psychiatrists did not separate mood from thought disorders, thus making it difficult to focus a spotlight on manic-depression. Jung had the advantage of working in comparative religion and in classical studies, and thus had a wealth of material pertinent to mood disorders. Mania was something that he understood well, and could recognize it in his patients.

For Jung, the concept of mania tied in with his concept of psychic inflation. He would define a manic attack as one in which material from the unconscious simply overwhelmed consciousness and used it like a toy. The inflation came from the delusion maintained by consciousness that it was the source of the material flowing through it. Self-divinization drove the poor fragile ego to the brink of dissolution. In thought disorders, this dissolution can become total, while in manic-depression the ego retains some autonomy, however weak. In the flight of ideas and rapid speech of the manic-depressive there is always some thread that connects the bizarre material. The clinician may have to work very hard to find this thread, constituted by signs and interpretants, but it will be there.

The object, dynamic in its energy, is the code that manifests itself through encoding and transmission. Decoding unfolds as the symptoms of the disorder. Where does all of this take place? Combining our two models of the sign/object/interpretant and the dialectic of consciousness and the unconscious, we can say that the unfolding of the manic-depressive gene takes place within the unconscious and then emerges into consciousness whenever the dynamic object is concresced into signs and codes. If the unconscious is pre-intelligible, consciousness is at least potentially intelligible. Psychic energy surges out of the unconscious into consciousness, producing psychic inflation in which many signs and interpretants whirl around with no seeming contour. At the other extreme, psychic energy can slip quietly out of the sphere of consciousness and leave it dry and desiccated. A long-term depression can deprive consciousness of even the *desire* for signs. Thus, if the manic state is too semiotically dense, with signs exploding off of everything whatsoever, the depressed state rejects the very possibility of signs and interpretants as they slink into oblivion.

Is there any value at all to this harrowing dialectic? We will say more about this in the next chapter, but for now we can say that some saving value can be rescued from this process. I am assuming that this dialectic exists whether or not one is on lithium or its equivalents, with the proviso that lithium does make the dialectic less violent. The dialectic itself can be understood to represent an accelerated rhythm that in normal proportions is found throughout the organic kingdoms. All living things experience some form of rapid expansion, combined with moments of contraction. In the human order this takes place across an astonishing continuum. The dialectic of mania and depression is thus an intensification of something that is built-in to the heart of the evolutionary process. My answer to this question is that the manic phase does allow for novel and powerful interpretants, while the depressed faze forces us to sift through them again and again to find some legitimate correlation between the interpretant and its object. Jamison presented an earlier version of this argument, from which mine derives, but tied it more directly to literary productivity. In her model, the poet or writer may create much useless material in the hypo-manic state (you cannot create much of lasting value in a full manic state), which then is pared down in the longer and more critical depressed state. As she puts it, "Depression prunes and sculpts; it also ruminates and ponders and, ultimately, subdues and focuses thought."[48] Artistic productivity is enhanced in the dialectic of hypo-manic semiotic excess, and the consequent weeding out of non-felicitous interpretants. From a survival standpoint, nature does not tolerate too many unpaid for signs. We pay for a sign by linking it back to its originating dynamic object.

William James coined the now well-known phrase of "cash value" as a way of showing the pragmatic link between a concept and a perception. In our terms, derived more from Peirce, this means that a sign or interpretant is like a check that needs to be cashed in and turned into hard currency (or gold, if you like the alchemical analogy). We take our check to the bank that has a dynamic object in the vault. If the signature on the check matches that on the object, then the exchange can be made. If it does not, we may be asked to leave the premises! Since manic-depressives can be notorious in their misuse of funds in the manic phase, the analogy has a special pertinence. I come to the bank with far more checks than can be converted into dynamic objects. Many of the checks must be returned or simply thrown away. The few that remain can be used to rebuild the edifice that has been damaged by the mood swings. The recovery depression can thus be likened to the slow and deliberate process by which the banker compares one check after another with their real or alleged objects in the vault. Assuming that this analogy is not too contrived or precious, we can conclude that our paid-for signs are the enduring touchstone that supports us in between the vagaries of mood.

I will detail some of the practical dimensions of this process in the fourth chapter, where I describe specific tactics that I have evolved to work my way back to the dynamic objects that support my genuine signs. At this point we need to look more closely at Jung's contributions to our understanding of the psyche and show how his general model illuminates the way that manic-depressive disorder upsets the balance within the psyche. As noted, he did not do a great deal with the concept of manic-depression per se, but his framework represents one of the richest for understanding its trajectory through the psyche. I think that one primary reason for this is his grasp of how psychic energy actually works. For Jung, psychic energy is neutral in quality, that is, it is not fundamentally qualified as it was for Freud with his model of psycho-sexuality. This energy *may* express itself in sexual form, but it may just as easily express itself as the will-to-power or as the quest for meaning.

Neutral psychic energy flows in and out of consciousness from the unconscious. The ego stands at the center of the field of consciousness and struggles to integrate the power of the unconscious into its own small world. There is a normal rhythm connecting consciousness with the unconscious. At certain stages of life the flow of energy will change of its own volition. Around mid-life, the unconscious becomes activated in a stronger way and compels consciousness to listen to its contents. This normal process can also become pathological. In a 1951 preface to a book on psychopathology written by John Custance, Jung makes one of the most complete statements in his writings about his own understanding of manic-depressive disorder:

> Although I myself have been studying the very same phenomena for years, and have repeatedly described them, it still came to me as a surprise and a novelty to see how the delirious flight of ideas and uninhibitedness of the manic state lower the threshold of consciousness to such an extent that, as with the *abaissment du niveau mental* [lowering of the mental threshold] in schizophrenia, the unconscious is laid bare and rendered intelligible. . . . The result [of this lowering] is a crude and unmitigated system of opposites, of every conceivable colour and form, extending from the heights to the depths. The symbolism is predominantly collective and archetypal in character, and thus decidedly mythological or religious. Clear indications of an individuation process are absent, since the dialectical drama unfolds in the spontaneous, inner confrontation of opposites before the eyes of a perceiving and reflecting subject.[49]

In both mood and thought disorders, the threshold separating consciousness from the great collective power below, is lowered. In the case of both schizophrenia and manic-depression, we now know that this lowering is genetic in origin. Earlier we used Jung's concept of psychic inflation as one way of describing how manic-depression works in the manic phase. In this passage, Jung puts strong emphasis on the archetypal and collective nature of the semiotic material that comes out through the inundated conscious mind. This material splits into strong binaries that cannot be reconciled, hence making individuation impossible. In untreated manic-depressive illness, individuation may still *be* possible but the struggle is immense. The opposites rush away from each other at such speed that no reconfiguration seems likely.

However, once the manic attack is over, and the recovery depression takes its place (as the energy from the unconscious withdraws) some rudimentary form of individuation can occur. With lithium treatment, of course, individuation can move along at an accelerated rate. In the next chapter, I will try to show how individuation can begin to take hold even with an untreated form of the disease. This will be most strongly manifest in the phenomenon of genius where other factors seem to be at play. In spite of the pessimistic tone of the above passage, Jung had an optimistic view of mental disease, namely, that it too was teleological in nature. The psyche uses both normal and pathological states as attempts at a cure. Hence a disease or a neurosis, perhaps even a psychosis, can be a means to an end, the highest end being individuation.

From a hermeneutic standpoint, we can even say that there is information when there is a complete breakdown of information. As the Austrian philosopher Ludwig Wittgenstein argued, the right kind of silence could be deeply illuminating of a situation. Wittgenstein, who *may* have been manic-depressive (I continue to ponder this possibility), understood that so-called straightforward forms of knowledge might have the least semiotic (not his word) value. Consequently, even in the case of a total manic explosion in which the universal archetypes stand apart in binary opposition, and there seems to be no reconciling third that brings meaning, we still have a *kind* of knowledge. Pathological breakdown has its own hermeneutic value and meaning, even if it may be reticent to show its face to the outside observer. In my own manic attacks, the meaning threads were radiantly clear at the time. Alas, I could not retrace them during the recovery depression.

To summarize our observations thus far, we can say that the psyche is constituted by consciousness, with the ego at its center, the unconscious, which is universal and rooted in our phylogenetic and evolutionary past, and psychic energy, which is qualitatively neutral, and which travels back and forth across the frontier separating consciousness from the unconscious. Manic-depressive disorder represents perhaps the most extreme manifestation of the dialectic of psychic energy across the lowered threshold between the two fundamental dimensions of the psyche. With the explosion of unconscious material into consciousness there is the resultant psychic inflation and the rapid fissuring of archetypal material. When this tidal wave has washed through the ego, there is the inevitable ebbing of the waters of mania and the consequent loss of energy to consciousness, which sinks into a longer-term depression. The receding waters of mania take all signs with them, and the ego is left with gray on gray as all life has fled.

One especially fascinating aspect of this dialectic has to do the personality changes in the individual. Above we described some of the social aspects of mood in the manic or hypo-manic phase, but said nothing about more fundamental typological variations. Jung, as is well known, developed a very rich and subtle theory of psychological types after his break with Freud. In his autobiographical reflections, he argued that he needed to discover why he and Freud had developed such different conclusions about the nature of the psyche, and tied this difference to typology with Freud being seen as extraverted, and he being introverted. This material was brought together in 1921 in his volume *Psychological Types*, and represents one of the most widely disseminated typological systems today.[50] Many readers will be familiar with it under the guise of the Myers-Briggs Type Indicator test. There are several popular forms of the test on the market today.[51] Since this may be familiar territory, I will only give the necessary reminders of Jung's basic system so that we can see how it might apply to manic-depressive disorder.

The fundamental distinction within the type theory is between the two basic attitude types. While Jung didn't invent the introvert/extravert distinction, he did bring it to prominence. It is important to note that this distinction is a directional one more than a behavioral one, although those elements will be present. That is, the distinction pertains to the direction in which psychic energy will flow.

For the extravert, psychic energy will move outward into the object world, thus leaving the inner sphere for the world of external connections. The introvert will use his or her energy internally, thus enriching the inner life of thought, intuition, sensation, or feeling. External reality will be less binding and compelling, while, for the extravert, inner reality will be less cultivated and honored.

The distinction between the two attitudes has become common currency, while the distinctions among the four psychic functions is less well known and understood. I will be either introverted or extraverted, along a continuum of course, but will also embody one of the four functions: thinking, feeling, sensing, and intuiting. One of these four will be dominant with another functioning as an auxiliary or back-up system. However, we must also distinguish between two parings of these four functions. Jung separated out the so-called rational functions (thought and feeling) from the so-called irrational functions (sensation and intuition). Thought and feeling are both rational because they make judgments across time about the objects under their purview. Clearly, thought is rational, but what about feeling? For Jung, feeling is as rational as thought because it works with realities that are good or bad, and can be seen as such by the feeling function. The irrational functions work by seeming leaps from one way station to another, thus avoiding the linear logic of both feeling and thought.

The dual axis between rational and irrational is important. If my main function is one of the rational ones, than my auxiliary must come from the irrational, or vice versa. I will thus have a basic attitude (introvert or extravert), a dominant function (from either the rational or irrational axis), and an auxiliary function (from the axis not expressed by the dominant function). My own typology is: Introvert, Intuitive, Feeling, and Perceiving, expressed as INFP. The final term refers to the distinction between modes of assessment of the world. Perceivers take in, while the opposite type, judgers, renders judgments on whatever is encountered. For example, I can go to a play with a judger and walk out of the theater with a very different mode of response. The judger will be full of all sorts of opinions: the staging was inferior, the actor who played so and so inflected too much on key lines, the other actor was sleep-walking, etc. My own response is to let the play sink in for several days, before rendering anything like a binary judgment. Needless to say, this typological difference can be quite frustrating to both parties.

The crunch point comes when we bring in the unconscious. The manifest functions and attitudes are all part of the world of consciousness. If I am intuitive, I interact with the world in the mode of the future with a strong interest in background patterns. If I am a sensation type, I live in present immediacy and go from particular to particular. If I am a feeling type I live in the past and seek out deep patterns of feeling that have an inner logical thread. If I am a thinking type I live across the time line and weight things in terms or true or false. Again, this is all in the sphere of consciousness. Now the unconscious, especially since it is compensatory to consciousness, works in the opposite direction. The conscious dominant function has its opposite in the unconscious, and it will be on the same axis. Thus, if my conscious attitude is feeling, then my inferior and unconscious function will be thinking. So too, if my conscious dominant function is intuition, then my inferior and unconscious function will be sensation. The plot thickens yet again because the function in the unconscious really will be inferior, that is, it will be far less developed than its twin in consciousness. The last of the four functions will also be in the unconscious, but play far less of a role. The attitude will also be contrary (and I am using this word in a double sense!) in the unconscious.

In my case, then, my conscious reality is introvert intuiting. In my unconscious, I am thus extravert sensing, but again, this dimension of my psyche is in an inferior mode. Whenever it comes out, say under the influence of self-medication, it comes out in an immature and problematic way. It has not had a chance to become integrated into the overall psychic economy. The reader can see where this framework is going. Our conscious attitude (extraversion or introversion) and our dominant function will be developed in a much richer way because of the pressures of social and personal survival. Unfortunately, this often keeps us from dealing with the contraries within, and with allowing them a more positive role in the psyche.

When we turn to the issue of manic-depression we see how Jung's type theory can shed some much needed light on the hermeneutics of mania, where the unconscious is bringing the inferior function to the surface in a violent irruption that cannot be integrated at the moment of the manic attack, but that can leave traces for the recovery depression to work over. We are fortunate in that Jung did reflect publicly on this issue. In 1935 Jung gave a series of lectures in London entitled *The Tavistock Lectures: On the Theory and Practice of*

96   Chapter Two

Analytical Psychology. At the conclusion of the first lecture he was asked the following question by Dr. E. A. Bennet, "Do you consider that the superior function in the case of a person suffering from manic-depression remains conscious during the period of depression?" Part of Jung's answer follows:

> I would not say that. If you consider the case of manic-depressive insanity you occasionally find that in the manic phase one function prevails and in the depressive phase another function prevails. For instance, people who are lively, sanguine, nice and kind in the manic phase, and do not think very much, suddenly become very thoughtful when the depression comes on, and then they have obsessive thoughts, and vice versa. I know several cases of intellectuals who have a manic-depressive disposition. In the manic phase they think freely, they are productive and very clear and very abstract. Then the depressive phase comes on, and they have obsessive feelings; they are obsessed by terrible moods, just moods, not thoughts.[52]

Here Jung nicely contrasts one pair of functions; namely, thought and feeling. In the first case he talks of a kind of extravert feeling self who suddenly, in depression, slips into an introvert thinking mode of relating to the world. The superior function, manifest during the manic episode, moves away during the depression. In the second case, Jung inverts the functions and describes the extravert thinker who becomes an introvert feeler during the depressed phase. So far the model seems fully consistent with non-pathological manifestations of typology. That is, mania heightens the superior function, while depression invites in the inferior one. I am not persuaded that this is all that Jung has to say, or that he is fully consistent here.

To illustrate my worry, let us look of the next question raised by Bennet after hearing Jung's answer to his first. Bennet asks, "Is melancholia not extraverted?" In Jung's answer to this query we get a little closer to the relation between type theory and psychopathology:

> You cannot say that, because it is an incommensurable consideration. Melancholia in itself could be termed an introverted condition but it is not an attitude of preference. When you call somebody an introvert, you mean that he

prefers an introverted habit, but he has his extraverted side too. We all have both sides, otherwise we could not adapt at all, we would have no influence, and we would be beside ourselves. Depression is always an introverted condition. Melancholics sink down into a sort of embryonic condition, therefore you find that accumulation of peculiar physical symptoms.[53]

I think that Jung spills the beans more fully in this answer. No matter what the individual may privilege in terms of introversion or extraversion, the mood swings characteristic of manic-depressive disorder have their own logic. I would reconstruct Jung's perspective in the following way: in manic-depressive disorder, mania must be extraverted, regardless of the individual's dominant or inferior attitude, while depression must be introverted, regardless of the individual's dominant or inferior attitude. However, when it comes to the four functions, I think that the model holds. If my conscious and dominant attitude is feeling, then the violent onrush of the unconscious will propel me into my inferior function, in this case, thinking. The disorder overrides the attitudinal structures, imposing extraversion on mania and introversion on depression. Yet it seems to work *with* the function types by the process Jung referred to as *enantiodromia* (the rapid conversion of something into its opposite). Hence, an extravert will remain an extravert in mania, while an introvert will become an extravert. An intuiter will become a sensor, while a thinker will become a feeler, etc. The introversion of depression may work with the auxiliary function, but this is less clear.

The issue is one involving the sheer power of a pathological condition over the normal functioning of the psyche. Jung often refers to manic-depressive disorder as a form of "insanity," namely as a psychotic condition that has its own autonomous rules of operation. His early monk-like years in the Burghölzli psychiatric clinic in Zürich showed him the devastation of thought and mood disorders, although the focus of the clinic was on thought disorders. By 1909 Jung came to understand these thought disorders in archetypal terms, namely, as manifesting great universal structures that in turn fascinated and dazed the spectator psyche.[54] The subject is a passive observer of things and powers that seem to have no hermeneutic meaning. However, by looking closely at the patient's symptoms, by tracing them back to personal traumatic events, and by carefully linking them to religious and mythological symbols, the beginnings of a cure could be affected, a cure that depended on a successful understanding of the patient's own hermeneutic circle.

In looking at his type theory we saw how he struggled, not always successfully, with bringing together pathological distortions with the basic underlying non-pathological laws. In terms of manic-depressive disorder, the general law of psychic compensation was found to work in one dimension but not in another. It works for the four functions but not for the two attitudes. Regardless of the normal compensation between introversion and extraversion, where the non-dominant attitude is manifest in an inferior way in the unconscious, manic-depressive disorder will subvert the basic structure and impose, as noted, extraversion on mania and introversion on depression. Jung saw this clearly. But the more complex issue of the four functions got muddied at bit. Here Jung overplayed his hand because of his genuine sense of the utter irrational power of manic-depressive disorder. As it turns out, so I would argue, the functions do continue to work in a compensatory way. You *will* be an extravert in your manic episode, but your function will be your inferior and opposite one. The thinker will become the feeler, the feeler will become the thinker, the intuiter will become the sensor, and the sensor will become the intuiter. In the depressed phase, you will revert to your normal dominant function, but of course, in much diminished capacity.

In my concluding remarks, I want to say a little more about how the quest for meaning enters into this extreme dialectic between consciousness and the unconscious. I am assuming a kind of parallelism here between psyche and soma, that is, between the inner reality of psychic energy, and the genetic code that is playing itself out through the drama of psychic energy. Philosophically we can talk of a parallelism between mind and brain, and, on a different axis, a causal relation that runs in two directions. In one direction, that most emphasized by the medical community, we have a causal relation running from the genetic code and its proxies in the mind (perhaps some enzyme activity)[55], toward the psyche. In the other direction, emphasized by the psychological community, the various trigger situations in the environment can send a signal to the genetic code, intensifying its prospects for activity. A balanced view will honor both causal trajectories and understand that they can synergize each other in fairly predictable ways. At the same time, the parallelism between both dimensions of the self must be acknowledged. I am using the term "parallelism" in a special way. For someone like Leibniz, for good reason a favorite philosopher among Jungians, the parallelism is read as a non-causal relation. In my use of the term, parallelism can be compatible with a causal analysis, namely, that the causal relation is symmetrical, i.e., going in both directions, all the while manifesting the ultimate depth connection between mind and brain. That is, the causal relations show that neither psyche nor soma can be what they are without a strict connection that keeps them on the very same parallel tracks at all times.

What then becomes of the issue of wholeness, that is, with the quest for an integral self? Since this will be a key issue in the next chapter, I will only lay out a few of the prospects that remain open to sufferers of manic-depressive disorder. We have seen how Jung was moved to deny any sense of individuation to the manic-depressive. This was, of course, in the pre-lithium era, but there is also a sense that even in psychosis the psyche is struggling with whatever resources remain, fighting for at least a fragmentary sense of meaning and wholeness. I am persuaded that the quest for wholeness runs so deeply in the human psyche that it will manifest itself again and again, regardless of the powerful resident conditions that seem bent on destroying it. And, given the teleological nature of the psyche, that is, its hunger for ultimate purpose amid the defeats of finite purposes, the goal of wholeness will remain present on the edges of the hermeneutic horizon, ready to be reawakened when the conditions are right.

Wholeness never entails the elimination of polar opposites within the psyche. On the contrary, the self is only whole when these tensions are present, under the guiding presence of the self archetype. For the manic-depressive this means that mood swings can be integrated into a larger and more capacious sense of the movement of the self. It is important, however, that this view of wholeness not be romanticized, as if any sustained tension between opposed forces will bring meaning and stability. Wholeness can only exist if the extremes each deliver some meaning and that that meaning can be integrated into the ego. In extreme forms of manic-depression this becomes close to impossible. I am taken by Jamison's description of Lord Byron in which his self is likened to a major geological collision:

> Notoriously a study in contrasts, Byron, with his divided and mercurial temperament, resembled less a cohesive personality than a field of tectonic plates clashing, and grating against one another.[56]

This is a profound description of the manic-depressive personality in its most extreme form. The contour of the self is hard to find. Any time you find a personality trait and see it as central, it slips underneath another one that seems to grind away at it as if it were an adversary. We hear the clashing and grating, while the individual sufferer feels the heat and friction that unsettle all established positions. Everything is depositioned and repositioned, and no position can become normative or guiding. Rescuing a sense of wholeness from such a reality will be difficult, but I continue to maintain the hope that it will not be impossible.

On the simplest level, a manic-depressive moves toward a fragmentary sense of wholeness whenever an episode is understood in the context of non-episodic reality. The manic attack can leave permanent deposits that contain their own forms of wisdom and meaning, even if there is a strong tendency to deny the riches of the boundary-shattering experience. The hardest lessen to learn is to take ownership for the psychotic dimensions of the illness, and to find their hidden semiotic values.

There is a continuum connecting moments of high creativity and increased output with the humiliating manic episode that brings shame and suicidal ideation. By the same token, there is also a continuum connecting the debilitating and career damaging depressions with those moments of clarity that refine and focus our hypo-manic products. My analyst kept coming back to the issue of self-acceptance, especially for anyone living with *this* disease. My first response was to see this as a kind of narcissistic indulgence, but I am slowly coming to realize that it is actually a part of survival. If one can accept the often-public humiliation of a manic attack as something that does not invalidate the self, then suicidal ideation is less likely to be too intense or overwhelming. It is all too easy to practice self-acceptance when the creative juices are flowing; it is much harder when you are waiting fearfully by the phone for some strong rebuke from the social super-ego, a rebuke that rarely comes.

Where, then, does this leave us at the end of our reflections on the medical and psychological aspects of this disorder?[57] We have made some progress in going from the irrational, meaningless and stunned sense that comes from this illness, toward a semiotic and depth-psychological understanding of the way this disease implants its code into the psyche and the outer life of the individual. We live as the decoding process. We live as a series of signs hungering to become interpretants. And we live as an open wound waiting some healing, both medically and psychologically. In a recent book I open with the following sentence, "At the heart of the self is a cleft, a wound that emerges with the first dawn of consciousness and remains with the self until its death."[58] I wrote this several months before my diagnosis, yet it points in a clear way to my post-diagnosis sense of self.

For the manic-depressive, this wound is merely intensified rather than invented anew. For the carrier of this disorder and its genetic code, there is a deep connection with the human condition shared by all persons, regardless of their genetic inheritance. This commonality provides grounds for hope, for a creative not yet that lies on the edge of every horizon of meaning. It is now time to probe into this liberating power and see how individuation can unfold even under the most extreme conditions. Creative force, whether manifest as genius or not, may be greater than the disease itself.

CHAPTER THREE: CREATIVITY AND GENIUS IN MANIC-DEPRESSION

The phenomena of creativity and genius are profoundly elusive, and often appear in a variety of guises, further perplexing inquiry into their origin, trajectory, and ultimate place within the human process. Yet we can shed some light on their manifestations within certain creative individuals and show how they and their gifts become transformed under the unique pressures of manic-depressive disorder. My argument in this chapter is fairly straightforward: while many manic-depressives have been highly creative in their lives in one way or another, only a few attain a culturally creative genius-level of accomplishment. On the other hand, an outsized proportion of geniuses have been manic-depressive.

Of course, manic-depressive disorder is not the only "pathology" associated with genius. Recently the historian of science Clifford A. Pickover has persuasively argued that many scientists suffer from obsessive-compulsive personality disorder, which tends to manifest itself in an extreme fastidiousness concerning order and number. It should be stressed that obsessive compulsive *personality* disorder (which is more global) is different from the more dramatic and familiar obsessive compulsive disorder which is manifest, for example, in constant hand washing to ward off germs. Pickover argues that there is some adaptive value in having the personality form of the disorder (a distinction that is not always carefully drawn) insofar as quantitative aspects of the world can become the focus of prolonged attention.[1]

An excellent example of a genius who suffered from obsessive compulsive personality disorder, or so I would argue, is the film director Stanley Kubrick, who only produced twelve feature length films because of his absolute obsession with detail and with total control of the innumerable variables in film making. He was notorious for his countless takes of each scene and with his control over sound, set design, cinematography, script writing (leading to many hard feelings with writers over the years), editing, marketing, casting, and even the physical features of the theaters where the films were to be premiered. Yet few would argue with the claim that he is among the two or three greatest filmmakers in the history of cinema.

Since the concern of this book is with manic-depressive disorder, the focus will be on its intense statistical correlation with genius, although in the case studies to follow there will be occasional reference to the often co-implicated manifestation of some form of obsessive-compulsive personality disorder. As in the case of manic-depression there seem to be certain brain anomalies associated with OCD, and it is to be hoped that scientific researchers with the phenomenon of genius will correlate these.

The philosopher, attempting to deal, then, with the ratio between manic-depressives and geniuses would put the same truth in more formal terms: the class of geniuses is much smaller than the class of manic-depressives, but most geniuses belong to the class of manic-depressives (and/or suffers of obsessive compulsive personality disorder). Were we to put this in the form of a Venn diagram found useful by logicians, we would have two circles, a large one containing a smaller one. The smaller one (class of geniuses) would be perhaps 3/4 inside of the larger one (class of manic-depressives), but would have perhaps 1/4 of its area outside of the larger circle (these figures are meant to be suggestive not empirically based). This iconic diagram should bring home the intimate correlation between the highest form of creativity, that of genius, and the pathology of this affective disorder.[2]

I want to present a theory of creativity first so that it can prepare the way for my theory of culturally significant genius, which will in turn facilitate the examination of two case studies of manic-depressive genius. I will be deliberately selecting persons from the pre-lithium era so that the rawness of manic-depression can be seen in its uncanny wedding with genius. As a larger horizon of meaning, the creativity question will be woven into the material of genius and manic-depression.

A. CREATIVITY: PRODUCT, PROCESS, AND COMMUNITY

We are all prepared to say that we know creativity when we see it. Yet it is another thing to ask, as philosophers do, for the necessary and sufficient conditions that must be in place before we will call a given phenomenon an instance of creativity. Invoking the strategy of the previous chapter, I am less inclined to look for sufficient conditions than

I am to look for necessary ones. This search entails working on several different axes simultaneously. Among the axes that show themselves most readily are: the product itself (however defined or shaped), the psychological dynamics of the creative process, and the location of the product within a given community for which it is held to be especially relevant.[3] Each is embedded in the other, although the importance of the third criterion is problematic. Hershman and Lieb place a great deal of emphasis on the recognition of creative genius during the genius' lifetime, "The work of those who die without reputation is usually lost to posterity."[4] This is a starker view than mine, yet they are certainly right about many such sad cases.

This third criterion, that of social recognition for the product, is problematic because there are two horizons of meaning that may or may not intersect. The product itself, and here we are only talking about works of high culture such as books, paintings, works of music, etc., will be a horizon of actual and possible traits. If the work has intrinsic greatness (I hope not a quaint notion in these postmodern times), then it will goad any potential assimilator into ramifying judgments and actions that enhance the product. By this I mean that someone reading a book, for example, will be compelled by the power of the book itself to make a series of novel and rich judgments that augment the work, that is, that bring its horizon into intersection with others. James Joyce's 1922 novel *Ulysses* is one such product because it compelled later novelists, playwrights, musicians, and painters to assimilate and expand upon many of its traits. This is the raw and intrinsic power of the work. The second horizon of meaning is that of the community. Suppose we have a product with intrinsic power, but its possible assimilators ignore it, perhaps for political, social, economic, or even psychological reasons. Are we prepared to deny genius to this work? Of course not. Yet many contemporary theories, even where they savagely deny the presence of a *Zeitgeist*, insist that without communal construction or reconstruction there is no "real" product. For such thinkers genius is only a social construction, which in turn makes the critic more important than the creator. This thinking is actually a form of *pseudo*-democratic reconstruction because it relocates power precisely where it has no intrinsic or natural basis. In its worst form it is a kind of theft. I am not persuaded that this thinking has a best form.

It should be clear that my emphasis is on the creator and on his or her product rather than on the cultural process of assimilation. How could we possibly know the ratio between well-assimilated products (which can always take place long after the death of the creator) and those that simply sink forever below the waters of awareness? Adding one more wrinkle to the plot, we must also recognize the powers of envy and inertia that frequently move communities toward the trivial and the easily assimilable. I believe that creativity is somehow a species-good, but that the species has a curious ability to ignore the goods that are often placed at its feet.

Let us examine in more detail the issue of the product, a necessary feature of creativity. The product doesn't have to be a normal space-time particular that endures with a steady cluster of traits. A dance can be a creative product, just as an artistic happening that is over almost as soon as it begins. Or consider a stage production that has a brief run (most actors consider a year to be the maximum desirable run on stage). Years ago I saw James Earl Jones and Christopher Plummer in Othello on Broadway. One critic at the time wrote that Plummer's performance was the "best Iago of the century." Just how one could know this, especially with the century then two decades from completion, is unclear. The performance, however, had entered a kind of hyperspace of value and meaning. Just "where" is their now past production located? It is located in its actual and still possible assimilations by actors, dramaturges, producers, and critics. It retains its potency to transform. There may come a time when all actualities and possibilities surrounding this product cease. Yet even so, it is clear that the scope of this product is far greater than any space-time parameters of the stage.

What does it mean to say that a product is creative? The first necessary condition is that it goes beyond antecedent products of its class. Novel and rich traits are added to the contour of the product, and past traits are transformed in their transmission into the new. What actor worth his salt would only say, "I want to be as good as Olivier in his Hamlet?" Olivier's version, whether the one in his 1948 film or the 1937 one at the Old Vic, must be transfigured into something with its own uniqueness and power. Of course, this is one of the Mt. Everests that haunt the actor, but the aspiration must be there nonetheless.

The second necessary condition for making a given product one manifesting high creativity is that the traits that it *does* have reinforce each other in a rich intensity of expression. There can even be incompatible and divergent traits within the same product, so long as they all add up to a cumulative force that distinguishes the product from others of its class. Dissonance in a piece of music can momentarily tear the fabric of the surrounding notes, but may add to the final integrity of a piece that embodies the shattering and recreation of forms. The genius of Hegel's writing is that he was able to create conceptual and historical horizons, only to rip them apart from within, only to reweave the fragments into a new but momentary whole. His students called him "Doctor Death" because of this propensity. In fact, one can argue that the greatest products of our traditions are precisely those that sustain harmony and dissonance and move both forward into a new transfigured integrity.

The third necessary condition for creativity within the product is what can best be called "depth." Of all of the words used to describe creativity, this one has become the most controversial. A number of philosophers have attacked any notion that there is a depth grammar or a depth structure to the world.[5] Everything is a mere play on the surface, a surface that is not covering anything beneath itself. My sense is that this denial of the depth dimension of the world is related to abjection of the unconscious. The power of the unconscious lies in its uncanny ability to shatter or transform anything on the surface level. Thus to believe in depth is to make oneself vulnerable to structures and dynamics over which one has no control. Unfortunately for these philosophers, our conscious beliefs have little power to protect us from that which is not conscious. In great works of art or science, there *is* a depth dimension that resonates down into the very heart of nature and history.

To be more precise, I want to use the word "depth" to refer to two realities: the human unconscious, and the "unconscious" of nature. A creative product, in addition to going beyond its antecedents, and combining harmony and dissonance in a new integrity, will also open up prospects onto the unconscious of the human process. The deepest traits of the self, such as the power of wholeness, the contra-sexual archetype, and forces of the spirit, will be manifest within any product that has been humanly contrived. Even if the assimilators do not immediately see these traits, they may exert an uncanny or haunting effect on those for whom the product is made. It is as if one unconscious (in the product) speaks to another (in the assimilator). The unconscious of nature, as constituted in its innumerable but unnamable potencies, will also speak in the product, linking it directly to what philosophers from the twelfth century on have called *nature naturing* (*natura naturans* or nature creating nature). [6] The unconscious of nature is the most difficult to approach, but its effects are strongly felt in our most creative products.

The fourth necessary condition for any product that can be called creative is that it contains a number of interpretants that are potentially public. In the previous chapter we worked through Peirce's famous triad of sign/object/interpretant as it applied to manic-depressive disorder.[7] Here we can see the same triad doing similar work to illuminate the phenomenon under study. The object is, of course, the product itself, while the sign is the immediate interpretation of that object, perhaps by its creator. The interpretant is the next step that may emerge from the correlation of sign and object. A truly great product will be able to generate a seemingly endless stream of interpretants that also serve to give the product scope. It must be stressed that the product *is* its actual and potential interpretants. That is, the novel interpretants that stream out of the object are not merely human contrivances, but have their origin in the work itself. There is a sense of bindingness (to use Heidegger's term *verbindlichkeit*) that guides the relation between the object and its interpretants. Interpretants make the product more efficacious within the world of other signs and interpretants.

Of course, there can emerge what Eco calls "hermetic drift" in which interpretants lose their connection with their originating object, but this moves us into a different domain of meaning and power and leaves the original product behind.[8] This situation is no longer a necessary condition for creativity in the product, but a contingent condition that actually violates the logic of the product. My formulation is meant to be very careful about invoking the social and political aspects of the assimilation of interpretants. The fourth necessary condition is not meant to say that a product needs to be socially recognized to be creative, but that the product must contain the potencies that *could* generate interpretants. It is as if the product nurtures these interpretants no matter how bleak the social situation. A weak or mediocre product would have few interpretants to sustain, and its social triumph would be lacking in depth and scope, both spatially and temporally. My belief is that most great works will show themselves to be such in the infinite long run, and that their interpretants will spring to life when the external conditions are right.

These four criteria for creativity in the product point directly to the creator of such products. Great works are not functions of drift, indifference, or mechanical contrivance, but spring from deep and often conflicting psychological roots. I am persuaded that works of genius, in particular, are over-determined in their origins within the self. By this I mean that the psyche must martial vast stores of energy and formal structure in order to break past the mediocre and predictable. If you ask the creator the question: why do you create, you may get an astonishing variety of answers. You are likely to hear such statements as: I had no choice, or my visions haunted me until they were translated into some medium, or my demons gave me no rest, or, finally, I was a medium through which something spoke. In most cases I suspect that several such motives are operating simultaneously. It may help to think of it this way. In much of our life we engage in a conscious or unconscious cost-benefit analysis. We want the benefits to outweigh the costs. For the most part, this is sound practice. But when we come to the creative process it seems as if cost-benefit analyses go out the window. The sheer work that goes into producing something of high value often outweighs the benefits, however measured. I do not know anyone who finds the act of writing pleasurable, nor do I know many people who get back from the world anything like what they put into writing their books. Yet the creative process continues, sometimes like clock work, and the hoped-for benefits are endlessly deferred. The only way that I can explain the process is to assume that something far deeper is at work than a cost-benefit analysis, and that this deeper reality is the over-determined momentum of the creative psyche.

I want to stress the point that creativity on its highest levels is to some extent a mystery. It does not follow from this that we cannot say something about the more available aspects of this mystery. As my late mentor and friend the philosopher Justus Buchler liked to argue, too much stress on mystery smacks more of "theoretical fatigue" than of insight! I hope to avoid such fatigue while honoring genuine mystery when it *is* manifest. With this in mind, I think that creativity seems more like a pressure from below than a conscious plan or contrivance. I am persuaded that the unconscious, both personal and collective, is absolutely necessary for the creative process. Much of the work on a specific product has already been prepared and energized in the unconscious before any media of expression are used. Let me give a homely example. I know a mathematician who was working on a complex problem in acoustical theory. He had developed a possible but inelegant solution that took up many pages of mathematical notation. In utter frustration of condensing the formula, he simply gave up all efforts. Some time later as he was returning from lunch, his foot hit the curb, and suddenly, the condensed formula appeared full-blown, as if out of the head of Zeus. The condensed formula was subsequently published and became a minor classic in its field. The unconscious seems to be "aware" of patterns and of purposive designs, that is, it "knew" that a solution was desired, and it had the means, based on years of conscious training that had filtered into its domain, to bring it about.

In less homely cases as well, the unconscious both goads consciousness into activity and provides needed clues toward the consummation of the project. This can happen via hunches or even in dream material. The bottom line is that people create because they are compelled, often against conscious will, to participate in the rhythms of the unconscious. In fact, will seems to be one of the least relevant players in the creative process. Perhaps the most dramatic anecdote we have of sheer creative passion is the image of Beethoven caught for posterity as he is composing his *Missa Solemnis* in 1819. The following oft-quoted description comes from Beethoven's friend and biographer Anton Schindler:

> From behind the closed door of one of the parlours we could hear the master working on the fugue of the Credo, singing, yelling, stamping his feet. When we heard enough of this almost frightening performance and were about to depart, the door opened and Beethoven stood before us, his features distorted to the point of inspiring terror. He looked as though he had just engaged in a life and death struggle with the whole army of contrapuntists, his everlasting enemies.[9]

This is a wonderful evocation of psychomotor agitation combined with either a manic or hypo-manic burst of creativity. Schindler goes on to describe the flight of the servants and the utter disarray of the apartment. The work is what is absolutely binding because it is the ultimate concern and the focus of almost all of his energies. Needless to say, the will-directed daytime consciousness is no match for the mania of the creative acts that course through the psyche with unabated intensity.

Of course, it is dangerous to overly romanticize the creative act, as if the Beethoven example is normative for all acts of creation, yet it represents one extreme to which the manic-depressive genius can be driven.[10] But even in its non manic-depressive forms, creativity puts profound pressure on the conscious will and bends it back toward the direction of the unconscious.

Creativity is its own end. It does not serve something higher than itself, excepting, of course, individuation, nor can it be reduced to its animating or motivating conditions. Even if I say that I create for money or love, the depth logic insists that I create because I create. There is no choice but to create or to suffer a unique kind of suffering. In my darker moments, I think that if one were given the choice between whether or not to enter into the creative process, most would elect to stay away from something that cannot bring pleasure or perhaps even lasting happiness. Put in the strongest terms: the psyche uses certain individuals for its species-needs, and all it gives in compensation is the elusive hope that the sacrifices will somehow cash out in the long run. Is the psyche cruel? My sense is that we cannot use such language, as much as we are tempted to. The psyche is beyond good and evil and will manifest its potencies wherever and whenever it will. The individual psyche is often an unwilling host for the creative virus, although creation can take place in more meditative states as well.

B. GENIUS AND THE *NOT YET*

Let us look more closely at how the phenomenon of creativity becomes quickened in the phenomenon of genius. We have seen how creativity is manifest in the product, in the creative psyche, and in the public reception, where pertinent, of the product. This reception is itself a creative act that involves the assimilation and manipulation of interpretants. Why are some products more generative of rich interpretants than others? The answer seems clear, namely, that they have emerged from a creative process of unusual intensity and complexity. These special products come from creators whose own motivations are over-determined and rooted in the surging potencies of the unconscious of the self and of nature. There has long been an awareness that these unique creators lived on the boundary where psychopathology and genius intersect. In fact, as we are now even more aware, genius is what it is because it is as a response to underlying destructive forces that cry out for a cure.

Above we noted Jung's view that the psyche is teleological, that is, it is moving toward an end, the goal of wholeness. It follows from this that even physical and psychic disease represents an attempt at a cure. In the case of unprecedented creativity, this basic wound of the psyche is even deeper than the norm, and, when combined with high talent, can call forth great works. It must be stressed again and again that the works produced by the genius are attempts at healing. The work *is* the medicine. One of the clearest statements of this correlation is found in the essay by Anthony Storr entitled, "Genius and Psychoanalysis: Freud, Jung and the Concept of Personality." Storr, a student of creativity and one of the best writers on the phenomenon of genius, states this relationship:

> Deeper anxieties, especially those connected with disintegration, lead to an especial concern with the search for order and coherence. The great abstract thinkers, for example, seem often to be people who do not form close interpersonal ties. For them, concern with finding some order and sense in the world takes precedence over human relationships. There is a connection between fear of close relationships, anxiety about disintegration, and a feeling that the world is an unpredictable, unsafe place over which some form of control must be exercised if any security is to be attained. . . . Given this intimate connection between inner and outer worlds, it seems to be reasonable to guess that those who are particularly strongly motivated to seek for unity and order, whether in the arts or in the sciences, are likely themselves to be particularly divided.[11]

One of the basic psychic facts in the genius is a deep bifurcation within the self. There is the fear and abjection of the outer world, combined with a split within the inner world. Each part self speaks with unusual intensity, thereby making the drive for wholeness that much more urgent. In Peircean terms, the creative act always seeks the healing "third," that is, the structure, image, concept, or process that will bring together the brute dyadic collisions of the inner and outer worlds. On one side, the genius is unusually sensitive to the returning bifurcations in his or her psyche. On another side, the genius also sees the way out through some form of creative transformation that is best related to his or her talents. Where there is no overarching need, there is no genius in response. Need and act belong together in a dialectic that is still only partially understood.

In many cases there seems to be a childhood scar that results in what has often been called a "wounded narcissism."[12] This concept denotes the reality of a psyche that was not allowed to develop a healthy narcissism over time, especially if the child must serve the imperial and omnivorous narcissism of the parent or parents. His or her own self-needs get buried under the continuing pressures of the parental lack of self. If this basic wound is combined with high energy and an intense drive for self-transformation, then some of the conditions of genius may be present.

Another long-time student of the genius phenomenon, Hans Eysenck, has detailed some of the necessary traits of the evolving self as it struggles toward a manifestation of its genius potential:

> I start with the assumption that genius, defined as supreme creative achievement, socially recognized over the centuries, is the product of many different components acting synergistically, i.e., multiplying with each other, rather than simply adding one to the other. Among these components are high intelligence, persistence, and creativity, regarded as a *trait*. Trait creativity may or may not issue in creative achievement, depending on the presence of the many other qualifications and situational conditions. Prominent among these additional qualifications are certain *personality traits*, such as ego-strength, i.e., the inner strength to function autonomously, to resist popular pressure, and to persist in endeavour in spite of negative reinforcement.[13]

The important point here is that the internal traits such as ego-strength, high intelligence, and creativity all interact through a synergy that is, for the moment, anti-entropic. That is, more order and "heat" are created rather than less; although in a strict sense the energy for this ordering comes from outside of the system, namely, from the unconscious. The trait of resistance to popular pressure is more complex. Many of the most inspired products in our culture represent a creative response to external social pressures and values; yet manage to simultaneously transcend these very pressures. Here one thinks of a manic-depressive genius like Charles Dickens who could sell more books in a month than most writers dream of selling in a lifetime. The books, often sold in serial form, clearly appealed to popular taste, yet they also generated powerful interpretants that could influence other geniuses of the stature of a Dostoyevsky. At the other extreme we have the example of Albert Einstein who was driven to assert the theories of both special and general relativity against the reigning paradigm of his discipline.

In a groundbreaking book on the phenomenon of genius, Dean Keith Simonton develops an evolutionary argument for what he calls "secondary Darwinian evolution" that applies the principles of random variation, natural selection, and adaptability to cultural evolution. Primary Darwinian evolution applies strictly to the physical order and is concerned with gene transmission, while the secondary form also works with what are called "memes," that is, with units of *meaning* that can be passed along within an evolving culture. The genius has a certain value for the species by adding to the stock of memes that can enrich the life of civilization.

Simonton analyzes the traits that geniuses have been seen to manifest throughout time and place and argues that these traits represent a reliable indicator that the person who manifests them will have productive success, the analogue to reproductive success in the strictly biological order:

> What is the typical creative genius like? According to the accumulated literature, creative geniuses are open to diverse experiences, display exceptional tolerance of ambiguity, seek out complexity and novelty, and can engage in defocused attention. They display a wide range of interests, including interests that extend beyond their immediate domain of creative activity. They are far more likely to be introverted than extroverted, and they may sometimes appear remote, withdrawn, and perhaps even antisocial. They also exhibit tremendous independence and autonomy, often refusing to conform to conventional norms — at time exhibiting a pronounced rebellious streak. They deeply love what they do, showing uncommon enthusiasm, energy, and commitment, usually appearing to friends and family as "workaholics." They are persistent in the face of obstacles and disappointments, but at the same time they are flexible

enough to alter strategies and tactics when repeated failure so dictates.[14]

The flexibility of the genius is manifest on the conscious level by a willingness to entertain a variety of stimuli that others might overlook as being irrelevant to more immediate plans and goals, while the desire to break through convention accelerates the process of bringing novel stimuli across more predictable boundaries.

The evolutionary value of genius should be clear, but the complex skein of motives that lead to enhanced productivity needs to be examined. Simonton notes that many geniuses come from dysfunctional homes and that very high percentages have lost a parent or caregiver before the age of fifteen, either literally or symbolically. This disruption can either produce a decrease in adaptive energy or, when the innate conditions are right, a rigorous struggle to compensate for instability by building an internal universe to replace the one that the hand of fate has taken away.

Some form of personal and cultural marginality is often part of the constitution of genius. Simonton notes, for example, that Unitarians, perhaps because of their marginal status within American religious culture, have produced a 100-fold number per capita of scientists compared to Roman Catholics, Baptists, and other so-called main line denominations.[15] Of course, it is also the case that Unitarians tend to be self-selective, that is, many are not members from birth but join the denomination in adulthood because of the premium it places on free inquiry in all of its forms.

From a cognitive standpoint, geniuses are highly tolerant of incubation states in which energy is lowered so that unconscious processes can take on some of the burden of creative transformation. This ties in with Jamison's previously mentioned argument that depression, the lowering of the energy threshold in consciousness, can indirectly aid the creative process by stilling the more manic processing of stimuli and ideas long enough so that the underlying principles can become welded into a new internal gestalt. Simonton puts this transformation in terms of Darwinian probabilities and their predictive values:

> Usually when people fail to solve a problem, their level of arousal increases — they experience excitement and

frustration. Such heightened emotion tends to constrict the width of attention. In addition, higher arousal tends to make high-probability associations even more probable and low-probability associations less so. Given that the solution requires the ability to look at the problem in an original way, the individual must attain a more relaxed state to allow the low-probability associations a reasonable chance to emerge. Hence, during the incubation period arousal may be lowered enough to make the person more able to take advantage of the sometimes subtle cues offered by the surrounding environment. In other words, the low-arousal state is more conducive to the Darwinian process needed to arrive at an insightful solution.[16]

The creative genius is thus someone who is capable of letting his or her arousal diminish to the point where novel and low-probability solutions can emerge. There is a kind of "variational blindness" that lets the psyche drift into broader and more capacious horizons of meaning and ideation. Consequently the noise of the more probable variations is not allowed to drown out the quieter signals coming from the unconscious where the lower-probability variations get played out. It follows from this model that genius functions according to standard Darwinian principles as they are applied to the creative generation of memes (public meanings and products) in the cultural sphere.

Moving toward my own definition of genius, I would assert that there are probably genetic elements (currently unknown), combined with deep psychological structures, quickened in most cases by manic-depressive disorder, and culminating in a creative power and energy that is over-determined and not to be out-maneuvered by the ego. There is a necessary dialectic between consciousness and the unconscious, combined with some kind of basic talent within some kind of discipline or craft. Finally, there must be a form of ultimate concern that rejects cost-benefit analyses as utterly beside the point.

We can ask the popular question: can a genius have a happy childhood? It is tempting to answer: no, out of the question. Of course, such an answer is simple-minded, but does point to some interesting possibilities. Happiness is itself an ambiguous phenomenon. We must ask: happiness in what respect? There is no such thing as "pure" happiness, although I am prompted to say that there is something fairly close to pure unhappiness. If genius, like non-genius, is a matter of drives and motives, then it follows that there is something unusual about the drives behind genius. Why are the drives so intense, and why are the motives behind creativity so tangled? The answer seems to be that childhood losses, whether literal like the death of a parent, or symbolic, like the loss of some psychic stability or connection, exert an uncanny and growing effect on the psyche of the genius. Where there is profound lack there is profound need to compensate for the lack. The French psychoanalyst Julia Kristeva talks of the lack that comes to every child when he or she must separate from the maternal and enter into the world of public language.[17] For the genius, something is added to this process, insuring that the loss of the maternal is felt more acutely.

The young nascent genius feels a double loss, that of the normal child as it moves away from the maternal ground, and that of the special circumstance of a unique inheritance, exacerbated by the pathology that is probably operating as well, i.e., manic-depressive disorder. This special circumstance may live only or partially in imagination, yet it has a peculiar force over the psyche. During adolescence, this lack is reinforced by the social order with its innumerable stings and forms of rejection. Since the young genius is most likely a manic-depressive, the sense of loss can assume almost psychotic proportions. Not only has the maternal presence fled, but also the cosmos itself seems an alien power that wishes to destroy the self.

This may seem a bit melodramatic, but my suspicion is that this is a very common experience among geniuses. The wound deepens and becomes what philosophers call an "ontological" wound, that is, a wound that is rooted in the very being of the world. The world is as broken asunder as the self, and the narcissistic hunger of the young genius manifests itself in a desire to heal this cosmic abyss through whatever means his or her talent allows. My formula is: first the wound, then the drive to heal it through the appropriate means, such as thought, pigment, words, sounds, etc. Genius is a response to unusual antecedent conditions, realities that seem to automatically call forth a response. The common piece of wisdom that asserts that all geniuses must suffer is on the mark. And the suffering is at both ends, in the tear that comes from childhood wounded narcissism, and in the creative process that always seems to be less powerful than the motivating conditions, that is, it repeatedly fails to heal the wound.

My sense is that the first manic or depressive attack works to tear open the wounded narcissism even more radically. What was once a human-all-too-human wound now becomes something almost greater than the human. Manic-depressive disorder provides the final condition for the drama of genius to unfold. If other conditions are not present, the disorder merely works out its savage logic in mute power. If ego-strength, high intelligence, trained talent, and other forces are also working within the psyche, the possibility of true genius emerges. Of course, genius must be paid for, and the cost is far higher than the host psyche realizes.

What do I mean by the high cost of genius? The answer is really quite simple. When the manic-depressive genius begins his or her project, there is the growing realization that the project is infinite in its demands while the psychic resources, no matter how fecund, are finite. Even with the presence of the anti-entropic unconscious, the creative process, which can only assimilate a finite amount of material at a time, must proceed in fits and starts to create an infinite that can never be realized. There is a kind of creative *not yet* that haunts the genius and that mocks all attained works. Geniuses are notoriously poor at assessing their own productions. For the manic-depressive genius, the work might be seen as truly great one moment, and mere dust the next. Even in hypomania there is the sense that the work and the objective will never fully converge. The lack manifest in the work is a painful reminder of the lack manifest in the psyche.

What of the issue of the correlation of genius and creativity with mental disorder? Neil Kessel argues for a kind of separatist position that asserts a disjunction between illness and great works. He states, "Talented people may turn to art because of madness therefore, or because of impending madness. But they achieve their greatness despite it, not because of it."[18] He sees mental illness as a reducing presence, one that lowers the ability of the self to create anything of social or lasting value. His view is rather one-dimensional and does not even begin to probe into the ways in which certain disorders can enter into the motivational soup. It is unfortunate that we are not only in an age that has a strong anti-genius bias, but one in which pathology is seen outside of the deeper teleological impulses of the psyche. If psychopathology were seen merely as a form of psychic entropy, then it would follow that it has no role to play in the anti-entropic forces of creativity. But this is a false view. Often a pathological condition can break through boundaries that can impede the creative act. It does not follow from this that pathology is always helpful to the psyche. For most individuals in fact, extreme pathology is simply destructive of possibility. But in the case of manic-depressive disorder and genius, there is a complicated synergy that is deeply teleological, even though there are also vast deserts of waste and emptiness.

Again it is imperative that we distinguish between thought and mood disorders when dealing with the genius question. The former, such as schizophrenia, are indeed less likely to help enhance creativity, except when the symptoms are in remission, while the latter disorders can be crucial in elevating talent into genius. The relation between the creative energies of the psyche and manic-depressive disorder is multi-layered and deeply ambiguous. There are gifts that come from mania and hypomania that cannot be attained any other way. And, as argued by Jamison, there are gifts that come from depression that are unique in their ability to sort through the abundant material that comes in through mania.

In the end, the thinkers of the early nineteenth century came closest to understanding the inner rhythms of genius, and its relation to ultimacy. The genius, according to such exemplars as Goethe, Coleridge, Blake, and Byron, stands in an original relation to nature, specifically, to the potencies of *natura naturans* (nature creating nature), and weaves this overwhelming material into finite but deeply resonating shapes that can enter into the conscious life of the species. The unconscious of nature enters into the unconscious of the creative psyche and pushes upward into the structures of consciousness that use the tools at its disposal to exhibit something that can only *hint* at the powers of nature. The contemporary abjection of romantic theory says more about envy and the abjection of greatness than it does about the creators and their work. Of the four figures mentioned, there is strong evidence that Coleridge, Blake, and Byron were manic-depressives.

What of skill and talent and its relation to genius? I am asking about the talent of the genius, not about the opposition between the two realities. More specifically, how does a young potential genius, perhaps before his or her first major manic or depressive attack, come to choose the talent or craft that will bring some relief from the pressures that come from the narcissistic wound? It seems clear that there may be a genetic component in many cases. One's medium of expression may be encoded within the individual system, although such encoding could be incomplete or fragmented in its unfolding. My suspicion is that there is also a strong reinforcement pattern at work. The Austrian philosopher

Ludwig Wittgenstein, who grew up in an extremely privileged family in Vienna, had the makings of a polymath. He was competent in music, some of the technical sciences, language, and, much later, architecture. Yet he recounts how he one day discovered that he could think, and think more powerfully and clearly than the people around him. When this tendency was reinforced, he made his choice for philosophy, although "choice" may be too weak a word. Since, as I have hinted, he may have been manic-depressive, he was compelled forward in his choice with great seriousness. He was also obsessed with the genius myth, and frequently endured periods of self-laceration because he felt that he did not live up to the demands of the myth. An excellent recent biography of Wittgenstein has the appropriate title, *The Duty of Genius* to denote this tension within his psyche.[19] Its author, Ray Monk recounts an experience of the young Wittgenstein that set its stamp on his psyche:

> Until he was fourteen, he was content to feel himself surrounded by genius, rather than possessed of it. A story he told in later life concerned an occasion when he was woken at three in the morning by the sound of a piano. He went downstairs to find [his brother] Hans performing one of his own compositions. Hans's concentration was manic. He was sweating, totally absorbed, and completely oblivious of Ludwig's presence. The image remained for Ludwig a paradigm of what it was like to be possessed of genius.[20]

Wittgenstein was also obsessed with the above-described image of Beethoven in the throws of his creative demons. The concept of "possession" is crucial for our definition of genius because it denotes a state bordering on psychic inflation in which the rich material from the unconscious, both of the self and of nature, enters into the conscious psyche. If that fiery magma (to use Jung's image) is met by measured and finely honed talent it takes on living form. The theologian Paul Tillich coined the phase "gestalt of grace" to denote that moment in the creative process when a living form encountered a kind of grace-filled ultimacy that established its link to the depth dimension of the world.

At this point, several necessary features of genius have emerged as central to my account. There is the experiencing of the almost inevitable narcissistic wound that comes when any child, male or female, must endure the imperial narcissism of one or both parents. This wound becomes deepened when the stirrings of the power of genius to create are felt. Kristeva argues that the child emerges into language (perhaps some other medium like music or paint) and begins to negotiate with this cultural code. As she puts it in her succinct way, "There is language instead of the good breast."[21] The loss of the breast, as a connecting link to the ground of the world, must be replaced by a variety of substitute strategies. For the emerging genius, these strategies take on a special fascination, and the conscious self seeks for that medium that will bring about the most healing power. This aspect need not be thematic, but it will be present as the adolescent probes into language, sounds, pigments, shapes, movements, etc. Once a medium is embraced, the training process begins. This too is teleological, that is, the self uses it's training not as an end in itself but to deepen the healing process in which the new medium becomes the substitute breast. The concept of "breast" could appear almost ludicrous here if it is literalized. The function of the breast is to connect the alienated self with the heart of nature; it is rarely a simple longing to return to the biological mother.

In addition to the psychological traits of the basic psychic wound and its exacerbation in genius, we have the presence of high creativity, centered on talent and medium. When the manic-depressive code starts to unfold in the self, we get an increase of energy combined with an almost messianic sense of mission. This messianic secret is common to all varieties of genius and is manifest in an awareness that one's work has been called-forth by forces greater than the individual self. The religious idea of a call is something that all geniuses understand, even if it may not be understood is a strictly religious sense. Where does the call come from? It comes from the powers of the unconscious that are responding to the deep wound within the psyche. Without the antecedent wound, the psyche would have no reason to enter into the dialectic of dynamics and form that can lead to genius.

Let me attempt to describe the creative process of genius as it moves into its maturity. This stage can exist at almost any point in the life history of the individual. It is a commonplace to talk of the early maturation of mathematicians, and the much later one of philosophers or writers, etc. There are, of course, intense periods of high creativity, and fallow periods in which almost nothing is accomplished. Jamison plots these phases on a series of graphs that show how productivity follows manic-depressive cycles in an almost one-to-one correlation.[22]

My description of the hypo-manic phase will assume that it can take place anywhere along the life history of the genius.

The inner and outer work goes something like this. Pressure intensifies from the original narcissistic wound, exposing incompleteness in the self because it could not develop its own healthy autonomy and narcissism. In the genius, who has by now had at least one manic episode, the initial pressure is increased by the sheer force of the affective disorder that tears open the original wound in new ways, perhaps through paranoia or strong libidinal surges. It has become clear to the genius that human relations cannot heal this doubled wound. The transference relation that alone could move toward the third reality of continuity cannot take place because of a lack of trust in what the transference brings. In my view, the genius refocuses all of his or her transference energy onto the creative work because it is here that the fundamental trust between self and other can take place. This rethinking of the transference should not be too jarring. Kristeva has argued that the proper reader can develop a transference relation to a text.[23] In my extension of her view, the transference is at the heart of the creation of one's own work.

The double wound is addressed by the transference to the unfolding work. The talent that goes with genius, and that is used by genius, takes its specific medium in hand to shape the energies that seem to be coming from the region of the wound itself. Both the wound and the creative surge are located within the unconscious. In another dimension, the wound is located in the space between consciousness and the unconscious, especially since the unconscious is seen to be other to the sovereign ego and its small kingdom of consciousness. To concretize this structure, I will focus on the emergence of language in the act of writing, where the "good breast" is replaced by a more generic power.

The transference in place, and the wound beginning to recede as language takes its place within the economy of the psyche, the task becomes that of shaping this powerful deliverer into a work that exhibits wisdom, power, and transforming energy. Within the heart of the momentarily stilled wound emerges a surging *not yet* that compels the psyche forward into a free space of creative energy.[24] The abyss of the wound gets transfigured into images, metaphors, names, and structures that give it a new kind of voice. The voice of the writer is multi-valent, and often labyrinthine in its subtle transformation of the lack that lies within the self.

From the lack, the wound that opens up the not yet, comes language that arches back to the origin while simultaneously moving in the opposite direction toward a kingdom of meaning that lies in the future. Put in more prosaic terms: the writing project is filled with a deep restlessness that comes from the lack within the self. The hope is that the completion of a rounded and whole work will fill in the lack and still its desperate rhythm. This hope is part of the sheer cunning of nature that spurs the genius on, full well "knowing" that there will be no stillness at the end of the journey. On one level, the genius knows the rules of the game that he or she has been forced to play, while on another level there is a wonderful kind of amnesia that makes it possible to hope against hope that this time the rules will change.

The product completed, it stands over and against the self as an autonomous, and often abjected, reality. Soon the product betrays its producer, and the full presence of the doubled wound returns, only to spur on yet another creative effort. There is a certain cruelty to this sport of nature. It would be like giving a gifted racehorse a shot of a dangerous stimulant (mania or hypo-mania) so that it can win a special race. As soon as the race is over, the prize is taken away and the horse may have to endure another injection of something that can elevate and damage at the same time. It is profoundly naive to think that genius is less driven than our hypothetical racehorse. The analogy breaks down, of course, because the genius is at least aware of the Faustian side of the bargain.

For me, the best literary expression of the demonic side of the ambiguous gift is Thomas Mann's 1948 novel Doctor Faustus. The protagonist, Adrian Leverkühn, a brilliant musician, makes a pact with the devil so that he can write the greatest music of his generation. Things get more complex because he is also a trained theologian, and hence is aware of the stakes involved in fulfilling his genius by entering into a transference with the demonic underside of the world. There is also the hint derived from the life of Nietzsche, that Leverkühn knowingly contracted syphilis so that his mind would be driven to new heights by the invading organisms. Mann long associated genius with physical and mental disease, and his literary formulations richly add to our current picture. It certainly feels as if some demonic forces are at work in the creative process, and that there is a covenant with something that could be malevolent to human need. However, as Tillich has so brilliantly argued, the demonic can only have power because it is rooted in the holy.[25]

This religious aspect of the genius phenomenon has not been explored enough, perhaps because the categories used from the religious side seem too denominationally burdened. But this sense is actually an illusion. All geniuses struggle with the "demonic" and the "holy," regardless of how they are named. The forces that come from the unconscious of the self and nature are demonic insofar as they shatter form. These forces are holy insofar as they create new form out of the ashes of the old forms. In language, the demonic and the holy are entwined, at least in the greatest works, precisely because language can house all contraries within one exhibitive array.

Is there any grace in this process? Grace does appear in fragmentary ways in the work itself. But grace is rarely an unambiguous gift. The creative process is given moments of grace-filled power, even if the genius is often oblivious to their presence. Again, amnesia is very much a part of both manic-depressive disorder and genius. Without some very specific forms of forgetting, the work could not continue to unfold. Grace moments would be too tempting, too likely to pull the creator back to the comforts of origin, the good breast. They must flash through the language, be briefly acknowledged by the creator who is always on the run, and then forgotten so that further work can unfold. Writing has its own unique form of restless melancholy.

This melancholy is well attested in suicide statistics. Of all the forms of creative activity, that of writing, especially poetry where the creator lives precariously on the very edges of language, has the highest suicide rate.[26] My own somewhat preliminary theory as to the correlation between language creation and a tendency toward suicide is that language is the most tenuous and yet omnivorous human mode of creation. It seems to promise us the world in a fully configured shape, yet it remains especially vulnerable to the counter-pull of the mute origin that can lure the creator toward death. Language is far less bound to space and time than other media of expression. It is as if all writers of stature have their own version of the death mother, waiting in the interstices of utterance to shatter carefully built form.

We have been rotating the phenomenon of genius through several horizons of meaning. In each case some traits have emerged as fairly recurrent. Preeminent is the inner tension between a lost power of origin and the surging and restless power of the not yet. This tension enters into the product as well. The work sustains traits that come from the longed-for period before the narcissistic wound, while also housing mobile traits that come from the open future. I strongly subscribe to the romantic view that all great works are fragmentary expressions of a longing that is religious at its heart. The finite/infinite correlation of the product is a concretization of the finite/infinite dialectic of consciousness and its relation with the unconscious. This harks back to the concept of "depth" introduced earlier.

If a great work speaks to a great interpreter, it is because the resonating power of the lost and hoped-for infinite speaks across time and place. Put in very stark terms, our species needs works of genius in order to find some way stations on the journey toward an infinite that remains elusive yet continues to make its ambiguous appearance whenever meaning becomes incarnate in a particular work. The infinite is found in the depths of the world rather than in some illusory vertical transcendence of the world. If the reader finds this too romantic, I can only ask once again about our human motives. Just why do we return again and again to those epiphanies and powers that come from great cultural products?

In answering this question, it is important that we ask the corollary question: just whom is the genius creating for? If "we," perhaps a small group, are the assimilators of this work, how does the great creator find this "we" and how is it housed in the mind as an ideal? The process of creation is not a simple one involving symmetry between the not yet surrounding the work, and some real or alleged audience waiting to encounter it. The transference relation between the manic-depressive genius and his or her work always takes precedence over the issue of audience. The genius develops something like an ideal assimilator, usually a projection of his or her whole self, for the work in process. That is, the creative process is first and foremost centered around the integrity of the product, and secondarily on the assimilator who turns out to be the future psychic state of the genius. The ideal reader, viewer, listener, etc, is the future self that comes out of the not yet. The genius creates both the work and its assimilator in the process of creation. The much talked about time lag between the work of genius and its recognition is a product of the gap between the ideal future self and the external world of potential assimilators. This may sound like a rather narcissistic and tight loop in which the genius creates out of a broken self for the self he or she would like to be, but the deeper logic is that the broken self and the ideal self are aspects of the larger corporate self of the community.

Manic-depressive disorder enters into this loop in a clear way. The genius begins the process of moving something potential into something actual and powerful, evocative of meaning and transforming energy. The disorder hammers away at the process of creation, calling forth counter-moves that can compensate for the ambiguous gifts of mania and depression. The psychic compensation, since it has so much material to deal with, makes it possible to create a work of unusual scope and richness. The ecstatic horizon opened up by hypomania can be trimmed and shaped in new ways that leaves a product that is clearly in the not yet. In the transference relation both the genius and the work condition each other in a dialectic that continues until either death or the victory of the disease over its host. The so-called closed loop between creator and product is actually open on all sides, and radiates out to potential assimilators.

Thus the ideal future self of the genius joins with the gifted assimilators who can participate in the traits of the work because they too are moving toward an unclarified not yet. In most cases, Dickens being one of the notable exceptions, this process is always slow and often painful. For the manic-depressive genius, the sheer inertia in the social body, causing it to ignore the work because of its own incomprehension or indifference, can lead to thoughts of suicide. The reason for this is clear. If the most precious product of the transference is rejected or ignored, while countless mediocre products find their way to publishers, concert stages, galleries, theater stages, etc., then the sense of betrayal is acute. The choice is to either redouble efforts with the help of psychic inflation, or to leave the stage entirely through suicide. Non-geniuses may find this bifurcation way over the mark, but that is because their lives are not totally invested in a creative and non-personal transference that allows for no others. Put differently, the creative transference allows for neither adultery nor divorce, only success, psychic inflation, or, in many cases, death.

The accumulation of products in a lifetime does not still the energy that comes from the not yet. It is as if the genius is caught in a no win form of works righteousness in which each offering, lifted up out of the transference, is the one that will win the approval of the gods, however envisioned. It does not. It merely stands as a way station on the way toward something that is always elusive. For Beethoven, for example, it was not enough to write nine brilliant symphonies, there also had to be highly complex string quartets, not to mention numerous other forms. And even here, there was the sense that this did not fill-in the not yet. Another way of putting this is to say that for the non-genius the not yet is much smaller in scope and in energy, while for the genius it seems to be both infinite and expanding. The paradox of a growing infinite is well known in mathematics. It is a central phenomenon in our study of the genius phenomenon. We will see its uncanny shapes in looking at the lives and products of two who served it, almost always against their will.

C. TWO CASE STUDIES OF MANIC-DEPRESSIVE GENIUS: NEWTON AND SRI RAMAKRISHNA

As we turn toward particular figures, individuals who were clearly in the genius category and who also suffered from manic-depressive disorder, we will see these features of creativity return in a rich variety of guises. The infinite longing for a healing that can transform the wound of the self is expressed in almost any medium or form of articulation. The creation of an encompassing theory of celestial mechanics can be as much a movement toward the infinite *not yet* as the shaping of color and texture, or the architectonic formulation of sounds in a symphony or string quartet. Creatures without the basic ontological wound, the abyss that separates the lost object from the promise of the *not yet*, cannot experience the firestorm of the creative act. Nor do they need to. Manic-depressive disorder does its uncanny work in our species alone, and only in our species, at least in the known universe, does genius join itself with this disease to wrest meaning from entropy and sheer drift. I want to stress the heroic quality of this holy/unholy wedding, this *mysterium coniunctionis*. The relation between genius and manic-depressive disorder has a sacramental core, even if the individual who labors under this marriage may ofttimes be oblivious to its presence.

I have selected two very different individuals for my case studies. Newton, who advanced both mathematics and physics as he created the first grand scientific theoretical edifice of the century of genius, was a profoundly neurotic genius who manifested a number of manic-depressive traits as his brilliance propelled to the forefront of European thought. At the same time he was a practicing alchemist, a theological heretic (adopting the Arian view that Christ was a unique spiritual body and not a person in the trinity), and a man capable of extreme emotional and political violence to his real or alleged rivals.

Lesser known to most readers is the nineteenth century Bengali saint Sri Ramakrishna who indirectly spawned the twentieth century Vedanta movement through his disciple Vivekananda. An illiterate peasant, Sri Ramakrishna from early on in his life had intense experiences of divine intoxication in which the power of *shakti* (the feminine principle of a kind of divine energy) coursed through his body and soul. He was quickly recognized as an *avatar* (incarnation of god) by a small but rapidly growing band of followers. Yet strong manic-depressive features also marked his religious and mystical states, which I consider to be quite genuine. He had an unusual emotional volatility and a highly charged but sublimated eroticism that colored his relationships with his disciples. His personal devotion to the female goddess Kali had features that are reminiscent of Newton's quest for the lost maternal in his scientific work. And like Newton he probed in an unrelenting way into the fundamental structures of the religious universe in order to find a treasure that time could not corrupt.

There are other striking points of comparison between the scientific and religious geniuses of Newton and Sri Ramakrishna that will unfold with our case studies. Throughout, my concern is to show precisely how manic-depressive disorder can, in certain rare cases like these, actually aid its carrier in the process of finding truths that can be of direct value to the rest of the human species. The case of Sri Ramakrishna is especially sensitive because he has a large international following today, and conversely there have been efforts to reduce his religious insights to forms of psychopathology. My concern is the exact opposite, namely, to show that his extreme psychological modalities may well have been a divine instrument by which the power of Brahman (the Hindu term for god in its guise as absolute indifferent ground beyond being and nonbeing) became manifest.

Further, I want to show that the concept of genius can be applied to a certain class of saints (but not all) who have an unusually intense and creative relationship to the energy of the divine. This relationship is manifest in behavior, utterances, writing (in some cases), leadership, and the creative reconstruction of the self. The collision between the archetype of genius with that of sainthood is perhaps the most fascinating in the human order. And it is my contention that Sri Ramakrishna, the simple uneducated worshiper of the goddess Kali, was in fact a religious genius of a unique order.

C. a. ISAAC NEWTON: COSMOLOGY AND DIVINIZATION

We will begin our case studies with one of the most perplexing and fascinating figures of the so-called Century of Genius, Sir Isaac Newton.[27] In the history of Euro-centric science, Newton is regarded as perhaps the greatest mind of the past several centuries. Yet few historians of science understand the role that manic-depressive disorder played in the development of his work, and in the shaping of his other concerns such as alchemy or the complex and then precarious finances of the Bank of England.

When examining the long life of Newton (he lived to be 84) it soon becomes clear that he had a prodigious drive to conquer both his inner and outer environment. He alternated between extreme depressions and mania or hypomania that propelled him to the forefront of the rapidly emerging world of the new physics. From his childhood on he often fell into violent rages, literally striking the people around him. Many of his moods could be characterized as mixed states, as is to be expected with this disorder, and drove his behavior in contradictory directions at the same time. He spent much of his life on the edges of society, almost always alienating the few people who chose to get close to him. At the same time, he showed an amazing integrity in his inner beliefs, refusing to compromise them even when his very career was at stake. The most famous example is that of his hidden Unitarian belief that the Christian trinity was non biblical and an invention of heretical minds in the early church. His academic position at Trinity College Cambridge was jeopardized because he was compelled, along with all other professors, to affirm the 39 Articles of the Church of England. He narrowly avoided this public debacle by having acquaintances connected with the Royal Court change the law itself so that holders of his prestigious Lucasian Chair of Mathematics (the same one now held by Stephen Hawking) would not have to take the same oath as the holders of other academic chairs. Had the law not been changed, he surely would not have made what to him was an unbiblical pledge. The happy result in this case shows both integrity and cunning, a combination we see in Newton again and again.

There is some indirect evidence that Newton's father was a manic-depressive.[28] His father died before he was born, leaving his genetic material but little else in the way of wealth. Newton was born prematurely on Christmas day in 1642 in a little village in Lincolnshire. He struggled for a week, hanging between life and death before he was out of the woods. His mother remarried when he was three, but Newton's stepfather showed him little love. He was both physically and psychically dislocated before he could get a real purchase on his life or environment.

His mother moved with her new husband to another village, and left Newton to be raised by his relatives. His mother rarely visited and his relationship with his stepfather was never warm or cordial. This dual abandonment, the death of his father and the seeming flight of his mother, is a motif that, as noted above, is often found in the lives of geniuses. The wound opened up by the loss of the maternal in particular marked Newton throughout his life and may have lead to his utter failure to establish an erotic relationship with any woman.

The pattern of loneliness that haunted Newton until his dying day emerged very early on in his life. Richard S. Westfall, perhaps the leading scholar on Newton's life and work, states the case quite forcefully:

> . . . Newton was a tortured man, an extremely neurotic personality who teetered always, at least through middle age, on the verge of breakdown. No one has to stretch credulity excessively to believe that the second marriage and departure of his mother could have contributed enormously to the inner torment of the boy already bewildered by the realization that he, unlike others, had no father.[29]

The loss of the power of origin, of the "good breast" in Kristeva's sense, provided the inner dynamic that accelerated the disorder. Newton's boyhood was characterized by periods of intense introspection and contemplation, punctuated with violent outbursts against the members of his household, especially servants. His mother betrayed him, in his eyes, by quickly marrying a disagreeable man who had more interest in the Newton estate than in the son.

Another perspective on these first few years comes from the brilliant psychoanalytic scholar Frank E. Manuel. His focus is less on relating Newton to the history of science and more on the inner dynamics of Newton the solitary thinker. Like Westfall, but with a different conceptual horizon, he stresses the centrality of abandonment in marking both the young and the mature Newton:

> The shakiness of Newton's self-esteem throughout his life may have one of its origins in an infantile failure to be satiated at the breast and in his littleness.... The loss of his mother to another man [Barnabas Smith] was a traumatic event in Newton's life from which he never recovered. And at any moment in his later experience when he was confronted by the possibility of being robbed of what was his, he reacted with a violence commensurate with the terror and anger generated by his first searing deprivation.[30]

Let us tabulate the losses in the young man before his fourth birthday. He loses his father to death before he is born. He arrives in this world early and must overcome his physical littleness and vulnerability. His beloved mother takes on another husband who is indifferent to him. His mother moves to her new husband's home, leaving him in the hands of older relatives who have no special attachment to him. His estate is in jeopardy, and his own way in the world is threatened by the sheer inertia of his environment that would see him tied to the life of the farm forever. He responds by sinking into an unbelievably complex inner world that has no connection with the worlds of the farm or the church. His stepfather is a clergyman who uses the church for his own ends, thus giving Newton a permanent dislike of the clergy. The only thing of value that he derived from his stepfather was the use of his large library.

Still, in spite of the wrenching loss of the conditions of origin, he moves forward by probing into the natural world around him. The transference energy that he might have given to one or more parents gets refocused with unusual intensity to the phenomena he observes around him. Like the young Wittgenstein, Newton was fascinated with mechanical processes and built a number of devices that he could use to learn about the forces in nature. He was particularly interested in experimenting with water clocks, kites, and sundials, i.e., in issues of motion and time.[31] It is almost as if the natural world, because of its astonishing regularity, can assume the powers of origin because nature will not betray like parents do.

The issue of his education certainly vexed the family. He wanted to pursue the life of scholarship, but not that of divinity. The family wanted him to remain on the farm, yet were pessimistic about his abilities to run such a complex affair. He went to a local grammar school, at Grantham, at age twelve. While there his work oscillated between an obsession with his gadgets, at which point his schoolwork fell behind, and an obsession with beating the other boys at the academic game, at which point his work flourished. In either case, the students and teachers were certainly astonished at the strange boy in their midst.

Upon graduation he set his mind on Cambridge. By age 18 he was ready to start work at Trinity College, which had one of the strongest reputations at the university. He was admitted on what today might be called a work-study grant, except that the work done in those days was not like that of working in the library or for a professor, but that of waiting on senior students in a highly demeaning capacity. The so-called subsizar was the lowest student on the social totem pole. Given Newton's anti-social yet haughty nature, this status must have been galling. Yet he had escaped the stifling atmosphere of Grantham and Lincolnshire for a world that was to remain central to him for most of the rest of his life. He remained deeply introverted around his own projects, and his roommates left little information about him, other than to note his propensity to spend days on end with little sleep. He rarely laughed and had nothing like a social life, especially, as noted, with women, whom he studiously seemed to avoid.

In the years between 1662 and 1664 (age 20-22), his strange work habits combined with the unfolding of his manic-depressive disorder to produce a severe self-lacerating depression, followed by hyper activity and a complete breakdown.[32] His super-ego pounded away at him with delusions of extreme sinfulness and corruption. He took little care for his health, often staring directly at the sun until he was partially blind. A kind of bodily masochism emerged in this period that served as an outward mark of the inner travail. In one infamous experiment he inserted a knife into his eye socket to create pressure on the optical nerve to see what light effects would ensue.[33] When in a manic or hypo-manic period he would totally ignore his food and spin out ideas in far greater abundance than could be integrated. Sleep became a luxury, not to be indulged in when ideas were afoot.

Supporting all of this work was his self-education in mathematics and physics. He rarely attended lectures and filled in any

Genius and Creativity 133

pertinent gaps in his knowledge by intense reading and analysis. He quickly evolved to the point where no one could teach him anyway. His physical experiments in optics set new standards that came to dominate work in England and on the Continent. He seemed to have an obsession with finding an encompassing conceptual framework that would put all uncertainty and ignorance to rout. Manuel provides his own theory as to the motive behind the emerging physics:

> A chief source of Newton's desire to know was his anxiety before and his fear of the unknown. When he learned the laws of his God he was able to allay those fears; but his anxiety often kept pace with his discoveries and was perpetually renewed.[34]

This characteristic is in keeping with the inner logic of genius. The world threatens to undo the imperial ego and its project by swamping the self with unknown content. This abjected unknown is, of course, the power of the unconscious as it gets projected on the matter to be thought. Yet, at the same time, the universe as disclosed by Newton's celestial mechanics, also embodies the unknown. But that in itself does not provide sufficient motive for the over-determined work of the psyche. Like all manic-depressive geniuses, Newton tried to wrestle the *not yet* to the ground by giving it immediacy and concrete shape. Each shape that emerged from his analytic work became protean and threatened to undo the security attained. He would track down optical structures as minute as a hundredth of an inch so that they would not get away from him.[35] There is a clear predatory quality to his scientific experiments that seem to show a profound ambivalence about nature. On the one hand, nature is the object of the great transference energy of his life, while on the other it is like some kind of coy lover whose coyness, in his case, ignites a desire to conquer by violence and control. For Newton, and I would not generalize to others, precision and violence go hand in hand.

In addition he manifested strong traits of obsessive-compulsive personality disorder, particularly in his insistence, whether working in astronomy, mechanics, optics, mathematics, or the manufacture of non-counterfitable coins, on complete control of any possible variable that might thwart his plans for total understanding or total power over men or materials. His alchemical experiments, which often took up far more of his energy than his work in science, involved the most exacting control of ofttimes volatile and dangerous substances. Whatever he tackled, he assaulted with a kind of military precision and the will to dominate. In his later years when he was appointed as Master of the Royal Mint, housed in the Tower of London, he applied what today would be called "efficiency management" to the labor process. In the words of Michael White:

> Newton's first concern was to increase the efficiency of this process by carefully watching each step and carrying out a time-and-motion study on the system. He calculated where and how improvements could be made, noting that, if the movement of the press and the action of the coiner were coordinated properly, a single coiner could flick out a coin and insert a new blank between fifty and fifty-five times a minute. Writing in one of his many notebooks covering the work at the Mint, he analyzed the processes to the finest detail: "Two mills with 4 millers, 12 horses, two horse keepers, 3 cutters, 2 flatters, 8 sizers, one nealer, three blanchers, two markers, two presses with fourteen labourers to pull at them can coin after the rate of a thousand weight or *300 lib* [pounds] of money per diem."[36]

This obsession with minutia was consistent throughout his long life, enabling him to validate his mathematical theories of the heavens with precise measurements of astronomical bodies, and making it possible for him to detail the reflecting and refracting properties of light down to the smallest details possible with the current technology. And he would quickly become angry with anyone who he thought was withholding crucial data from him concerning subjects he wanted to quantify.

In 1665 Newton made a momentous decision to return to his maternal home in Woolsthorpe. A plague was descending upon Cambridge, and the officials of the university were slowly advocating that students and faculty withdraw. For two years Newton, then in his early twenties, worked with manic intensity on the foundations of his calculus. By the end of this period, referred to as his *anni mirabiles*, he had moved to the front ranks of European mathematicians. While he remained unknown, it seems that in his own mind he knew that he had no serious competitors. The evidence points to at least a sustained hypo-manic period with little sleep and with fasting. At the same time, his work and writing were punctuated with periods in which little or no work was done. A tentative guess is that he was a rapid cycler, and that his manic or hypo-manic states moved him toward grand religious ideas that served to augment, but not necessarily support, his work on the calculus. He retained a fascination for both alchemy and the biblical prophecies, working out schemes in both fields that show some marks of psychic inflation.

This is also a period of self-discovery. Newton was an autodidact of the highest order and drew little inspiration or help from the people around him. His mentor relations were deeply ambiguous and tenuous, as his own inner drives propelled him past and through any possible teachers. It has been noted that Newton's return to his mother's house played a powerful role in enabling him to probe into the most recalcitrant and multi-layered problems in mechanics and calculus. The return to the "good breast" was also a movement forward into the maternal analogue within an absolute space and time that enveloped and protected all things subject to change. Insofar as manic-depressive disorder often confers a sense of private destiny, Newton was able to gain access to his true role and to his standing within the world of ideas. His disorder and his genius reinforced his sense of his stature. Westfall gives a wonderful capsule description of this realization:

> In 1665, as he realized the full extent of his achievement in mathematics, Newton must have felt the burden of genius settle upon him, the terrible burden which he would have to carry in the isolation it imposed for more than sixty years. From this time on, there is little evidence of the futile efforts to ingratiate himself with his peers that appeared intermittently during his grammar school and undergraduate days. Accepting as sufficient his one close relationship with his chamber-fellow Wickins, he abandoned himself, as he had always longed to do, to the imperious demands of truth.[37]

What I find especially pertinent here is the correlation of hypomania, psychic inflation, and an accurate self-understanding that would transform his social relations for the rest of his life. The power of the disorder is one that can have positive fruits, both in terms of the work, and in terms of self-images that have some evidential force. Psychic inflation can always cut both ways, on the one hand filling the ego with undigested and unearned unconscious content, while at other times, or in other selves, bringing the whole self into an awareness of both its manifest and latent powers. Needless to say, this is extremely tricky terrain to negotiate. Yet Newton seems to have made the right decisions about his work and stature based on the wealth of psychic and scientific material presented to him by his hypomanias.

But one should not place too much emphasis on his stay in the maternal home at this time. While he continued to make headway toward the theory of universal gravitation, he was still two decades away from writing the great *Principia*. He returned to his rooms at Cambridge after the plague had left London and the surrounding areas and continued with his work in optics and alchemy. One of the central psychological facets of Newton's personality became solidified in his twenties, namely, that of keeping an intensely private and somewhat intellectually dangerous world to himself and a small circle of trusted acquaintances. Earlier, I noted his Arianism, which disqualified him for any academic position, let alone the one he attained at age 27, the Lucasian Chair of Mathematics. But in addition to this arch heresy was his interest in alchemy as a spiritual discipline that could unlock the secrets of nature. Scholars like Michael White have argued that some of the inspiration for Newton's mature conception of gravity as action at a distance (rather than being a function of Descartes' vortices) had its roots in the kinds of chemical attractions he observed in his alchemical retorts. Yet alchemy was, even in Newton's time, politically and theologically suspect and many of his letters were penned using a pseudonym.

Newton also, as noted, had an obsession with biblical prophecies and constantly worked and reworked the biblical material to see if he could gain access to the time-line that would predict the end of the whore of Babylon (the Roman Catholic Church which he loathed) and the return of Christ. He continued with these arcane speculations right up to the last weeks of his life and would on the very rare occasion share some of his speculations with others. For some reason he lighted on the idea that the ground plan of the Temple of Solomon contained a code for the time-line that God had established for the world. The curious feature of Newton's mind, to us at least, is that he did not seem to see any contradiction between his alchemical studies and his biblical research, let alone a conflict with either of these and his work on the calculus and celestial mechanics.

One of the most significant features of manic-depressive disorder is that its carriers have a tendency to exhibit psychic inflation in the hypo-manic or manic phases. Newton went way beyond having a strong ego or secure self-image into a state that could sometimes come close to self-divinization. Michael White gives an intriguing, and I think convincing, argument as to why Newton rejected the trinity, an argument that ties in perfectly with the issue of psychic inflation:

> But why was Newton so fanatically opposed to the concept of the Trinity? Such obsessiveness could not be based only upon a distaste for the illogical. Would it be unreasonable to suggest that he wanted to identify himself with Christ? After all, was he not the only child of a dead father, born on Christmas Day and (so he believed) possessed of unparalleled ability and unique talents? And could it be that identification with his long-dead father — a man he had never known, but whom he knew was uneducated — was so repugnant to him that he could not contemplate the notion of a Trinity, a concept involving not just attachment to 'the Father' but the sharing of identity? Newton, the man who had adopted the pseudonym 'One Holy God,' [in his alchemical correspondences] was a perpetual loner. He could not even show love towards his mother; he felt only disgust at her betrayal. The possibility of unity or amalgamation could only engender feelings of abhorrence in this most individualistic and private of men.[38]

It is surely astonishing how much energy Newton poured into proving, from biblical and church sources, the fallacy of the doctrine of the trinity. His interests were over determined and went way beyond the need to establish his theological claims in the context of the contrary views of the Church of England. Of course, had the sheer radicalness of his views become known outside of a small select circle, his career could have been shipwrecked.

Newton also exhibited the manic-depressive trait of paranoia, even though the shifting political context of his time has to be taken into account. The period after the English civil war and the eventual Restoration of the Monarchy brought some stability, but with each succession to the throne the theological climate changed. In a certain sense, Newton served at the discretion of both the University and the King or Queen, although the true ratio of power was often contested, for example, around the issue of admitting a Roman Catholic student to

Cambridge for advanced study, with the King (the Roman Catholic James II) pushing for admission and the University attempting to hold firm against the King. (The King won.)[39] Whatever religious tolerance was practiced was only done so within very narrow limits, and Arianism was *never* accepted during Newton's lifetime.

But beyond some justified paranoia about his theological and alchemical views, Newton developed suspicions toward many of the men who were actually trying to help him with his career. He was capable of sustaining resentments and fears of rivals for decades at a time, for example, in the case of the flamboyant astronomer and self-promoter Robert Hooke who claimed to have invented both the inverse square law and the reflecting telescope before Newton (neither claim being true). He could work tirelessly behind a rival's back and marshal forces against him while in public maintaining an image of aloofness from such petty matters and tactics. This sheer ferocity to protect what he thought was his god-given intellectual property and priority reached its sad peak in his highly public feud with the German philosopher Leibniz.

Genius, especially when it is intensified by manic-depressive disorder, is not noted for welcoming challenges to its sovereignty. One need only think of the Freud/Jung relationship (neither of whom, however, were manic-depressive) to see a contemporary version of the perhaps inevitable clash that occurs when two persons of equal talent and raw intellectual power try to occupy the same cultural space. When Leibniz came upon the scene with his own version of the calculus that proved so crucial for celestial mechanics, Newton could barely contain his rage, marshaling all of his friends in the Royal Society, of which he was president in his later years, to discredit Leibniz and to establish his absolute priority. He succeeded in stacking the deck against Leibniz, with the "impartial" Royal Society establishing Newton's priority, but history took its revenge by using Leibniz's system of notion rather than Newton's. But again, Newton's response went beyond simple professional rivalry or jealously and showed the same traits of self-divinization that Michael White has described.

Throughout his long life, Newton was a hypochondriac, and used his knowledge of chemistry and alchemy to develop his own unique forms of self-medication. For the manic-depressive, self-medication almost always comes with the territory, as the lack of control over feeling states can sometimes be intolerable. White quotes from Newton's long-time chamber-mate Wickens:

> Wickens was witness to some of his methods in Cambridge: "He sometimes suspected himself to be inclining to a consumption, & the medicine he made use of was the Lacatellus Balsam which, when he had composed himself, he would now & then melt in quantity about a quarter of a pint & so drink it." This, it turns out, was a delicious combination of turpentine, rose-water, beeswax, olive oil, sack [sherry] and red sandalwood. Newton considered it so powerful that, as well as drinking it, he often applied it externally, finding it useful for "green wounds" and "the bite of a mad dog." He also wrote in praise of the curative powers of opium.[40]

It is not clear how often Newton medicated himself, but the use of opium gives pause. He suffered from extreme insomnia, sometimes staying awake in a working mania that could last a week or longer. Even when he slept, it was often only for a few hours at a time. Perhaps his use of opium was an attempt to slow down his manic energy long enough for him to gain equilibrium. The irony is that Newton had fairly stable good health throughout his 84 years and only failed right at the end.

The issue of psychological types was developed in the previous chapter in the context of a discussion of Jung's views on manic-depression. There it was argued that in the manic state the inferior function becomes activated in a crude and chaotic form, often producing serious complications for the individual involved. It is possible that Newton was an introvert (consistent with Simonton's theory of genius) of the thinking type with sensing as the secondary or auxiliary function. From this it follows that extraverted feeling was his inferior function and the one most likely to appear during a manic attack. His highly emotional rages, often out of all relation to their stimulus, took over his psyche and lowered the quality of his mental and emotional life. When he was in a more balanced or only slightly hypo-manic state, his thinking function could operate smoothly. How did his type function in his work?

Newton was capable of a level of sustained concentration and focus that is almost unparalleled. He could hold a complex problem in his mind for decades and return to it when internal and external conditions, like the threat of competition, warranted. His introversion can be seen in the usual anecdotal evidence about his utter detachment from his surroundings and in the more subtle form, which is manifest in the retention of psychic energy for internal tasks. He would rotate a problem in his mind, such as the complexity of determining the mathematical properties of the ellipse as it relates to the inverse square law of gravity, and examine it from every conceivable angle. If the mathematical tools were simply not available, he would invent them and apply them to the issue at hand. He also had what would be called a strong judging function, as opposed to a perceiving one that is more concerned with acquiring data than with rendering a verdict. Newton never rested until he had judged and tested the merits of his internal conceptual world against the world of experience.

His sensing function is clearly evident in his extensive and minute work with optical phenomena. He had a vaguely corpuscular theory of light (which we now know is half right) and exerted an astonishing care with measuring and calibrating the ways in which it reflected off of solid bodies and was refracted through prisms. In a letter written in his twenties to his friend Henry Oldenburg, he states his view of proper scientific method so as to quell any doubts about the means by which he developed his optical theories:

> I cannot think it effectuall for determining truth to examin the severall ways by which Phaenomena may be explained, unlesse where there can be a perfect enumeration of all those ways. You know the proper Method for inquiring after the properties of things is to deduce them from Experiments... The way therefore to examin it [the Theory] is by considering whether the experiments which I propound do prove those parts of the Theory to which they are applyed, or by prosecuting other experiments which the Theory may suggest for its examination.[41]

Here we see the notion of rotating an experiment through deductive pathways that should reinforce the original power of the observations. There is no hint here of a kind of intuitive probing of a hidden background, as would be the primary strategy of an intuitive type, but much rather of a straightforward process of going from antecedent to consequent, the process by which a thinking type approaches data. Even in his alchemical work and his early and late speculations on the ether (what he called "aethereal spirits"), he used the combination of thinking and sensing to wrest control from his data.

As an introverted thinking/sensing type he would not be in a position to gauge the feelings others had toward him, a fact that resulted in innumerable misunderstandings, some exacerbated by his paranoia. Again, when his feeling function did surface, it was unmodulated and ofttimes out of control. In a famous letter of 1693 to the philosopher John Locke, Newton exposed his paranoia and expressed his consequent remorse:

> Sir
>
> Being of opinion that you have endeavoured to embroil me with women & by other means I was so much affected with it as that when one told me you were sickly & would not live I answered that it was better if you were dead. I desire you to forgive me this uncharitableness. For I am now satisfied that what you have done is just & beg your pardon for having hard thoughts of you for it & for representing that you stuck at the root of mortality in a principle you laid down in your book of ideas & designed to pursue in another book & that I took you for a Hobbist. I beg your pardon also for saying or thinking that there was a design to sell me an office, or to embroil me. I am your most humble & most unfortunate servant.
>
> Is. Newton[42]

Several paranoid themes converge in this strange missive. First is the fear that he is to be entangled with the worst of all possible creatures, a woman (or women). Second is the belief that Locke was trying to procure him a post (another kind of pimping), while third is the belief that Locke was a follower of the philosopher Thomas Hobbes, of which nothing could be further from the truth. Hobbes was a strict monarchist while Locke was a Whig and a strong supporter of parliament and democracy. Even more damning, Hobbes was a materialist and neither Newton nor Locke could envision a world without some kind of providential hand, however elusive.

Returning to our chronology, Newton worked with his usual mighty fury to complete his great life work the *Principia*. In a period of eighteen months he wrote the First and Second Books (in Latin so as to keep it out of the hands of the vulgar) and completed work on the more speculative Third Book. By 1687 the work was completed. Newton was 46 years old and at the height of his powers. Getting such a massive work published proved to be a challenge, but with the help of friends in the Royal Society, he was able to get it into print and to insure that it would be "properly" reviewed in the *Transactions* of the Society. Within months Newton went from the Cambridge boy wonder to the status of an international star. He had clearly earned the fruits of his unique harvest.

What had he accomplished in the *Principia* and why was it ground breaking? Of primary importance is his unification of all celestial phenomena under one mathematical formula for universal gravitation. In book III he tackled the issue of comets and also found a place for their orbits within his scheme. Specifically, according to A. Rupert Hall, he brought:

> ...the Moon and the satellites of Saturn within the scope of celestial mechanics, only partly because of his wanting appropriate information, but he was able to demonstrate to a high degree of accuracy how the known parameters of the orbits of the remaining planets and satellites could be derived from mechanical principles and shown to conform to those derived by astronomers from observation.[43]

Yet even in this scientific treatise he had a place for an absolute god who maintained the equally absolute structures of space and time, preserving them against collapse. The perfection of the universe is a divine gift that lies at the foundation of all scientific inquiry, and the investigator of celestial phenomena must never ignore this providential hand of god. If we accept White's argument of Newton's self-divinization, then it is not an egregious deduction to assume that Newton assumed that he had fathomed the mind of god in a way that no one had done before him.

Of primary importance is his statement at the beginning of Book I of the three laws of motion. He was able to reconcile the worlds of Kepler (the concept of ellipses) and Galileo (the concept of uniform motion in a straight line) and bring greater precision to our understanding of celestial and planetary motion. The Laws assert:

Law I. Every body perserveres in its state of being at rest or of moving uniformly straightforward, except insofar as is compelled to change its state by forces impressed.

Law II. A change in motion is proportional to the motive force impressed and takes place along the straight line in which that force is impressed.

Law III. To any action there is always an opposite and equal reaction; in other words, the actions of two bodies upon each other are always equal and always opposite in direction.[44]

The first law is the famous law of inertia that rejects Aristotle's notion that bodies tend naturally to be in a state of rest unless acted upon by another force. In Newton's worldview, god started each particle moving along straight paths and these paths only change through the effect of gravity, which deflects them from their straight lines. The second law quantifies the first and takes the mathematical form: $f=ma$ where "f" is the force that interacts with an object while "m" is the mass and "a" is the acceleration. To plot the force required to move an object in a certain way one simply multiplies its mass times its acceleration. Using this second law it is possible to quantify the amount of force required to put a satellite in orbit (a possibility that Newton envisioned). The third law is an implication of the first two and shows how objects must interact within space and time.

When looking at the moon, Newton came to the conclusion that it was the force of gravity that deviated it from what would have been a straight line movement had the earth not been there. So he concluded rightly that the moon is falling toward the earth according to strict mathematical principles. His calculus was developed to show how ellipses functioned with a large mass object at one of its foci. Thus the sun sits at the foci of the ellipses that the planets travel. As a planet gets closer to the sun in its journey it accelerates its motion due to the increase in the amount of gravity it encounters, while it slows in its motion, as it is further away from the sun. Newton's genius was to find a way to bring terrestrial and celestial mechanics (the science of motion) under one mathematical structure.

From these basic laws Newton went on to derive more complex phenomena such as the role of centripetal forces in an ellipse and the mathematical properties of curvilinear figures. The entire work (550 pages in its original Latin edition) is set up as a series axioms and deductions from basic principles showing how any body will behave under any gravitational, inertial, centripetal, or centrifugal condition. Descartes' mysterious vortices play no role and the entire conceptual edifice posits a mechanistic, if still divine, universe operating according to known mathematical principles.

At the beginning of the Third book, Newton lays down three general philosophical principles that ought to be imposed on the scientific study of nature. The first rule is especially interesting because it contains some hint of what some have seen as the quest for the lost maternal in Newton. Nature, like the eternal womb, is simple and reliable:

> No more causes of natural things should be admitted than are both true and sufficient to explain their phenomena. As the philosophers say: Nature does nothing in vain, and more causes are in vain when fewer suffice. For nature is simple and does not indulge in the luxury of superfluous causes. [45]

The last clause reminds us of Newton's Puritan roots, namely, that god's handiwork must be as simple as possible in order to make it accessible to our penetrating gaze. As noted by Manuel, Newton was profoundly uncomfortable with anything that could not be explained, that could not be wrestled to the ground. One immediately thinks of the biblical story of Jacob wrestling with the unnamed stranger by the river. Like Jacob, Newton will not let go until nature has given him her secret, and he is pleased that this secret is one that can be understood without "superfluous causes," as such causes would continue to mock him by their very reticence to be brought under the force of his pan-mathematicization of the world.

If White is correct that Newton identified with Christ, perhaps unconsciously, and I am right that he may also have lived through the archetype of Jacob and the unnamed stranger, then surely the *Principia* represents his emblematic marking of his cosmic triumph over the absent father and his return to the ontological mother (since the biological mother is not sufficient or perhaps even necessary for his purposes). He gives the father voice, unlike his biological father, who was uneducated, and brings his mother back in the much more reliable form of the nurturing laws of nature. And regardless of his over determined motives, he still got nature right, and this again should remind us that so-called psychopathology can often be a surer route to the truth than ordinary states of consciousness.

An interesting sub theme that runs throughout Newton's writings is the desire to tie together his celestial mechanics with an atomic theory that would show how the microscopic constituents of nature operated according to the same principles of attraction and repulsion as planets, satellites, and comets. Scholars have noted the parallels to his alchemical work, and this quest for a unified theory haunted Newton throughout the post-*Principia* period.

But as is so often the case, the result of such manic energy is a compensatory depression that can be as devastating as the initial mania or hypomania was exhilarating. He certainly had little trouble in accepting his hard-won fame, or with jousting with his interlocutors on the Continent, some of whom were at first reluctant to abandon their Cartesian philosophy for the Newtonian corpuscular theory and its mysterious invocation of action at a distance. What caused his breakdown?

Obviously, such monumental intellectual effort always comes at a price, a kind of postpartum depression that certainly has physiological corollaries. Yet there are also trigger events in the environment, both internal and external, that can accelerate the downward spiral. Internally, Newton was already restless as the book was in press. He felt dissatisfied with some of his calculations and conclusions and immediately started filling his notebooks with planned revisions. His drive for perfection, related to his obsessive-compulsive personality disorder, gave him no rest even with such a towering intellectual achievement. Externally there was a personal relationship that floundered at this time and may have been the most important factor in his period of madness as it reached its crescendo in 1693.

Newton was not noted for intense personal friendships, but he did have two relationships that have led to some reasoned speculation that he had homosexual affairs with his chamber-mate Wickens and with the flamboyant and charismatic autodidact Nicholas Fatio de Duillier. Both relationships were intense, and both broke off abruptly and without any lasting reconciliation. As to his relationship with Wickens, little is known, while we do have a number of letters between Newton and de Duillier that indicate at the very least an intense homoerotic attachment between the older Newton and the younger Swiss scientist. White makes a great deal of this relationship and argues that its sudden rise and equally sudden denouement may have precipitated the crisis of 1693. White further argues that de Duillier was a manic-depressive who used his own hypochondria to manipulate Newton and to exert a kind of emotional blackmail.[46]

Hence the internal doubts about his great work and the external loss of what to him was the most intimate and secretive relationship of his life combined to drive him over the edge. He shared his deepest alchemical and religious speculations with de Duillier and must have felt the loss of that connection acutely. After this period Newton hardened his heart toward the world and slowly began to manifest a studied cruelty toward others that can only be called sadistic. We will bring our case study of Newton to a close by examining the main features of his post-*Principia* and post-Cambridge life.

Newton was finally drawn out of Cambridge by the offer of the post as Master of the Royal Mint, a duty he assumed in 1696 at the age of 53. He very quickly astonished the Warden of the Mint by assuming absolute control of all operations connected with coinage and started on a fairly ruthless campaign to find and prosecute any and all counterfeiters, sending some of them to the gallows. Again, in the words of White:

> As well as providing him with the means to pursue his new passion, this internal battle [to find funds for the operation of "his" mint] had whetted his appetites. Having already cut the umbilical cord to academia to submerge himself in the world of high finance and economic theory, he now leaped into a new role — that of private investigator and prosecutor.[47]

He showed no mercy to those who were convicted and went so far as to use spies and informers to bring villains to book. He became so notorious for his methods and his obsession with convictions that he had a price on his head, all of which he ignored in his single-minded quest to purify the realm.

Intellectually, Newton remained busy with his optical theory and with his work in the Royal Society, which he also took over in his growing quest for power. It was during the later period that his infamous struggle with Leibniz took place, bringing disgrace upon himself (in hindsight) and the Royal Society. Yet he also advanced into new scientific territory with the revised editions of his *Principia* and with his *Opticks* of 1704 (with a second edition in 1717). The *Opticks* proved to be more accessible to readers, and hence more popular. He had been working on optical phenomena since his time as a student at Cambridge and his eventual publication of his researches, which he had delayed until the death of his arch enemy Robert Hooke, again brought him to the forefront of English and Continental science. As with the *Principia* he vigorously defended his views on refraction and reflection against his critics' attacks.

In the *Opticks* Newton probes into the complexity of refraction and details the experiments he had done back in his twenties while still a student at Cambridge. His descriptions are for the most part very easy to read, an excellent example being his proof of how a prism refracts the light of the sun:

> In a very dark Chamber, at a round Hole, about one third Part of an Inch broad, made in the Shut of a Window, I placed a Glass Prism, whereby the Beam of the Sun's Light, which came in at that Hole, might be refracted upwards toward the opposite Wall of the Chamber, and there form a colour'd Image of the Sun. The Axis of the Prism (that is, the Line passing through the middle of the Prism from one end of it to the other end parallel to the edge of the Refracting Angle) was in this and the following Experiments perpendicular to the incident Rays. About this Axis I turned the Prism slowly, and saw the refracted Light on the Wall, or coloured Image of the Sun, first to descend, and then to ascend.[48]

He also details how refraction works by candle light and when water is applied to the prism. Throughout there is a mathematical analysis of the various properties of light and an interest in understanding how light may relate to the "aethereal spirits."

At the conclusion of the *Opticks* Newton allows himself a kind of final summing up of his general philosophical and theological perspective. He reiterates his belief in atomism and his belief that the universe must have an inner logical and divine cause:

> Now by the help of these Principles, all material Things seem to have been composed of the hard and solid Particles above-mention'd, variously associated in the first Creation by he Counsel of an intelligent Agent. For it became him who created them to set them in order. And if he did so, it's unphilosophical to seek for any other Origin of the World, or to pretend that it might arise out of a Chaos by the mere Laws of Nature...[49]

So at the end of his long scientific and philosophical journey, we see Newton still affirming the faith of his Puritan heritage, a faith that the universe makes sense and that its basic laws are available for circumspection by the enlightened. The laws of gravity and light are but part of the eternal mind of the creator who set the infinite world in motion so that it could exist in its undimmed splendor. And Newton was the loyal son who pried open the secret and gave it to humankind.

His intellectual energy only slightly dimmed, Newton succumbed to illness on March 20, 1717 in his home in the Kensington section of London. Unlike Leibniz who was buried with no fanfare, Newton received the equivalent of a State Funeral, coming to rest in a prominent place in Westminster Abbey. A monument was erected in the Abbey after his death showing in sculpted relief his various accomplishments during his long lifetime. The Arian heretic, the alchemist, the closet homosexual, and the manic-depressive scientist was interred in the holiest site of the Church of England. Shortly after his death, his disciples forged the myth of the pure intellect, the man devoid of worldly ambitions or vanities. It has taken scholars almost three hundred years to destructure the myth and see the man in all of his complexity.

We have seen a towering genius who still sought the power of the maternal ground in his celestial mechanics governed by an absent father deity who merely sustained absolute space and time against disillusion. We have seen a man whose uncontrolled rages wounded many of the people around him and sent some to their death on the gallows. We have seen a man who tortured his body in his early optical experiments, forcing nature to give up her secrets. We have seen the process of self-divinization emerge through his alchemical speculations and his unique Christology that somehow placed himself at the center of the self-revealing cosmos. We have briefly peered into the mind of a man who could find astonishing (to us) biblical prophecies that pointed to the conquest of the whore of Babylon and the return of Christ/Newton. And we have seen a man who, both aided and cursed by his manic-depressive disorder, managed to give to all of us a picture of the universe that did not have to be modified until the advent of the twentieth century and the work of the young Einstein.

It is clear to me that had he not been manic-depressive, his legacy would have been far less than it was, but it is also clear that his illness both shattered and transformed many around him. In the face of such a contradiction it is impossible to do a simple cost-benefit analysis of what his genius exacted and what it enabled. And it is this ambivalence, to use Freud's profound concept that stays with us as we continue to ponder this eruption from nature's still reticent ground.

C.b. SRI RAMAKRISHNA: DIVINE ENERGY

Since my high school years I have been fascinated with the sages of India, not only because I felt that they had opened up vistas that my rather straightforward Methodist training had not seen, but that they were also creatures who had lived on the cusp where psychopathology and sainthood intersect. While the correlation of genius with psychopathology is a shop-worn truism, the correlation of sainthood with thought or mood disorder is an area that remains less well explored. I suppose that my first guru was Paramahansa Yogananda. His best selling book, *Autobiography of a Yogi*, made the inner India come alive for me, even if I couldn't then or now accept some of the magical thinking and miracles that he describes. But here was a man who had *seen*, who had penetrated into the ground and abyss of the world and had discovered that it was "existence, consciousness, and bliss," rather than chaos and blindness.

But as my thinking evolved, I turned away from India and threw myself into European and Euro-American thought. I vividly remember having an emotionally painful conversation with one of my closest friends during my college years who had decided that India was his spiritual home. He accused me of being enchanted by mere "professors," i.e., people who wrote books but who had not tasted the godhead directly. He left for India, and I left for graduate school, and our paths have never crossed since. Perhaps it is with some irony that I now find myself, after almost twenty years of being one of those "professors," returning in my mind to the India that I left behind so long ago. Yet the debt has been partially paid. I have been to Southern India twice now and have found a new center for my spiritual life.

But I return to an India that, try as I might, is now filtered through a different lens, one deeply colored by my commitment to psychoanalysis and depth psychology. In what follows you will see my ongoing struggle to both honor this lens and yet transcend it, to let something other than my lens speak to me. The German philosopher Gadamer once put it very succinctly: you must let the text or alien horizon grasp you and put you into question rather than the other way around. This is what I shall try to do in wrestling with the complex and multi-layered life of Sri Ramakrishna, whose inner journey was far more intense and "manic" than almost any of the other sages of India.

One of the most striking facts that recurs again and again in the literature is that Sri Ramakrishna, whose boyhood name was Gadadhar (which means "Bearer of the Mace"), was early on seen as an avatar or incarnation of god. He was born into the Brahmin caste and thus had high expectations placed upon him by his family and his community. Before his birth, his father Kshudiram had a vision in a temple that he would the parent of a special avatar of Vishnu who would revive his religious tradition.[50] He was born on February 18, 1836, in a small village outside of Calcutta in the province of Bengal. From the time he could walk and move about in the world he assumed a dreamy air and would often sink into deep trances from which he could not be awakened. The women in the village were especially drawn to him, and he spent most of his time with them, often dressing in women's clothing and acting in "feminine" ways. This was a practice that he continued late into his life, and it drew a considerable amount of attention, even though many religious saints of India had done the same. He was most comfortable when he could cross dress and take on the role of the divine feminine.

If we can talk about mystics being precocious in the same sense that scientists or mathematicians are precocious, then Sri Ramakrishna was indeed in that category. Swami Nikhilananda describes a pivotal event of early life that occurred some time during the 1840s:

> At the age of six or seven Gadadhar had his first experience
> of spiritual ecstasy. One day in June or July, when he was
> walking along a narrow path between paddy fields, eating

the puffed rice that he carried in a basket, he looked up at the sky and saw a beautiful, dark thunder-cloud. As it spread, rapidly enveloping the whole sky, a flight of snow-white cranes passed in front of it. The beauty of the contrast overwhelmed the boy. He fell to the ground, unconscious, and the puffed rice went in all directions. Some villagers found him and carried him home in their arms. Gadadhar said later that in that state he had experienced an indescribable joy.[51]

What a striking visual image! Here is the young semi-literate Brahmin boy walking across a field who sees the stark contrast of the flying birds and the brooding cloud overhead. The overload on his senses was so great that he was knocked unconscious. This is a characteristic trait that appears over and over again in his life, namely, that some outer or inner experience is of such magnitude that he simply cannot endure its power of being and must alter his state of consciousness to bear it. As his mystical path unfolded and matured, he was able to integrate such experiences without losing literal consciousness. Instead he shifted to a different dimension of consciousness.

When Gadadhar was seven years old, his father unexpectedly died and he felt the blow deeply. Again we are reminded how it is so often the case that geniuses lose a parent in their early years, and that this sense of loss propels them forward to find some kind of replacement for the gap that has opened up. His mother decided that extra pressure now had to be put on the boy to make sure that he could fill his father's shoes.

His mother was fully aware of his mystical tendencies and was worried lest he be diverted from the true path of a Brahmin. A Brahmin male was expected to make his way in the social world, probably in the employ of the British East India Company, which controlled all civil service jobs. With this in mind, at age sixteen Gadadhar was sent to Calcutta where his brother Rumkumar was running a school that taught Sanskrit. But try as he might, his brother could not get him to pay any attention to the worldly issue of finding a career or taking on the training that would be required to succeed. Gadadhar much preferred to engage in theatre where he could assume the roles of the Hindu deities like Krishna, Radha, Hanuman, or Shiva. He could be so enveloped in a role that he would be unable to speak his lines and would stand on the stage with tears streaming down his face, again lost in a spiritual ecstasy.

Ramkumar's Sanskrit school failed, but Gadadhar's brother was offered a position as priest at a Kali temple outside of Calcutta in the village of Dakshineswar. Gadadhar reluctantly went along but deliberately stayed away from the priestly duties that his brother was asked to perform, perhaps from an innate fear that getting too close to the goddess would be dangerous and from his Brahmin sensibilities that made him feel it would be unclean to participate in worship in a temple that, in this case, was owned by a woman of a lower caste. The goddess Kali is often seen in the West in her more terrible aspect as the black-skinned devouring ogre whose body is festooned with human skulls and whose mouth drips with the blood of her victims. In some Christian caricatures of Hinduism, Kali is isolated as being the premier example of what is wrong with Hindu belief systems. But in actual practice she is a much more complex deity. Certainly she has her aspect as the devourer of the world of manifest things, but she is also the Great Mother, the preserver and protector of her children. To understand Kali is to understand the eternal play between the necessary destruction of all things and the eternal renewal of the world. She is also an embodiment of the great power of *Shakti*, which can be defined as the divine energy that courses through all things, not unlike the *drala* of Tibetan Buddhism. Such energy is universal and underlies everything. In the words of Ajit Mookerjee:

> Shakti means power, force, the feminine energy, for she represents the primal creative principle underlying the cosmos. She is the energizing force of all divinity, of every being and every thing. The whole universe is a manifestation of Shakti. A Shakta, a follower of Shakta-worship, regards her as the supreme reality.[52]

Already we get a sense of the fluidity of Hindu concepts. In talking about the ultimate, one can invoke an energy, or a principle, or a deity, or vision. The power of shakti can concresce into a goddess or can be manifest on its own, but from one perspective, all that is and that has being is quickened and empowered by the energy at its heart.

Slowly Gadadhar overcame his caste aversion to the owner of the temple. With the sudden death of his older brother he was asked to take over the position as head priest. At the heart of the temple was a statue of Kali that would be the focus of daily devotions and ministrations. In the Hindu belief system, the statue is an incarnation of its deity and it should be treated exactly as one would treat the deity him or herself. One can choose to see this as primitive animism or one can become sensitive to its deeper logic and see it as a powerful means for establishing *connection* between the devotee and his or her deity. As his devotion accelerated, Sri Ramakrishna's mystical states grew more and more intense and frantic as he caught a brief glimpse of the Great Mother, only to see her disappear again. His anguish was so great that he would throw himself on the ground and rub his face in the dirt, always crying out "Mother, Mother."

His French follower Romain Rolland, who had the advantage of interviewing a number of still living direct disciples of Sri Ramakrishna, gives a vivid account of the period of anguish leading up to his first overwhelming experience of the Great Mother:

> To touch Her, to embrace Her, to win one sign of life from Her, one look, one sigh, one smile, became the sole object of his existence. He flung himself down in the wild jungle-like part of the garden, meditating and praying. He tore off all his clothes, even to the sacred cord, which no Brahmin ever lays aside; but love for the Mother had revealed to him that no man can contemplate God unless he has shed all his prejudices. Like a child lost in tears he besought the Mother to show Herself to him.[53]

We are reminded of the anguish that faced St. Augustine before his conversion to Christianity. He had made his intellectual conversion years before, but his heart was still closed to the deeper realities that he sought. One day in his garden Augustine heard someone say "take and read," and he turned to a biblical passage that spoke of his sinful condition, at which point he fell to the ground in a fetal position and had his true depth-conversion. For Gadadhar the tumult leading up to his conversion was even more painful, more fraught with a great and soaring longing that could not be stilled. Those who witnessed his anguish were convinced that he was mad, and experts were even brought into the temple to see if he was insane or a true avatar (incarnation) of god. All of the scholars brought in decided that Gadadhar, who was by now being called Sri Ramakrishna, was indeed an avatar and that his strange manic behavior was a sign of the difficulty he had as a divine being living in a human form.

Sri Ramakrishna pushed and drove against the walls that were keeping him from embracing the Great Mother fully. He would shout, cry, roll on the ground, petition Kali's statue, meditate, cite verse, and do everything in his power to pierce beyond the veil of illusion. Finally it all came to a head. He describes in his own words what happened:

> One day I was torn by intolerable anguish. My heart seemed wrung as a damp cloth might be wrung. I was racked with pain. A terrible frenzy seized me at the thought that I might never be blessed with the divine vision. I thought if that were so then enough of this! A sword was hanging in the sanctuary of Kali. My eyes seized upon it and the thought raced through my brain like a flash of lightning — "The sword it will help me put an end to it." I rushed up to it and seized it like a madman. . . And lo! The whole scene, doors, windows, the temple itself simply vanished. It seemed as if nothing existed anymore. Instead I saw an ocean of spirit, boundless, dazzling. In whatever direction I turned, great luminous waves were rising. They bore down upon me with a loud roar, as if to swallow me up. In an instant they were upon me. They broke over me, they engulfed me, I was suffocated. I lost all normal consciousness and fell to the ground. . . How I passed that day and the next I know not. Round me rolled an ocean of unspeakable joy such as I had never experienced before. And inside me was an immediate knowledge of the light that is the Mother.[54]

Only the most churlish imagination would want to see this as an example of a psychotic state rather than a vision of a deeper reality, yet there are features that force one to pause for reflection. There is a state of overwhelming anguish that speaks of the loss of something primal, something dimly sensed on the edges of experience. Before, Sri Ramakrishna had encountered such sacred folds, small epiphanies (like the cranes against the dark cloud) that pointed to something even deeper in the world. Here he left behind all sense of name and form, all connection with three-dimensional reality. Perhaps a Freudian would see this as a perfect example of the death drive in action, the need to return to oceanic immediacy, to loosen the bonds of the all too demanding ego.

But the complex of experiences that Ramakrishna had on that fateful day point in several directions. There is nothing wrong in saying that he was trying to replace his lost father through a substitute, if displaced, religious vision. After all, a great mystical vision, termed *samadhi* in Hinduism, can be doing a number of things at once, from wrestling with personal unconscious complexes, to solving social and relational problems, to fleeing from worldly obligation, to opening out a genuine vision of *Brahman* or god. What is especially telling is how the world dissolved into light, sound, and bliss. The Great Mother returned with her full force and magnitude, blasting through the structures of ego consciousness.

Not everyone is comfortable with the idea that mystical states should be understood in terms of the religious ideas that surround them. One of the sharpest critics of Sri Ramakrishna is the Bengali scholar Narasingha P. Sil who uses psychoanalysis in a more reductive way to probe into the role of childhood trauma in shaping his states of *samadhi*. He takes the sage to task for a deeply seeded misogyny that only talks about the Great Mother as a way of sublimated his real abjection of mortal women and all that he sees them standing for. Where I am more inclined to see a genuine avatar, or at least a god-infused mystic, Sil sees a schizophrenic:

> Quite possibly he was, in the terminology of psychologists, an "unknown psychotic" in that he remained outwardly a normal individual, while "forgetting" or "repressing" his childhood experiences and traumas, and grew up to be a severely neurotic individual, imagining himself in his mystical state (*madhura bhava*) to be God's bride — Radha to Krishna — leading to his subsequent conviction that he was "other," unique, and therefore "divine."[55]

Sil has a thorough knowledge of the primary material (the various sayings of Sri Ramakrishna) and has worked through his thesis with some care. While I see psychotic features in Sri Ramakrishna, I believe that they are tied to a manic-depressive syndrome rather than to any form of schizophrenia or even childhood sexual traumas. His adolescent ability to enter into the roles of the Hindu deities, a process that he continues in later years, marks him as a strong intuitive type who was able to reshape external material in an internal way.

My sense is that Sri Ramakrishna was an introvert intuiter with a strong feeling function, which would mean that his extravert sensing function was in the undeveloped mode. Unlike Newton, he was far more in the perceiving mode than in the judging, and this is marked by his astonishing ability to enter into other religions on their own terms. He had a strong intuitive grasp of Islam, at least in its mystical form, and developed a (brief) relationship with Jesus. When his sense function was activated, he found it too chaotic and would be forced to retreat from its onslaught. Jeffrey J. Kripal notes this feature, "Ramakrishna might be described as hyperassociative. Almost anything he saw or heard could awaken powerful forces that often overwhelmed him."[56]

Is being "hyperassociative" the same thing as being manic-depressive? I think that one can make a strong argument that a special vulnerability to lightning-like associations is a strong trait of manic-depression and that Sri Ramakrishna was especially open to these invasions. We saw how the sight of white cranes against a black thundercloud literally rendered him unconscious, and we saw how his vision of Kali's sword drove him outside of his own three-dimensional ego world into a realm of pure undulating light. If I am right that a mania or hypo-mania compels one into extraversion and brings about the rise of the inferior function, then Sri Ramakrishna was driven into his extravert sensing function which in turn overwhelmed him and caused him to short circuit. In his own theological reflection there is a tension between what is called *bhakti yoga*, or the yoga of love, devotion, and fervent worship, and *jnana yoga*, or the quiet contemplative and philosophical yoga that seeks the god beyond the god or goddess that is worshiped by the *bhakta*. The *bhakta* sees the particular and worships the incarnation of the divine in some form, for Sri Ramakrishna that being Kali.[57] The philosophical or Vedantic (nondualistic) yoga seeks the divine beyond all name and form. It is interesting that Sri Ramakrishna created the modern movement of nondual Vedanta while in his heart being more of a *bhakti* worshiper, or even, as Kripal argues, a secret Tantric practitioner. The Tantric yogi is someone who tries to unite divine *Shakti* with bodily energy, sometimes sexual, as in the "left handed" school, and sometimes sublimated, as in the "right handed" school.

The tension between his love of the particular and his sense of an enveloping ultimate beyond the three-dimensional universe remained with him. This dialectic is expressed by Richard Schiffman, who has a much more appreciative attitude to the struggles undergone by Sri Ramakrishna than does Sil:

> Sri Ramakrishna was the ultimate connoisseur of these Avatars of the Divine. He savored each one with a fresh thrill of discovery, and marveled at all that they revealed to him of the compassion, the power, the inscrutableness, and the whimsical playfulness of the Absolute. He adored God, the Artist of Worlds, and watched Him at work behind the scenes with His palette of many colors. If it had been left to him, he never would have stirred from this privileged and rapturous vantage point at the very threshold of relative consciousness, where the white light of eternity spreads out in all of its marvelous perfection.[58]

This expresses the well-known dilemma facing those who have seen a vision of the ground of being itself. Should they return to the world of relative consciousness and bring others with them to the state of *samadhi* or should they remain totally enveloped and outside of space and time (however this latter concept is understood)? Sri Ramakrishna was not prone to promote public works, the domain of *karma yoga*, but continued mining his psyche for more and more complex experiences of divine energy. In a sense, he left no stone unturned in his quest for the Great Mother and, like a hungry actor, was more than willing to take on any role that was offered to him, especially if it involved the infusion of a deity.

But my affirmation that Sri Ramakrishna was truly god-infused does not contradict the view that he was *also* in the grip of his manic-depressive psychosis. One is never sure where to draw the line between a hallucination and a vision that pierces the veil of illusion. Swami Nikhilananda gives this account of what might pass for a series of hallucinations:

> When he sat to meditate, he would hear strange clicking sounds in the joints of his legs, as if someone were locking them up, one after the other, to keep him motionless; and at the conclusion of his meditation he would again hear the same sounds, this time unlocking them and leaving him free to move about. He would see flashes like a swarm of fireflies floating before his eyes, or a sea of deep mist around him, with luminous waves of molten silver. Again, from a sea of translucent mist he would behold the Mother rising, first Her feet, then Her waist, body, face, and head, finally Her whole person; he would feel Her breath and hear Her voice.[59]

Are these flashes of light some kind of projected internal imagery, perhaps caused by meditation, a kind of random optical noise that can come from bodily denial and sheer exhaustion, or are they portals onto another dimension of the world? Is the mist that rises up and provides the clearing for the appearance of the Mother a thinly disguised complex that gets projected out onto a world that is utterly indifferent to the complex's existence?

I have come to the conclusion that there are ways to tell the difference between a genuine mystical state, especially as undergone by a manic-depressive, and a hallucination. Two features strike me as important: 1) that the genuine mystical state involves a reintegration of the self after the firestorm of the state has passed, and 2) that paranoid features are absent. The status of the ego during a genuine mystical state, perhaps a Western concern, is more problematic. Western conceptions of religious or spiritual individuation insist that the ego, as the center of the field of consciousness, remains fully intact and reality oriented before, during (perhaps), and after a major religious experience, while in the Hindu context the ego is seen as an impediment to letting the deeper self (*atman*) know that it is *Brahman*. When the ego and its external senses are shattered, the divine *Shakti* can radically transform the whole person. To cling to the ego is to lose god.

Sri Ramakrishna continued to probe into the source of the great *Shakti* energy that surrounded him. As his fame grew, other sages and ascetics started to appear at the temple in Dakshineswar. A female initiate introduced him to Tantric right-handed practices, which he mastered in an astonishingly short time. But his commitment to the particular was still stronger than his awareness of the universal *Brahman*. Perhaps his strangest visitor and teacher was the wandering monk Tota Puri, who wore no clothing at all, the state known as being "sky clad." It was Tota Puri who secretly initiated him into the truths of Advaita (nondual) Vedanta, and helped him to find and secure the sense of the ultimate. Before saying more about this complex and important relationship, I want to say something about the two ways in which *Brahman* can be apprehended.

The Western scholar of Hinduism Eliot Deutsch analyzes the historical and conceptual strains that go into the most advanced form of Indian religion, that of Vedanta. The two ways of understanding the ultimate are clearly delineated:

Advaita Vedanta thus distinguishes two aspects or modes of Brahman, *nirguna* and *saguna*. *Nirguna* Brahman — Brahman without qualities — is just that transcendent indeterminate state of being about which ultimately nothing can be affirmed. *Saguna* Brahman — Brahman with qualities — is Brahman as interpreted and affirmed by the mind from its necessarily limited standpoint; it is that about which something can be said. And it is also a kind of spiritual experience.[60]

Most of us, insofar as we are spiritual at all, gain some glimpses of *saguna* Brahman, the god with name, form, and qualities. The technical term for the mental act that shrinks the ultimate down into its manifest form is "superimposition," in which we impose human traits onto that which has none. The act of superimposition is unconscious and is not even known as such until heroic efforts are undertaken to break free from *maya* or illusion. For Advaita Vedanta, not only is *saguna* Brahman an illusion, so too is the entire manifest universe, although it is also affirmed that even the illusion is god.

When Sri Ramakrishna came under the tutelage of Tota Puri, he still had to work through some of his superimposition, and to leave Kali behind so that he could separate out the two dimensions of the ultimate. But unlike his new mentor, Sri Ramakrishna was a true religious genius and was able to break through to *nirguna* Brahman with only three days of intense effort, something that had taken Tota Puri forty years (by his own account). Here is how Sri Ramakrishna describes his illumination under the instruction of Tota Puri:

> The naked man, Tota Puri, taught me to detach my mind from all objects and to plunge it into the heart of the Atman. But despite all my efforts, I could not cross the realm of name and form and lead my spirit to the Unconditional state. I had no difficulty in detaching my mind from all objects with the one exception of the too familiar form of the radiant Mother, the essence of pure knowledge, who appeared before me as a living reality. She barred the way to the beyond. I tried on several occasions to concentrate my mind on the precepts of the Advaita Vedanta; but each time the form of the Mother intervened. I said to Tota Puri in despair: "It is no good. I shall never succeed in lifting my spirit to the 'unconditioned' state and find myself face to

face with the Atman." He replied severely: "What! you say you cannot? You must!" Looking about him, he found a piece of glass. He took it and stuck the point between my eyes saying: "Concentrate your mind on that point." Then I began to meditate with all my might, and as soon as the gracious form of the Divine Mother appeared, I used my discrimination as a sword, and I clove Her in two. The last barrier fell and my spirit immediately precipitated itself beyond the plane of the "conditioned," and I lost myself in Samadhi.[61]

Yet Sri Ramakrishna had some lessons of his own to teach! He insisted that Tota Puri also learn of the Great Mother and see her in all things, even if she is not the ultimate. Tota Puri, in some despair over the inferiority of his own powers, decided to drown himself in the Ganges river, which flowed next to the ashram. He waded into the water but found much to his dismay that it was not deep enough in that season of the year for him to immerse himself fully. As he turned around and looked back at the temple he too had a mystical awakening, this time of the Great Mother herself, showing him that even the advanced nondual Vedantin needed *saguna* Brahman. This mutual sharing of visions marked a watershed for both sages, and from what we know, colored each of their lives from then on.

Earlier to this period Sri Ramakrishna, following family tradition, took on a child bride. The marriage was never consummated, and his wife later became one of his disciples (itself an issue ripe for analysis). Tota Puri's initiation of Sri Ramakrishna had to be conducted in secret because he was actually asking him to violate his marriage vows by becoming a renunciate, that is, a celibate. Sri Ramakrishna wanted this to remain secret so as not to offend his own mother, who was living in the ashram. His fear of his mother's wrath and his indifference to the needs of his wife provide evidence for Sil's thesis that Sri Ramakrishna had profound difficulties dealing with female power and sexuality.

Like most manic-depressives, Sri Ramakrishna had very strong erotic drives, which he sublimated in an elaborate framework that involved homoeroticism, cross dressing, and a strong identification with the mother/child relationship in which he played the mother to his disciples, most of whom it should be noted, were males. It seems clear that he did not understand these dynamics in anything like psychoanalytic terms, and always cast them in the guise of the great roles of Hindu mythology, such as the love of Radha for Krishna. He would play the divine lover so as to merge with Krishna and become one with the ultimate. At the same time he would experience a longing for his "boys" or young disciples that had clear (to some scholars) homoerotic aspects. The feminine was a metaphysical principle, not a concrete person. Sri Ramakrishna makes this clear to his disciples:

> A man forgets God if he is entangled in the world of maya through a woman. It is the Mother of the Universe who has assumed the form of maya, the form of woman. One who knows this rightly does not feel like leading the life of maya in the world. But he who truly realizes that all women are manifestations of the Divine Mother may lead a spiritual life in the world. Without realizing God one cannot truly know what a woman is.[62]

Perhaps, when in the grip of his hypo-manic states Sri Ramakrishna needed to distance himself from the object of temptation by theologizing it, that is, by converting it into something far less dangerous, so that the underlying sexual energy could be cathected elsewhere. This is both a traditional strategy and an injustice to the actual women in his world. But I say this with some trepidation because of the long and rich history of ascetic practices in all of the major religions. However, I am also persuaded that these very practices, designed to speed the seeker toward the divine, have powerful, negative implications for gender roles, and that a more integrated pattern of living with sexuality is called for. Instead of negating the sexual energies of the body, the seeker might accept and learn to integrate such energies as part of the religious path.

We noted how in his earlier years, from his late teens into his twenties, he would roll in the ground crying "Mother, Mother." During his later period when he had attracted a following he would often climb to the roof of the temple and cry out in anguish for his boys to come to him, to be in his presence. I am not persuaded that any of these relationships were consummated, but they do seem to be over determined and to have served the function of some kind of erotic connection with the world.

The most important disciple to appear at the ashram was the young, academically brilliant and proud scholar of both Hindu and Western ideas, Narendranath Dutta, later given the name by which he became famous, Swami Vivekananda. He was a talented singer, and one can say that he swept Sri Ramakrishna off his feet. He immediately seized on the idea that Vivekananda was a divine being with whom he had been in communion in the heavenly plane before this earthly incarnation. Vivekananda was at first greatly disturbed by the attention he was being given and tried to pull away from Sri Ramakrishna's rather insistent presence. But all of this changed rather dramatically:

> During his second visit to the Master, Narendra had an even stranger experience. After a minute or two Sri Ramakrishna drew near him in an ecstatic mood, muttered some words, fixed his eyes on him, and placed his right foot on Naren's body. At this touch Naren saw, with eyes open, the walls, the room, the temple garden — nay, the whole world — vanishing, and even himself disappearing into a void. He felt sure that he was facing death. He cried in consternation: "What are you doing to me? I have my parents, brothers, and sisters at home."[63]

This experience has all of the hallmarks of the one that befell Sri Ramakrishna when he held the sword of Kali. From a psychoanalytic perspective it points to the power of the transference to ignite a countertransference and to bring about a sudden and catastrophic change in consciousness. From a classical Hindu perspective it shows the power of the guru, who is the incarnation of god, to infuse divine energy into the disciple with a simple touch (the so-called *shaktipat*). From this point on Sri Vivekananda started on his own mystical journey, which was to be far more extraverted and public than that of his teacher.

Swami Vivekananda became famous in the West in 1893 when he attended the World Congress of Religions in Chicago as an unofficial delegate of Hinduism. His commanding presence, handsome looks, and total command of the English language captivated his listeners. He brought with him Sri Ramakrishna's universal religion as an antidote to the Western monotheisms and their endless internecine struggles. In finding Swami Vivekananda, Sri Ramakrishna found the man who would bring Vedanta to the world stage and make it a global movement.

As I have argued, Sri Ramakrishna, like many manic-depressives, had a genius for entering into the mind of another person or perspective. He had an unusually generous attitude to other religions, even though he was in many other respects a fairly conservative orthodox Brahmin. In one of his conversations he gives an indication of how capacious his religious horizon became:

> Mother, Mother, Mother! How I long to pray with sincere Christians in their churches and to bow and prostrate with devoted Muslims in their mosques! All religions are glorious! Yet if I display too much freedom, every religious community will become angry with me. I might even be forbidden to enter your Temple again, O blissful Kali. Therefore take me secretly into the sanctuary of every tradition without exception, and I will worship ceaselessly with all humanity, night and day.[64]

Two themes strike me as interesting in the context of manic-depressive disorder: 1) the drive toward universality, and 2) the need for secrecy. Both themes were strongly present in the lives of Newton and Sri Ramakrishna. Newton's Unitarian Christianity was truly universal and rational, while it also had to remain secret, along with his alchemical speculations. And the mystical experiments of Sri Ramakrishna moved toward a pan-Hinduism that could also birth a world religious consciousness. He kept secrets from the inner circle, not as a controlling device but as a way of saving deeper teachings for those ready to assimilate them.

Sri Ramakrishna did no writing himself, but many of his conversations were taken down verbatim in the original Bengali. He had his Boswell in a man who has come down to us with the simple name of "M." "M" records innumerable conversations between "the Master" and his disciples, and this record is a treasure of information on the inner struggles of Sri Ramakrishna as he fought against his own extreme mood swings and the lures of the world (the realm he called "gold and women"). As recorded by "M," toward the end of his life Sri Ramakrishna grew more and more detached from the world and had a strong sense of his impending death (He was to die of throat cancer in his fiftieth year.) In conversation with a disciple he gives the following advice:

> Give up worldly talk altogether. Don't ask about anything whatever but God. If you see a worldly person coming near you, leave the place before he arrives. You have spent your whole life in the world. You have seen that it is all hollow. Isn't that so? God alone is Substance, and all else is

illusory. God alone is real, and all else has only a two-days existence. What is there in the world? The world is like a pickled hog plum: one craves for it. But what is there in the hog plum? Only skin and pit. And if you eat it you will have colic.[65]

The world makes one sick and should be avoided at all costs. Sri Ramakrishna remained profoundly conflicted about erotic issues, never coming to grips with his strong libido and his homoeroticism, not to mention his dread of actual women in the flesh, whom he either idealized as incarnations of Kali or demonized as manifestations of lust and temptation. He had strong physical appetites, especially around food, but in his denial of food could almost be seen (by some) as a male anorexic. Food, along with woman, represented the lure of *maya* which must be overcome in spite of their enjoyable qualities, at least of the former.

Sri Ramakrishna was a deeply divided soul, a man pulled back and forth between highly eroticized particulars (his "boys" and the Great Mother) and the abyss of *nirguna* Brahman. Some scholars, like Kripal, see a dissociative consciousness that is the result of childhood sexual trauma.[66] On this reading, Sri Ramakrishna entered into mystical states as a way of dissociating himself from his hidden transgressions and their secret guilt. My own reading moves in a different direction, assuming that his experiences of *samadhi* were genuine attempts at finding wholeness even with and against his conflicted sexuality. His hypo-manic states were often overloaded with strong sexual and visual content, driving him in the reverse direction toward his more natural introverted function. But in this process he was actually probing into the divine itself, not merely filling the void with his own projected content.

Sri Ramakrishna, the manic-depressive sage of Dakshineswar, died on August 15, 1886, from the final effects of his throat cancer. Romain Rolland describes his last moments as his disciples surround him, especially his chosen heir Swami Vivekananda:

> In the afternoon he still had the almost miraculous energy to talk for two hours to his disciples in spite of his martyred throat. At nightfall he became unconscious. They believed him to be dead, but toward midnight he revived. Leaning against five or six pillows supported by the body of the

humble disciple, Ramakrishnaananda, he talked up to the last moment with Naren, the beloved disciple, and gave him his last counsel in a low voice. Then in ringing tones he cried three times the name of his life's Beloved, Kali, the Divine Mother, and lay back. The final ecstasy began. He remained in it until half an hour before noon, when he died. In his own words of faith: "He has passed from one room to the other."[67]

His body was cremated on the temple grounds and his ashes were carefully gathered and placed in an urn. Later they were interred in a small temple created in his honor where they remain today. The disciples who remained started the process of bringing his message to the world and with establishing ashrams and teaching centers throughout India and in North America.

What are we to make of the life of this religious saint who was both god-infused and manic-depressive? We saw how he was vulnerable to religious ecstasy from his early youth and how rapidly he was able to assimilate the various practices of his traditional culture (bhakti, tantrism and Vedanta). At the same time his intuitive genius, which made him not only a gifted actor but also a gifted reader of souls, enabled him to enter into the spiritual worlds of Christianity and Islam. His hypo-manic sexuality, always very strong in its outward play, bedeviled him in the form of abjections, misogyny, and homoerotic fantasy. Yet even here he was able to take this primal energy and weave it into the cosmic *Shakti* in true sublimated, or right handed, Tantric fashion. My growing conviction is that the visions he experienced were made possible by these internal pressures, and that he was able to take his playful and astonishing energy and direct it toward an ultimate *samadhi* that can become normative for others.

It is a shame that students of Sri Ramakrishna, and there are many both in India and North America, seem divided between hagiography with its adulation of the Master and what could be called biopathography with its psychosexual reductionisms.[68] Clearly, he was a man who had not fully integrated his strong libido. Yet he was also a man who was unusually sensitive to the presence of sacred folds and their calming intervals (concepts we will examine more fully in the next chapter). He advanced our understanding of the divine energies and their potential correlation with sexual energy.

In bringing to a conclusion these two case studies I want to ask a final question: what traits distinguish a manic-depressive genius from a manic-depressive religious saint (who may also be a genius)? Several possibilities have already suggested themselves, and I now want to lay them out in a more linear way. I see five pairs of contrasts: 1) the genius wants to generate a series of products in public space, while the saint is far less concerned with a body or corpus of works, 2) the genius struggles to remain firmly in the domain of "name and form" insofar as it is the place where the creative act takes place, while the saint pushes beyond the particulars of space and time into the ultimate ground and abyss of the world, 3) the genius expresses the quest for wholeness through a drive to dominate and shape others in some fundamental way, while the saint struggles to dominate his or her internal visions, 4) the genius insists on constant feed-back and external reinforcement because of the heroic quality of the work itself, while the saint can derive feed-back through internal means, and 5) the genius rarely looks upon his or her work ironically or with disdain (except when depressed), while the saint can be indifferent to whatever issues from his or her life. We have seen the five contrasting points in our case studies, and I would argue that they are fairly universal features of each human type. Of course, in a given individual who is both a genius and has some qualities of the religious visionary (e.g., Augustine), these oppositional parings can blend in complex ways. Yet they can also cut across each other longitudinally. Here one thinks of St. Thomas Aquinas who dropped all work on his magisterial Summa Theologica after having had a mystical experience. From that day onward he referred to his voluminous writings as mere "straw," and did not take up his pen again.

CHAPTER FOUR: INTIMATIONS OF WHOLENESS

Wholeness is not something that can be experienced as a static or unchanging state. It is a process of movement in which the various players in the psychic drama must be given specific roles to play, and in which each player will inevitably come into conflict with others. It often helps to personify these psychic forces because they have a degree of autonomy that has to be honored if there is to be any success in balancing oppositional forces within the self. Jung, as noted, referred to the unconscious powers that shape our lives as complexes, a concept that has entered into the public vocabulary. The complexes of the unconscious are like planetary systems with their own systems of gravity and with strong magnetic fields that can affect whatever comes within the sphere of their influence. Not to take them seriously as autonomous powers is to risk becoming the passive victim of their effects.

Manic-depressive disorder dramatically complicates the quest for wholeness because it pushes psychic structure and psychic dynamics to the extreme edges of experience. The boundary between the conscious and the unconscious, part of the structural integrity of the self, is compromised by both depression and mania. Psychic energy is accelerated and intensified in mania and drastically withdrawn into the unconscious in depression. Normal ratios between consciousness and the unconscious and between the upward and downward movement of psychic energy are disrupted, and the ego, always fragile in those grappling with a major thought or mood disorder, is fragmented and reconstituted in an endless variety of ways. The romantic vision of psychic wholeness seems to be a mockery to those who must ride the Windhorse of manic-depression.

I want to make clear in what follows that the quest for wholeness is not only built-in to the human psyche, but that it is even manifest in extreme states of psychopathology where there seems to be slender hope of achieving a balance among energy surges and their ideational contents. The human process has an uncanny ability to forge meaning even when the support conditions for doing so are broken or in absence. One of the most important insights to be gained from the study of manic-depressive disorder is that there are meanings embedded in those volatile feeling transitions that carry the finite ego along with them as if it were a piece of driftwood in a churning river. From the immediate perspective of the driftwood the riverbanks may be unseen through the swirling waters that surround it, yet they are there nonetheless; permanent structures that hold the entire movement of water and debris within circumscribed bounds. Our goal is to find access to these structures from the standpoint of our finite existence.

The image of the Windhorse can work in concert with that of the churning river, especially when the focus is on the immediate surrounding conditions of manic-depressive disorder. Whether you prefer the image of violent air currents or that of whirlpools and eddies in a river, the upshot is the same, namely, that the ego is compelled to engage in a heroic struggle if it is to negotiate its way through the extremes of shipwreck or self-divinization. In depression psychic energy is withdrawn back into the unconscious where it becomes unavailable to consciousness and its immediate survival needs. In mania or hypomania psychic energy blasts through the ego and carries unconscious material with it into consciousness, generating that psychic inflation in which all boundaries are transgressed. In those calm states between depression and mania the ego struggles to regain some sense of its integrity and moral coherence.

The language that makes the most sense to me in this context is that of the dialectic between finite and infinite energy and meaning. The ego and its "container" consciousness are deeply finite and perspectival, always tied to a personal history and conditions of origin like race, class, gender, and language group. Most people when asked the simple question, "Who are you?" will answer in terms of their specific conditions of origin. You might answer that you are a North American female whose primary language is English. One's ego structure, which is never a static thing like a rock or table, is tied to these conditions of origin. They represent one's finite position within the world, and shape one's perspective on all that is said, done, or made. For persons who do not suffer from a major mood or thought disorder, the structures of origin and the integrity of the ego are not an issue, they can be relied upon to secure identity through the vicissitudes of life. For those who do have a thought or mood disorder, finite ego structures are deeply ambiguous and rest on shifting terrain.

The infinite energy that courses through the self can be seen as deeply disruptive, deeply healing, or more usually, both simultaneously. It is this last possibility that I want to focus on. Put in the form of a question, I ask: how can someone with manic-depressive disorder learn to wrestle with the infinite energy that inundates consciousness from all sides and still retain the wholeness not only of their ego but of the entire self? We have seen the effects of this energy in the lives of Newton and Sri Ramakrishna, and the moral ambiguities that it produced for them and for those of us who share this disorder. And we have seen that this infinite energy, when channeled through a finite vessel, leaves many meaningless shards in its wake as well as intimations of something more profound.

The theologian Paul Tillich developed the concept of "ultimate import" (*gehalt*) in his early writings in the 1920s to point to the religious meaning that lies at the heart of all great works of art and culture. For him, religious meaning did not have to be "religious" in the doctrinal or traditional sense. Rather it pointed to the quality of grace-filled depth within cultural artifacts, a depth that we can participate in when we too are willing to enter into the axis of that grace. Hence the infinite can be found in any finite object that simultaneously points to and participates in ultimate import. Most people remain blind to this depth until they experience a transforming event, such as the encounter with death or nonbeing. For the manic-depressive, the encounter with ultimate or infinite important is too laden with unconscious content, that is, it is too over determined with meaning and threatens to unloosen the bonds of the ego.

My contention is that manic-depressives, whether they recognize it or not, are compelled to explore the realm of ultimate import through extraordinary means. That is why it is not uncommon to find many religious ideas, some of them clearly delusional, in manic-depressives. But it does not follow, contrary to what some in the psychiatric profession might assume, that all religious ideas are pathological or delusional. It depends on the quality of integration by which the impulses of the infinite are woven into the ego structure over time. In the case of Sri Ramakrishna, we saw someone who was able to use the powerful and well-delineated concepts of Hinduism to shape and mould his mystical experiences and to convey them to others. When his ego might have failed him, his religious framework provided the meaning-filled gestalt that protected him from total dissolution. In the process he revived his own tradition during a time in which it was moribund and under siege from Christianity and provided a structure that could be carried forward into the wider world.

We have seen how a classical psychoanalytic conception of mystical states can often be at odds with the one that I am presenting. For Freud, any such experience represented a kind of primitive narcissism, a desire to return to the womb and to a state prior to the Oedipal conflicts of adolescent and adult life. He referred to this state as containing an "oceanic feeling," akin to floating in the warm amniotic fluid of the mother. In a series of letters, written between 1923 and 1936, he works out his notions of mysticism in dialogue with Romain Rolland, whom we briefly encountered in our discussion of Sri Ramakrishna. Rolland had sent Freud his biographies of Sri Ramakrishna and Swami Vivekananda and pressed upon Freud his idea that mystical states were truly of another world beyond this one. One letter from Freud to Rolland sharply expresses his disagreements. It was written on January 30, 1930:

> We seem to diverge rather far in the role we assign to intuition. Your mystics rely on it to teach them how to solve the riddle of the universe; we believe that it cannot reveal to us anything but primitive, instinctual impulses and attitudes — highly valuable for the embryology of the soul when correctly interpreted, but worthless for orientation in the alien, external world.[1]

It is interesting that Freud takes his typical backward-looking tactic of tracing mystical states to the "embryology of the soul" rather than looking teleologically, as Jung had done, toward the future states of integration made possible by those very mystical states. Earlier in the same letter, he tars Rolland with the same brush that he used on the now despised Jung who, ". . . hasn't belonged to us for years."[2] For Freud, Rolland's biographies of Sri Ramakrishna and Swami Vivekananda were little more than case studies of pre-Oedipal regression and longing.

A more generous psychoanalytic model would struggle to define mystical states insofar as they genuinely differ from both the death drive and the hunger for a return to the mother. Such a model would be sensitive to the religious traditions within which mystical experiences are embedded. At the same time, a more capacious psychoanalysis would be open to the movement toward wholeness that mystical states seem to express. I suspect that Freud's negative countertransference toward Jung kept him from exploring the positive aspects of religiosity and the human need for contact with the infinite. In his own mind, as argued by William B. Parsons, Freud began to equate Rolland with the heresy of Jungian analysis, and thereby placed Rolland's positive mystical model outside of the pale of true psychoanalytic science.

Moving past Freud, then, we can say that the infinite is beyond good and evil, consequently it makes no sense to ask of it that it satisfy our moral longings and aspirations. The Western monotheisms, I would argue, have been mistaken in assigning moral predicates to the ultimate, and have thus limited access to the infinite by shaping it in a human all too human guises. While the infinite must be filtered through the finite, it must also be honored in its terms rather than our own. We cannot dictate to the winds on which we ride what name they shall take or what form we prefer they assume.

From the standpoint of our ego, our unconscious complexes also seem to be infinite, that is, to be larger than consciousness and its intentional acts and plans. A complex can disrupt and deposition consciousness whenever it is activated. Part of the wisdom of living with manic-depressive disorder is to recognize that these complexes have even more force than they would have for someone without a mood disorder. Therapy can help in naming one's complexes and with understanding those external trigger events that activate them. Trigger events do not operate in a vacuum. They are always tied to specific complexes in specific respects. If I know, for example, that I have a mother complex, then I will be especially careful in my dealings with those women who may trigger my complex, especially since they may be innocent of playing into the hands of the complex (although not necessarily so). And if my mother complex is also intensified by mania or depression, then I must be even more careful in avoiding those situations that will send their reverberations through my unconscious.

When infinite content inundates consciousness, psychic inflation and self-divinization occur. Yet this is only part of the story. For there is a deeper and uncanny logic at play, which involves the quest for the wholeness that can only, come from ultimate import. The manic-depressive gets it half right. The ego needs to understand that it is a finite and culturally inscripted product, from which it follows that it must also come to recognize an infinite background within which it is situated. The problem is that the infinite is too strong, too unmediated to sustain and transfigure the ego. The ego has little chance of finding the right ratio between infinite energy and finite means of living.

This is why medication is absolutely crucial to the spiritual quest for wholeness. By readjusting the relevant chemicals in the brain it is possible to give the ego more strength to withstand and ultimately accept the powers of the infinite. Yet here a dilemma emerges. For those of us who have been treated by lithium, anti-depressants, or the anti-convulsants, there remains the fear of what went before, a deeply seeded fear of the very infinite that was so devastating in the first place. My suspicion is that very few people have even considered the spiritual aspects of this fear and its implications for religious life once medication is applied to the disease. What I want to do is to lay out my own conception of the spiritual life especially as it relates to manic-depressive disorder and the quest for wholeness.

A. SPIRITUALITY, SACRED FOLDS, AND INTERVALS

I am persuaded that the human animal is fundamentally religious, although I would also argue that this religiosity almost always gets sidetracked into doctrines and frameworks that represent systems of patriarchal control. The movement of ultimate import is anti-systematic in its heart and the dialectic that most honors this fact is the one that recognizes that all finite expressions are merely means to briefly contain that which can never be contained. The Chinese Taoists have a simple expression that honors this fact: "The Tao that can be named is not the real Tao." In Hinduism, this insight is put in a similar fashion: "Brahman is beyond name and form." Yet as finite creatures, tied to our conditions of origin, we need names and forms if we are to enter into community with others and to give some shape to what can otherwise be so frightening.

For some years I have been looking for the right language to talk about the more concrete aspects of the infinite/finite dialectic and its relation to the self. I have decided to use simple language that remains open to the infinite varieties of religious experience that we see in our species. The term that I prefer for referring to the object of religious or spiritual experience is that of the "sacred fold." The concept of the fold comes from the mathematics of catastrophe theory where the idea is that certain shapes in nature can be reduced down into a set of basic geometric shapes or folds. For me, the concept of fold refers to an infolding of meaning that takes place in nature, such as a sacred grove or an unusually striking landscape. It is as if meanings fold in on themselves over and over again, giving the object an extra depth of meaning.

We encounter these sacred folds in innumerable ways even if we do not consciously know that we are doing so. In an intense friendship, perhaps activated by mutual unconscious complexes, we encounter a sacred fold. In a great piece of music we encounter a sacred fold. In a transforming idea, like Newton's conception of universal gravitation, we encounter a sacred fold. In bodily movements we can encounter a sacred fold. In all of these examples, what matters is that ultimate import be manifest through some object and that the sacred fold interacts with some complex in our own unconscious. We participate in its sacredness even if we are only dimly aware that we are doing so. The unconscious can be understood, among other things, as a great silent scanning system that lights on sacred folds and brings them, through whatever means, to the attention of consciousness.

Connecting the sacred fold to the complex in the unconscious is the transference relationship that can operate outside of the analytic context (analyst to analysand). In fact, the transference that is the central player in psychoanalysis is a more ubiquitous phenomenon that is manifest in a variety of ways in psychic life. At its heart the transference is religious and remains restless until it finds a sacred fold upon which to fasten its focus. In a positive transference, whether consciously accessed or not, the sacred fold is allowed to unfold its implicate content and to become manifest in a fulsome way. In the negative transference the sacred fold is distorted and turned into a mere semblance of its deeper meaning, yet it is still binding on the self nonetheless. And the same individual will certainly have positive transferences to his or her "chosen" sacred objects and latent or manifest negative transferences to the sacred folds of others. As is so often the case, the most significant issues for psychic growth often come from probing into the negative transference and its objects.

Manic-depressive disorder heightens the ability to experience and understand sacred folds. In the hypo-manic state the entire world can become regnant with sacred folds, each pulsating and demanding attention. When hypomania explodes into mania there is an immediate overload of sacred folds, the world has too much numinosity, too much meaning, too many beckoning prospects. This enveloping horizon of sheer sacredness has no place for finite meaning, for the nonsacred. What is left of the discriminating ego is emptied into pure undulating radiance, a manic mysticism that refuses to be tied to particularity. In it's most pathological form the self becomes divine, the center of the universe. Such an experience leaves profound and haunting traces long after it has passed.

In the other extreme of suicidal depression all traces of sacredness dissolve. Earlier I used the image of an astronomic black hole to point to this state. A black hole is so gravitationally dense that even light is pulled into it. In fact, anything that arrives at its event horizon is destructured and pulled inside. An overwhelming depression takes away any and all structures of the adaptive ego and leaves consciousness with a meaning vacuum that can only be understood by those who have experienced it. No experiences within normal or even neurotic life even comes close to that of seeing one after another of one's meaning structures collapse and vaporize in turn. The body becomes leaden and bereft of all life giving energy, while the mind slows to a crawl, surrounded with but the barest hints of the plenitude that went before. For the potential suicide, only self-initiated death can have meaning. For those among us who have been there, this statement, unfortunately, makes perfect sense. For meanings must be had and if external meanings are unavailable then some internal heroic act seems to be the only alternative. It is as if the suicide is saying, "My fragmented ego can still control being and nonbeing, and I choose nonbeing."

It is not enough to say that the return from a suicidal state should make life that much the sweeter. Would that the inner cunning of manic-depression were so simple. Amnesia is a constant companion of the manic-depressive. In the quest for hypomanias, certainly a form of addictive behavior, the depressions and their consequences are forgotten. The abyss beneath one's feet is ignored as the open and radiant world of artificially enhanced meanings exerts its lure. The only sweetness that comes is like the sugar high of a diabetic, evoking disaster and a crash worse than the previous dimly remembered one. And what is even more uncanny is that the often more devastating effects of the highs are themselves forgotten. Forgetfulness marks both ends of the manic-depressive spectrum.

But where do the sacred folds come into play in this ofttimes-tragic dialectic? It is my contention, certainly one that will be contested by some, that the manic-depressive is on a spiritual quest with tools that are simply too crude and too inept for the job. Yet these are the only tools at hand. Even with medication, mood swings will over determine the ways in which sacred folds are encountered, and there is no life, no matter how "flat" that is bereft of sacred folds. The deciding question for us becomes: how do we enter into the quest for wholeness without on the one side sacrificing those peak experiences that most people will never be able to undergo without at the same time foundering in the abyss of nonmeaning and potential death?

Sacred folds do not occur by themselves, this is only one aspect of the sacred dimensions of nature. Each fold is surrounded by what I have come to call an "interval," namely, a clearing within which the more manic energy of the fold can be unfolded and some of its energy drained away. In theatre the interval is the time when the audience can step back and distance itself creatively from the intensity of the drama and prepare for a fresh encounter after the break. The Oxford English Dictionary defines what I am talking about, "The space of time intervening between two febrile paroxysms, or between any fits or periods of disease (1634 use)." This seventeenth century definition points to the space that surrounds the paroxysms that can punctuate the organism. It is a resting period that reempowers the organism for a new encounter with something shattering or transforming.

Another image that might help is that of the electrical transformer that steps down the voltage of electricity before it enters the house. The interval is like this transformer, taking the more manic energy of the sacred fold and making sure that it doesn't overwhelm the psychic house. Each sacred fold, whether a person, event, physical location, work of art, liturgical object, or anything that is numinous, will have its own interval. Consider, for example, the role of the words of religious liturgy as they surround a sacred act such as the drinking of wine as the blood of Christ. The cup and its contents represent a sacred fold for the Christian, but alone, without mediation, they would be too powerful, too strong in their archetypal force. Consequently, there are well known surrounding conditions that both locate the sacred fold and make it more manageable, more continuous with the rest of psychic life. Hymns, the sermon and the words of the liturgy all serve as intervals protecting the self from the overwhelming power of the sacred fold. It does not follow that communicants are aware of this logic, but it is part of the necessary reality sustaining the central sacred fold.

Hinduism has its own wonderful myth for showing the necessary dialectic between sacred folds and their intervals. Many of you will be familiar with the figure of the dancing Shiva who is surrounded with a large enveloping circle from which flames emerge. Shiva is standing on top of the figure for ignorance and dancing his cosmic dance through all eternity. His hair is spread out in wild strands that surround his head, going in all directions at once. The power of his hair actually serves as an interval for the energy that it helped to disperse. According to the myth, the great cosmic energy wanted to descend to earth in the form of a rushing river, but Shiva realized that this energy, which is meant to be healing, would actually destroy everything in its unbridled path. To disperse the energy and make it more manageable he forced it to flow through his long hair so that it would be channeled into several streams and lose its manic energy. When the cosmic energy finally arrived on earth it was able to assume the forms of the sacred rivers of India, such as the Ganga (Ganges). Hence, the hair of Shiva served as the interval for the divine *Shakti* that would otherwise have been too powerful for the earth to bear.

Sacred folds and their intervals have a natural history and are subject to entropy, by which I mean that they do not last forever and are subject to the loss of meaning over time. Try as I might, I cannot revive the classical Greek world, even if I go to Delphi and call upon Zeus and his eagles to make an appearance. That sacred fold, insofar as it has any lingering presence at all, has dimmed almost beyond recognition. Nor can I simply sit down and create a sacred fold and its interval by an act of will. Sacred folds emerge in their own way and by a logic that is deeply tied to unconscious (probably collective) currents. The fold and the interval seem to have an autonomous existence, and from our finite human perspective there is little we can say about the matter.

All of this may sound reasonable, but the question soon emerges: how do I, in practical terms, negotiate among these sacred folds and find their dampening intervals so that I can live the creative life in all of its richness? It is much easier to understand the concept of a sacred fold than that of an interval. After all, a sacred fold grasps you and transforms you in an absolutely unmistakable way, but the interval seems to be far too subtle, too hard to see and gauge. Perhaps an analogy will help. When looking at the night sky thorough a telescope or good pair of binoculars we often come across what is called a "deep space object," that is, something that is outside of our own Milky Way galaxy. The most famous perhaps is the Andromeda galaxy, known as M 31. It is very faint and hard to see if you look at it directly. However, if you shift your focus and look at it out of the corner of your eye, it comes into view as a distinct nebular shape. The side of the eye has more light sensitive rods and cones and can see more dimly lit objects. I would argue that the same sort of special sideward glance helps us to see intervals.

But are there specific things we can do psychologically that help us to see both folds and their intervals? This is tricky terrain because we are beginning to probe into the mysteries of the spiritual dimension of nature and with a form of natural grace that makes our encounter with this dimension possible. How can be combine technique with grace? We seem to be at an impasse. If we use a conscious technique, then we have usurped the role of grace, while if we simply wait around for grace we have failed to avail ourselves of real human tools. But this paradox is not as confounding as it might seem. For there are techniques that are in themselves grace-filled and that have the force they have because they are supported by something larger than consciousness and its intentional acts. It is not so much a vicious circle as it is a creative dialectic, with technique helping us to enter into the axis of grace, and grace helping us to master and secure technique. In what follows we will see this dialectic at work.

B. CREATIVE DISTANCING AND COMMUNAL TESTING

If it is impossible to eliminate the winds on which the Windhorse rides, then the only alternative is with finding the right way of riding those winds, of steering a course through often conflicting and overpowering energies that come from outside of the ego and its need for control. I have come to recognize that I will never be able to control my mood swings, and that I will always be subject to my complexes and my cravings for alcohol. I have seen the need to continue in therapy and to stay sober, but it is also important, perhaps more important, to understand the spiritual energies that I can rely upon to work with the demons and angels that are as much a gift as they are a curse. I want to be well, but not at the expense of a deeper and more tension-filled wholeness that calls forth greater effort.

I have learned from Vedanta, the more universal form of classical Hinduism as expressed in the *Upanishads*, that the infinite, while not a person or a moral agent, is a source for life transforming energy. Time and again I have returned to a reading of the major *Upanishads* when I have been most in danger of fragmentation and despair, and have come to see these works as perhaps the greatest religious texts ever written. Within them one finds the deepest wisdom of our species concerning how to both encounter and live with divine energy, the *Shakti* that for me has a feminine face. They have provided a means for me to deal with my death mother (as discussed in the first chapter) by transforming her into the Great Mother that is the preserver of the world. At the same time, they have taught me, in however tenuous a form, the lesson of what I call the "creative distancing" from the ambiguous fruits of my disease.

In the *Upanishads*, probably composed between 1200 B.C.E. and 500 C.E., the goal is to unite the true depth-self, termed *Atman* with the ultimate which is beyond all name or form, termed *Brahman* (concepts we saw in our discussion of Sri Ramakrishna). In the second chapter of the famous *Mundaka Upanishad* this insight is presented:

> The luminous Brahman dwells in the cave of the heart and is known to move there. It is the great support of all; for in It is centered everything that moves, breathes, and blinks. O disciples, know that to be your Self [*Atman*] — that which is both gross and subtle, which is adorable, supreme, and beyond the understanding of creatures.[3]

The self, like god, is both gross and subtle, which means that it has a manifest form in body and space and an unmanifest form that is outside of shape, name, texture, or attributes. At the same time the self *is* Brahman, is the divine source of the world of name and form. However, and this is an absolutely crucial point, the identification of self and god in the *Upanishads* has nothing in common with the pathological self-divinization of the manias in manic-depressive disorder. The fundamental difference between these two experiences is that the genuinely religious one entails that one has already worked through one's complexes and unconscious powers through creative distancing, and has thereby encountered the intervals that protect the self. In mania, on the other hand, the self is still the victim of momenta that partially tear it away from the divine.

Theologically, Hinduism has arrived at a brilliant dialectic in which it finds a place for both the particularity of gods and goddesses (for example Sri Ramakrishna's obsession with Kali), and a place for the absolute ground that silently radiates prior to even being and nonbeing. The contemporary Hindu scholar Raimundo Panikkar has well described the ultimate abyss within which even the gods and goddesses disappear:

> They [the writers of the *Upanishads*] plunge thus into a darkness enwrapped by darkness, into the Beyond from which there is no return, into that Prelude of Existence in which creatures of any type; the traveler himself is volatized, has disappeared.[4]

The movement of the self into the abyss of Brahman can be characterized as a centripetal movement toward pure radiance in which the various stands of the self are creatively rewoven and brought into harmony. Manic experience can be seen as centrifugal in which the shards of the self are thrown outward into a great chaotic arc that has neither center nor circumference, only an over determined pulsation of nonintegrated meanings. Further, unlike genuine religious experience, manic experience quickly degenerates into paranoia and fears the infinite energies that course through it. In creative distancing, infinite energy is worked through with the help of divine grace and the power of the spirit. Sacred folds and intervals achieve their proper measure with each other and envelop the self in nondestructive ways.

Mere distancing, mere detachment, entails a deadening of life energies, a turning away from the ground and abyss of the world in an effort to protect the self from the infinite. Creative distancing, on the other hand, embraces the dialectic of being and nonbeing, of the sacred and the demonic, but does not identify fully with their powers. It is a way of distancing that at the same time works in and through complex unconscious material as it buffets the ego and threatens it with dissolution. To be creatively detached from one's moods and complexes is still to honor their necessary being in one's life and to find a means for bringing them to expression.

This process is not the same as that denoted by Freud with his concept of sublimation in which psychosexual energy is channeled (cathected) into something safer. Psychosexual energy is allowed its play *as* psychosexual energy, but other forms of energy are also brought into the creative matrix. The winds upon which the Windhorse rides take many forms, and it is a species of reductionism to assume, as Freud did, that one form is ultimate in all respects.

The problem is that of returning to those energies from which medication has partially freed the self. Clearly, sexual energy is the most problematic, especially for the manic-depressive who acts out sexually in the hypo-manic or manic state. The repercussions for failing to handle this seemingly infinite power are the great insofar as it can tear at the fabric of the family or the community. It is not uncommon for the manic-depressive to abject or deny this bodily form of the *Shakti* when in a more stable state. We do not have to accept Freud's version of the ideal solution to this dilemma to recognize its centrality to our lives. But a deadening detachment is not the answer.

In creative distancing it is possible to reenhance bodily and sexual energy and to find the right foci for its expression. One's partner becomes more than a means to release overwhelming manic energy and can be seen as an end in him or herself. It is not so much that one becomes detached from the body and its needs as that one recognizes that the body is one of the places where ultimate import can come to rest and find expression. It has been a tragedy, and here I would agree with Reich, that almost all of the major religious have driven a wedge between spirituality and sexuality, producing in their wake innumerable forms of pathology than honor neither. The issue becomes that of spiritualizing sexuality, but perhaps more importantly, of sexualizing spirituality.

When the powerful currents of sexuality course through the body the ego can regain its strength and integrity, provided that sexual energy is used to enhance meaning and ensure participation in the depths of another self. All of this would sound like a banal truism were it not so hard to achieve, especially for the manic-depressive for whom sexual energy is over determined and represents the danger of manic inflation. For some, medication can impede the flow of sexual energy and this fact needs to be integrated into problem of the quest for wholeness. In the act of creative distancing, the touch and feel of the Other can become the gateway to the right correlation of the finite and the infinite.

In social interaction, another treacherous terrain for the manic-depressive, there remains the problem of public validation for the ambiguous gifts of creative work. In the previous chapter I worked through the relationship between products of genius and the nature of communal life that can sustain such products. Here I want to examine how the individual creator learns to intersect with the social structures that are often so baffling, recalcitrant, or seemingly perverse. The strategy of cognitive testing is one of the most helpful in both intrapsychic work and intersubjectivity.

In cognitive therapy the goal is to work through one's ideation and feelings to test them against as much of reality as it is possible to access at a given time. For example, it is a common experience that those with a mood disorder are most depressed when they wake up and find that their immediate assessment of the impending day is darkened by depression. The tasks that are looming in the present often seem overwhelming, and one can feel self-loathing. The first thing I do in this common almost daily experience is to list in my mind those things that must be done and to do a kind of cost-benefit analysis of how much of my carefully guarded energy will be spent and how much will be held back for me and how much given over to my community. I weigh each option and work through those that have the most positive outcome for me and for those who are dependent upon me for their own work. If something can be tackled immediately with little effort, I select that for my first task. At the same time I know how my energy flows move through the day and set aside my best hours for my most important work.

Things get more layered when we deal with the emotional aspects of the cost-benefit analysis. Like most manic-depressives, I am always concerned to minimize any trigger events that might disrupt the flow of energy into more profitable pursuits. I cannot always avoid all stressors of course, but I can minimize their impact by working through in my mind the worst aspects that could happen in a given situation. The point, however, is that I do this in a *realistic* rather than a paranoid manner, precisely to eliminate unnecessary fears about social interaction. With trusted colleagues I have even come to the point where I can share my fears, especially if they know about my disease, and can, through them, do further reality testing.

Cognitive therapy is thus both a personal and a social means of constructing various scenarios for the day so that some meaningful parameters emerge that can be trusted. If a situation becomes too fraught with tension, I have learned to absent myself even if that places an extra burden on others who must complete a given task without me. But this simply cannot be helped if I am to survive the mood swings and latent or manifest forms of paranoia that still do persist even with medication. There is a kind of higher selfishness that goes with creative distancing that insures some penumbra of protection around me as I negotiate with external reality and internal negative voices.

The relationship between the individual and the community is always complex, especially since there are innumerable communities embedded in every individual whether they are consciously known about or not. I can have an unconscious identity with a seemingly distant community that I am not aware of until a traumatic or transfiguring event occurs that suddenly shows me that I do belong to that community in a host of ways that I did not suspect. My decision to enter into the divestment campaign against companies practicing in South Africa, as discussed in the first chapter, represents one such example where I was brought into intersection with a world many thousands of miles away because of prophetic voices, such as that of Archbishop Tutu, that spoke to me in my seeming isolation.

It helps to see the individual as the place where innumerable communities intersect like so many ellipses around a gravitational body. For the manic-depressive it is often profoundly difficult to discover the *actual* trajectories of these communities because the power of manic projection or depressed abjection is so strong. Yet with ongoing internal and social cognitive therapy it is possible to find some way of feeling the pull of these ellipses as they enrich or challenge the self.

Creative distancing, higher selfishness, and cognitive therapy are all tools that the manic-depressive can use to find some lasting stability in the world that so often seems just out of reach. Yet all of these finite strategies can have little power, can have little purchase on the self unless there is something deeper that supports and guides them. In my final reflections I want to probe into this depth-structure and power that makes it possible for the manic-depressive to move toward some sense of wholeness and to provide a model for individuation for those who are not subject to intense mood swings.

C. INDIVIDUATION AND THE SPIRITS

It is my belief that all profound spirituality starts in the experience of melancholy, in the sense of mourning for a lost object that is still dimly remembered around the edges of consciousness. On the simplest level this is the sense of loss for the biological conditions of origin in the mother from whose womb we have fallen into the world of pain and confusion. It is almost literally a fall from paradise. Yet on a much deeper level it is a fall from the divine origin of meaning that beckons to us from a domain that I have called the pretemporal. It is outside of the flow of time, as we know it in our three-dimensional world, where time is measured as movement through space (the view of Newton). The pretemporal is the domain or dimension of nature that is the eternal womb (what Plato called the *chora*) for all things. It is a domain that on some unconscious level we know to be there, even if we have no means for rendering it into words, or even of wanting to do so. Yet it exerts its uncanny presence nonetheless.

How do I know enough to make what may seem like an astonishing and nonempirical claim? After all, manic-depressives are often accused of just such leaps into religious fancy when their manias are on the march. And it is surely not enough to simply cite ancient texts like the venerable *Upanishads* if the very concept of religion or spirituality is held to be a holdover from antiquated ways of thinking, or much worse, to be forms of delusional self-justification. What then are the marks or traces of this ultimate ground and abyss that can be seen in the self? Asked differently: what does melancholy actually reveal about the hidden support conditions for psychic life?

The first thing that must be done is to let thought and experience slow down long enough to enter into the rhythms of the real itself. In the technical language of philosophy there is a strategy, developed originally in Germany in the twentieth century, called *phenomenology* that has as its simple motto, "To the things themselves." The creator of this still vital and evolving movement, to which my own thinking belongs, Edmund Husserl, argued that philosophers were far too ready to import presuppositions into their work and to dictate to the world the ways in which it must appear. As a counter to this rather arrogant stance he proposed that we take the time to carefully examine the ways in which consciousness actually goes about its business of letting objects appear to it in their *own* terms. The very word "phenomenon" means the act of self-showing that is the way in which the object comes to us. And this "object" can be anything from a thing, to a thought, to a feeling, to a possibility, or to a sacred fold. What I want to propose is that for the manic-depressive, who is by definition in search for both stable and ultimate meanings, the method of phenomenology is invaluable (even if it is not named as such).

Let us then look (phenomenologically) at the phenomenon of melancholy and see if there is anything about its unique form of self-showing that can point to the ground and abyss of meaning. We need to let this phenomenon, which we have all experienced even if in a muted form, enter into our awareness and trace out how it moves and follow where it leads us. We must let go of all of our presuppositions and theories about what we *think* melancholy is and let *it* be the lead in our investigations.

In turning our attention to melancholy the first thing we notice is that it is *all-pervasive*. It is not a mood that is about this or that particular but is about *all* particulars, about the world as a whole. In the experience of melancholy the world is illuminated as a totality over and against the self, a totality that is opaque in its very illumination. This is a paradox. On the one hand melancholy lights up the world, that is, makes it manifest as a totality in a certain way, while on the other hand it also cloaks the world in darkness. The world of the melancholic is both manifest and unmanifest, hidden and unhidden. The sheer power of melancholy is that it illumines the utter loss of the meaning the world as a whole.

The second thing we notice about melancholy is that it carries with it a *sense of loss*, again, not about this or that particular but about the world as a whole. The meaning of the world as a whole is lost; it recedes into an abyss that is dimly sensed on the edges of awareness. There is a sense of a *no longer* that goes with melancholy. What once was obtains no more and the self feels an uncanny absence at the heart of the world. Of course this is another paradox, namely, that the absent is also present but *as* absent. This paradox is not so hard to understand. We all have the experience of missing someone who is absent from us, but the very fact that we miss *him or her* is a presence, something we can feel in the present. Combining our first two phenomenological observations we can say that the mood of melancholy reveals to us that the world as a whole is bereft of meaning and is a curious blend of absence, with its sense of loss, and of muted presence.

The third thing we notice about the phenomenon of melancholy is that it contains a seed of *restlessness* at its heart. That is, melancholy wants to move forward or backward, to step away from itself in some direction. In suicidal ideation melancholy wants to deliver the self from itself through death. But even more primal that this suicidal ideation is a stirring that wants to move from the great *no longer* to a greater *not yet*, to an open world in which meaning may once again emerge not just for this or that particular but for the world as a whole.

It is absolutely crucial that the potential suicide be understood as someone caught in the dialectic between the two directions that melancholy can take. On one level is the direction that leads to the sudden, total, and complete extinction of all meaning, while on another level is the direction that leads to a slow opening into the *not yet*. It is the totality of meaning that is at stake, not this or that relationship, this or that economic dilemma, or this or that regret. And the quest for wholeness founders or succeeds at just this nexus.

Here there is a splitting within the experience of melancholy. One path leads downward into ultimate closure and the other into a nascent hope. The fourth thing we notice about melancholy is this *opening potential* into the *not yet*. At the very heart of the restlessness of melancholy is the possibility that meaning will return and transfigure melancholy into hope. How do we experience this in concrete terms?

If melancholy is a totalizing experience about the loss of meaning in the world as a whole, and if melancholy is also in mourning for a lost object, then the movement of melancholy must change directions and look for its lost object elsewhere than in the *no longer* (i.e., the past). Again we see a paradox. For the attempt to return to the *no longer* pulls the self into closure and death. The lost object, in that dimension, is truly lost and can never return. But what is most uncanny about melancholy is that the lost object can return from the exact opposite direction, namely, out of the open future in which meaning returns to the world as a whole. I can regain a sense of the power of my being and of the supremacy of meaning over nonmeaning, say in a resurrected relationship that had seemed lost beyond repair.

The fifth and final thing we notice about melancholy is that it contains within itself the seeds of the *return of meaning* in the *not yet*. How does this meaning come about? My sense is that if we carefully listen to what melancholy is telling us, rather than imposing a theoretical structure onto it, we find that it intersects with an energy that has traditionally been called the spirit. What then is the spirit that slumbers within the heart of melancholy and how do we know that it is present?

In traditional Christianity the spirit is seen as a quasi-person who completes the work of Christ in history after the drama of the resurrection has taken place. It blows where it wills and cannot be tamed by any human hand or agency. In this sense it is like the *drala* that I referred to in the Preface, or like the *Shakti* that I referred to in the context of Hinduism. It is an energy that is larger than human and that can intersect with the human in a variety of ways. It is the energy that works in those great between spaces (the intervals) where meanings can open out and become available to the self.

In the restless heart of melancholy the spirit can be seen as it leaves a moving trace or clearing that invites meaning back into the opaque totality of the world. The spirit is not so much a noun as it is a verb, a movement of opening awaiting the emergence of the *not yet*. Again, this is an experience we all have felt, for example, when a conversation suddenly turns in a dramatic new direction and opens up a deeper sense of the person with whom we are speaking, or when there is an epiphany in the context of ordinary routine. What was once closed now becomes open, what was once opaque suddenly takes on a new radiance.

But why have I used the plural form of "spirits" in the subheading of this chapter if I am really talking about the spirit? Am I regressing to a primitive form of animism in which the world is seen as the locus for all sorts of energies and magical powers that swirl in and out of consciousness? Or is there another logic at work here? My growing sense is that it has become increasingly difficult to talk of *the* spirit in these postmodern times, where so much attention is being paid to difference and discontinuity within experience. And while I do not share all of the philosophical presuppositions that go with postmodernism, I do agree that we are at a turning point in human history in which it has now become necessary to honor the various guises that the higher energy or power can take. Partly this comes from my initial AA experience, partly it comes from my sense that the Vedanta thinkers have it right about the dialectic between the particular and the universal, and partly it comes from my simple pragmatism that insists that all of us, regardless of what we might *think* we are doing, name our spirits in deeply private ways.

For the manic-depressive, especially when caught in the grip of melancholy, there are hints of a higher energy that come out of the restlessness within the world-eclipsing mood. But this energy is personal, is tied to a personal horizon, a personal center of meaning. The spirit that plays across the face of the deep, the swirling abyss of chaos in the Jewish *Torah*, emerges as a light in the personal center, promising meaning in the open future. If there is a universal spirit, it is manifest in personal forms, and this personal manifestation is part of its very being.

The individuation process, as so carefully described by Jung, involves the encounter with one's personal spirit, however named. It is a gift, a manifestation of grace that is found within each self, especially when psychic dissolution threatens. Is this to say that the gift of the spirit can take away the need for medication and chemical intervention? Certainly not. To say that would be to be guilty of magical thinking, and would strip away one of the necessary support conditions for the spirit's work. Again let me reiterate my hard won insight that without proper medication all talk of spiritual renewal or individuation is vacuous and in fact quite dangerous. And after all, the personal spirit is always incarnate in the body, and is not some free-floating apparition.

Each of us, then, encounters a spiritual presence that is deeply personal. It can assume "name and form" but these are never ultimate. The spirit that is ours will light up sacred folds but also manifest the intervals that protect us from those very folds. The Windhorse rides on the breath of the spirit and can, when the conditions are right, enter into the complex interplay of sacred folds and intervals and enrich spiritual existence. But we must not romanticize this process as if our spirit can somehow solve all of the dilemmas that go with living through our mood swings. Like any other product of nature the spirits are deeply finite. Perhaps they are less finite than other things we encounter, but they are certainly not omnipotent. There always remains some sense of mystery as to why my spirit "decides" to appear one day and retreat into silence the next. And even when it does appear it must always do so in ambiguous and fragmented ways. Ambiguity goes all the way down into the heart of nature's mysteries, and no conception of the spirit can be long maintained against the blows of fate that does not acknowledge this sobering fact.

Clearly, it is tempting to assume that the spirits of the world are always salvific and deeply concerned with my personal needs. But again, this is a kind of magical thinking that is unfortunately encouraged by institutional religions. The spirit that I encounter in the great between spaces of my life can and does aid in reading the signs, in finding the real in the midst of the ofttimes blinding panoply of signs and meanings that can inundate me. But it is neither omnipotent nor omniscient, that is, it is not some kind of ultimate data bank that holds eternal truths that I can withdraw when in need. It is more like a movement or clearing in which certain things come to light that I *can* use in salvific ways.

Above, I used the concept of "natural grace" to talk about one part of the dialectic between technique (e.g., creative distancing or cognitive therapy) and grace. The prefix "natural" is important. In my own sense of the life of the spirits, grace is not something that comes from a supernatural realm or from some divine act of a supernatural being, but from the momentum of nature itself. My own philosophical perspective of *ecstatic naturalism* insists that there is nothing discontinuous with nature, that there is nothing that stands outside of nature and its orders. This does not mean that nature can be understood only in scientific terms, nor does it assume an insidious reductionism or materialism. On the contrary, *ecstatic* naturalism takes mystery and sacredness very seriously. The important proviso, however, is that all mysteries and all manifestations of the sacred are *in* and *of* nature in its sheer plenitude (cf. appendix).

Consequently grace must be *natural* grace, a grace that is found within the orders of the world that surround us. It is the grace that secures our life against nonbeing, the grace that gives us a new sense of the power of our own being to overcome the forces that tear into our fragile ego. My personal spirit can quicken that natural grace, and insofar as it does so we are entitled to talk about a grace of the spirit. But again, this grace, if we wish to see it as a second and special form, is fully natural, as natural as my personal spirit, which must always work with and against recalcitrant and ambiguous material.

I remain persuaded that the last thing a manic-depressive needs is some kind of watered down and unrealistic form of spirituality, as if rhetoric and good feeling can help us struggle with this powerful psychosis. Our spirituality must be realistic, sober, cognizant of ambiguity, and open to the possibility that there will be failures, and that the energy of the spirit may withdraw. Ralph Waldo Emerson, while not manic-depressive, was far more profound than many of his readers realized when he spoke of the feelings that can overwhelm the self when the spirit suddenly disappears:

> Where do we find ourselves? In a series of which we do not know the extremes, and believe that is has none. We wake and find ourselves on a stair; there are stairs below us, which we seem to have ascended; there are stairs above us, many a one, which go upward and out of sight. But the Genius which, according to the old belief, stands at the door by which we enter, and gives us the lethe to drink, that we may tell no tales, mixed the cup too strongly, and we cannot shake off the lethargy now at noonday. . . Ghostlike we glide through nature, and should not know our place again. . . We are like millers on the lower levels of a stream, when the factories above them have exhausted the water. We too fancy that the upper people have raised their dams.[5]

Emerson was prone to deep depression and experienced forms of conversion hysteria while a divinity student (partial blindness). He was well aware of the strange trajectory of moods as they weave themselves in and out of the self and chronicled these moods as well as anyone in the Euro-American tradition. His imagery here is precisely reminiscent of what it feels like when spiritual energy recedes into the background, and we are left without enough sacred water to turn the water wheels of consciousness. No amount of positive thinking, no display of rhetorical power, and no amount of self-coaxing can force the waters of the spirit to return if they have decided to remain dammed up. Even with technique we sometimes have to learn to wait, to endure the dry spell that can come without warning.

The spirituality I am calling for is one that knows full well what the quest for wholeness can cost, both to the self and to the community. Wholeness is neither an antecedent state nor a state of total completion. We can only have intimations of what this state might be like, a state in which the fiery magma and chilling depths of our disorder are brought into some kind of tension-filled harmony. But we are not alone in this struggle. We have the power of medication and the insights of therapy. We also have the powers that circulate in and through sacred folds and their intervals and the momentum of the spirit that can help us find the right forms of measure among competing powers within our own life.

In a very clear sense, of course, many of these powers are of our own making, the result of projection and transferential longings that color and shape whatever sacred folds we encounter.

I have often wondered if we can apply the concept of the countertransference to the sacred folds in nature. This might sound like an absurd idea, especially since both the transference and the countertransference are deeply *human* responses to the world, not something that the *world* could generate outside of consciousness. I am stretching a concept to its breaking point, but I want to try out a speculation that just might help us live spiritually in the midst of those intense pockets of meaning that become so important whether we have manic-depressive disorder or not.

I can understand how I can have a transference relationship to another person and he or she to me. And I can also understand how I can have a transference relationship to a sacred text like the *Bible* or the *Upanishads*. So far so good. But what relationship can these latter types of things, especially since they are things and not selves, have to me? Can they exert some kind of pressure back on me that could, at least analogously, be called transferential? Could a sacred fold even be aware that I exist, that the same "I" that fills it with my projected content is part of it's inner logic? Aren't we falling into some kind of anthropomorphic trap here in importing human traits into nature, the very thing that I warned about before when talking about the ultimate? Or is there a special *kind* of countertransference that psychoanalysis has thus far failed to acknowledge or understand?

I want to propose the idea that sacred folds and their intervals are in some important sense capable of resisting our most flagrant projections, of throwing them back at us by "refusing" to take them on. In a further sense I want to say that this is a kind of ongoing energy that functions very much like a countertransference, namely, as an openness (which is not conscious of course) to the original transference that came to rest on the sacred fold. Consider the case of a painting that we encounter in a museum. We may be baffled by it at first, especially if it is nonrepresentational and uses strange forms and structures, that is, strange from the standpoint of what we usually mean by Newtonian three-dimensional space and its objects. Perhaps the painting is functioning like a large Rorschach blot that calls forth projections on our part. We can't help but project upon it some unconscious complexes of our own, whether the artist intended them or not. What happens to the social history of this painting if it is truly a sacred fold, a work of great power and scope?

My interpretations must enter into some kind of public space, however minimal. My projections will be compared with those of others, or I may engage in an internal conversation with myself alone, but both structures will be communal in some minimal sense. The space within which these conversations occur is actually the interval that surrounds the painting, that provides the clearing within which the sheer power of the painting can be encountered in finite ways. My contention is this: that this space, this enveloping and vibrant clearing is the locus for the countertransference that measures and challenges the transferences that come to meet the sacred fold of the painting. It is a counter move that will "encourage" some interpretations and "discourage" others, not, of course in a conscious intentional way. But the interval will come to meet us and provide a place for our transference.

I consider this idea so important that I want to rotate it on a different axis to see if it can be further illuminated. Think about reading sacred scripture. In the Jewish tradition such reading is not for the purpose of proclamation but for creative argument and interpretation, the process known as Midrash. A Midrashic reading is one that enters into the to-and-fro movement of the text and its historical commentaries. We read the text in order to be drawn into a dialectic in which the text, as mediated through its great interpreters (whose commentaries actually appear around the text), enters into the movement of our own longings and projections. But the text and commentaries do not simply stare back at us in mute indifference. They answer us, they challenge, and they call our transferences into question. They can say "yes" and "no" to what we want to throw over them, and I want to say that this process of saying yes and no is a countertransferential process. It is a response to what we have sent, to our particularity, our immediacy as projecting beings whose complexes are ever restless until they land on some sacred fold. And the space that surrounds the Midrashic activity is the interval that brings transference and countertransference together.

Living in the spirit, then, is living in and through our own transferences, which are at heart religious, and in the strange ways of the countertransference that can come to meet us where we stand in our struggle. For the manic-depressive nature will always be alive with meaning, more meanings in fact than most people will ever know. In our mild hypomanias we can understand the ways in which the countertransference operate. Objects speak to us, if not in the tongues of the *Bible*, then in ways we can still feel in the deepest recesses of consciousness. There is a kind of intimacy with the world that is peculiar with this disease, an intimacy with its own forms of terrible grace.

What, then, can we conclude at the end of our journey through the many byways of manic-depressive disorder? I have said what I can about practical strategies such as avoiding trigger events, the use of medicine, creative distancing, communal testing, cognitive therapy, avoiding substance abuse, negotiating the transference and countertransference currents of life, and establishing relationships of trust. I have spoken of the need to be honest with one's own demons and one's past transgressions, and with making amends in the present (strong AA principles). I have myself tried to look at the world through the eyes of fellow sufferers like Newton and Sri Ramakrishna. And I have revealed much of my own journey, being cognizant of what I have lost and what I have gained as I have been forced to reshape my self again in my post-diagnosis universe.

APPENDIX: MY PASSAGE FROM PANENTHEISM TO PANTHEISM

There is a difference between being on a philosophical passage across uncharted waters, and being on a pathway through known hills and woodlands. In the latter case it is easy to see natural and conventional sign posts that indicate the whence and whither of the journey, while in the former case there is always the uncanny awareness of a hidden dialectic at play; namely, between a deliberate embarkation on a goal directed sea voyage, and the uncanny sense of being driven by some taciturn force across waters whose surface and depth contours have failed to reveal themselves. In philosophical query there may come moments in which a certain subtle kind of clarity begins to emerge as to the hidden whence and whither of such a lonely journey, even if these moments of understanding soon fade back into the mists and fogs of the enveloping sea.

Having arrived at such a moment, I feel the need to exhibit some of its contours before the mists return to shroud what has emerged as a sign of the passage I have taken from the ordinal panentheism shaped in my writings in the late 1980s and early 1990s toward a pantheistic ecstatic naturalism that is now coming more fully into its own in this new century. The earlier works struggled toward a post-monotheistic understanding of the *one* nature and its innumerable orders, yet my theological articulations remained too closely related to the forms of twentieth century panentheism coming out of process thought to truly reflect the depth-categories of *nature naturing* and *nature natured* that have continued to serve as a leitmotif throughout my thinking.[1] Further, my hope was that a rethinking of the categorical legacies of Alfred North Whitehead and Charles Hartshorne with the aid of the ordinal metaphysics of Justus Buchler[2] would free philosophical theology from any taint of atomism and a doctrine of internal relations, not to mention the seemingly anti-naturalist perspective of panpsychism.[3] I now realize that I was only partially right. My use of the powerful method of ordinal phenomenology[4] was occasionally misdirected by some implicit and unthought transcendental arguments derived from liberal Christianity. For my continual thinking, this creative tension between phenomenological descriptions and transcendental strategies remains inevitable and goads further query toward that elusive place where transcendental arguments will no longer be needed.

Clearly there is something soothing and mythological about process metaphysics, this last gasp of liberal Protestant theology. This mythos is hidden behind a cosmology of optimism and unending growth into complexity and wholeness. The more austere perspective of ordinal metaphysics seemed at the time to be the right antidote to the optimistic cosmology of actual occasions, with *its* contrary insistence on sheer complexity (all the way down), ordinal location, anti-eschatology, and pan-naturalism. Yet it too fails to probe deeply enough into the implications of the ontological difference between *nature naturing* and *nature natured*, a distinction that does operate in a highly muted way in the underside of ordinal metaphysics.

My naturalist critics have argued that I sell naturalism to the religionists because I affirm the view that nature has room for an ontologically thick spirit (or spirits), while my theological critics have argued that I am only a halfway process thinker because my antiquated naturalism holds me back from a full articulation of panpsychism (panexperientalism) and of the unique traits of the divine. Are both sets of critics curiously right but for very wrong reasons? Clearly, they have not grasped the entirety of ordinal panentheism (a strange post-monotheistic monotheism), and their readings are textually limited, even truncated, while falling into well-worn grooves of interpretation. However, the possibility of an internal conceptual problem in my perspective, as raised by my critics, emerged more starkly for me through my dialogue with Robert Neville in the mid-1990s. In his review of my 1992 book *Nature and Spirit*, he asserts that my commitment to exploring the distinction between *nature naturing* and *nature natured* does not logically entail that any "middling gods" (or divine dimensions) are needed to connect the two dimensions of the one nature together. I have now come to see that he is correct, especially because his critique comes from a sophisticated reading of my work, and that my carefully drawn four-fold dimensionality of the divine, while, perhaps evocative in certain respects, may be conceptually cumbersome, un-phenomenological, and even in tension with the basal insights of my perspective.

In retrospect, I now see that this four-fold view of the divine natures was an important way-station on the passage to a more fully self-aware ecstatic naturalism. It made it possible to envelop and locate theism with its list of anthropomorphic (and patriarchal) traits within a more generic perspective that envisioned the potencies of the unitarian and universalist spirit as occurring *within* an ordinal nature. At the same time, it brought out some of the tensions among the various activities that we demand from the divine and struggled to coordinate them within a dialectical unfolding that was fully open to these tensions. Further, the four-fold articulation of the divine made it possible to correlate finite and infinite traits in a way that had not been developed before, a way that may still have much intrinsic merit as a pointer and goad. Finally, the ordinal reconfiguration broke the link between atomism and panpsychism that has been the bane of foundational query into nature.

But what exactly is this (earlier) view that most of my interlocutors fail to understand, or so I continue to think, and what within it can be transliterated into a more capacious perspective that will honor the deepest impulses of this ongoing probe into the heart of nature? More precisely, how do perhaps compulsive, yet hidden, transcendental arguments veer into and deflect the much slower process of ordinal phenomenology? Are there forceful traces of a tribal Christian perspective, no matter how liberal, which operate to blunt the generic momenta of phenomenological insight into *all* of nature? Should the word "God" be gently purged from fundamental query into the ontological abyss between *nature naturing* and *nature natured*? And if so, as I now believe it must, can we still honor the primary phenomenological intuitions of the then nascent perspective of ecstatic naturalism and its probes into the ordinal traits of the sacred?

NATURE AND SPIRIT: THE FIRST EMBARKATION

A writer is frequently asked if she or he has a favored book, even if its perspective is in need of amelioration. When asked this question, I answer that *Nature and Spirit: An Essay in Ecstatic Naturalism,* remains the text that brings back the strongest memories of both composition and of the many struggles that had to be undergone before it could be written. It is the text of self-discovery on the way toward an ecstatic naturalism—a metaphysical commitment that is perhaps too boldly and prematurely proclaimed by the book's sub-title. It was written in several places, under very different personal and professional circumstances, and in ongoing dialectic with a number of pertinent traditions. My way of engaging in philosophical query is through a series of dialogues with living or deceased interlocutors.

In my own truncated self-history I can list six figures with whom I co-thought the perspective leading to the writing of *Nature and Spirit*: Martin Heidegger, Charles Sanders Peirce, Justus Buchler, Karl Jaspers, Paul Tillich, and Charles Hartshorne. Among these six I had the honor of knowing and working with Buchler and Hartshorne, neither of whom was especially fond of the other's categorial scheme. To be even more compressed I can say that Heidegger taught me the absolute bindingness of the craft of unrelenting thinking in and through the receding ground (*Ab-grund*). From Peirce I learned of the power of semiotics when grounded in an expansive metaphysics. From Buchler I learned the liberating power of thinking generically. As a thinker he was capacious, generous, and almost totally free from tribalism of any kind. From Jaspers I learned how to enter into the movement of different dimensions of the self and thereby to sense the Encompassing shining through them. Through Tillich I was able to remain within liberal Christianity somewhat longer than was perhaps wise, but I also learned how to use the symbols of a tradition in the richest possible ways. Finally, from Hartshorne I learned the strengths and profound limitations of optimism and of process metaphysics. His friendliness to Peirce gave us an initial point of connection through which we could discuss aspects of nature and the divine.

Yet all of these thinkers seemed to be fleeing from something I instinctively sensed at the heart of our encounters with *the* nature that we also *are*; namely the confrontation with the diremption of *nature naturing* as it both spawns and recedes from *nature natured*. Even Tillich used his regnant concept of the ground and abyss of being as a means for covering over an even deeper prospect into the darksome passages of the heart of nature. That he came closer to embracing this awareness than any of my other interlocutors puts him in an honorific category, although his categorical delineations are more prosaic and standard than those developed by Buchler. The question returns: was my thinking in *Nature and Spirit* able to face into the heart of nature while also unfolding a compelling metaphysics?

Here the term "metaphysics" shall denote the enterprise of thinking generically about anything whatsoever insofar as such thinking seeks to exhibit recurrent and fundamental traits of nature and 'its' orders. On this definition, one can no more overcome metaphysics than one can overcome nature. Each metaphysical perspective, whether it takes ownership of itself *as* metaphysics or not, says something about the way, how, and whats of nature, in however successful or blundering a fashion. To call one's own framework "anti-metaphysical" is merely to narcissistically parade a weak and wounded/wounding pseudo-metaphysics in front of those who would, in contrast, dare to make more bold and encompassing conceptual moves. This culturally expensive farce has now been played out fully and it no longer should concern or stifle the craft of genuine thinking.

The primary concern in *Nature and Spirit* is to develop a generic perspective that affirms that there is no supernatural realm, while also acknowledging that there are places within nature where something like the divine operates. The perspective of naturalism has too often limited itself to some kind of materialism, as if the word "matter" has more than a polemical value to begin with. Surely, we are told, one cannot be against good old trustworthy matter with its stable and knowable cluster of traits. But why privilege matter, whatever 'it' turns out to be? True naturalism does not seek nor designate any primary trait as being fundamental in all respects for the orders of and as nature, whether that alleged universal trait is seen as spirit, matter, monads, actual occasions, energy, actuality, potentiality, possibility, sense-data, form, or simple stuff. In fact, it is not even the task of *philosophy* to designate generic traits in *this* sense, but to do so in the very difference sense of providing categorial clearings onto how the *various* kinds of "whats" obtain or fail to obtain. Determining the nature of the more specific whats falls to the subaltern disciplines, each of which will name its field-specific "whatnesses" in its own ways. Hence, the task of *Nature and Spirit* is seen to be that of providing access to the openings within/as nature that let innumerable traits emerge on roughly their own terms. The point of tension comes when the divine dimensions are held to be among these natural traits.

In the fourth and final chapter of *Nature and Spirit* the four divine dimensions are articulated as they operate in 'themselves' (an impossible precinding from relationality) and as they correlate with each other and with nature (remembering that they must also be fully 'part' of the one nature and never in a mere "with" relationship to 'it'). The first two dimensions of god are understood to be natural complexes with limited scope and efficacy within the innumerable orders of *nature natured* ("creation" for the Christian). The first dimension is manifest to the human process as epiphanies of power that enhance, and sometimes assault, the self in its trajectory toward some kind of culmination of experience. These epiphanies emerge from conditions of origin in nature that are fragmentary and elusive, thereby denying anything like an extra-natural teleological ordering or any ultimate governing epiphany-of-all-epiphanies. They come and go by their own hidden logic, are subject to entropy, and ride on the currents of the human unconscious, whether personal or collective.

The second divine dimension, like the first, has no grand teleological structure, but comes from the opposite domain to that of origins; namely, from fragmented realistic utopian expectations that hold open a creative *not-yet* for struggling selves and their communities. There is a conflict between these first two dimensions:

> While the first dimension emerges out of a fragmented origin, the second appears from the fragmented powers of expectation. In this second dimension, God is still to be understood as a natural complex, and thus retains its plurality and fragmented quality. The goals of the divine life are fragmented because they must become efficacious against the backdrop of an inert and often hostile world. Finite purposes, as components within developmental teleology, work within and against powers that would like to see all purposes flattened into antecedent habits. God struggles against personal and social inertia by providing goads toward creative transformation.[5]

Against all of my intents and purposes, this language of a struggling god who must confront its own warring tendencies, imports a traditional Job-like personified pseudo-deity into the heart of nature. If nothing else, an unrelenting naturalism is strongly opposed to any form of anthropomorphic thinking that would write human traits too largely onto the face of the one nature. What could have been seen here as a tension between spirit-infused and unconsciously projected human traits, became solidified into a more finite but fulsome counter-model to the process notion of the much larger consequent nature of god. My phenomenological intuitions into the dialectic between the pull of origins and the pull of expectations was deflected into categorical posits of a divine puller and a divine pulled. The act of substituting a smaller, often pain ridden, consequent nature of god for the more tender and infinitely capacious process version failed to let the phenomenological self-showing of traits proceed along its own way and at its own pace. The process mythos had not yet been overcome, in spite of my rhetorical claims to the contrary.

To be truer to ordinal phenomenology it would have been necessary to enter into the bindingness of what shows itself here while also refusing to name these curious facets of nature in advance. This is especially so insofar as they are concresced in the human process and its pertinent orders of relevance. Further, such a continual rotation of relational and 'internal' traits would have utterly avoided any honorific language that would give these traits some special status within the innumerable traits of nature *and* the subaltern human orders. To call the extra-human, but never extra-natural, pull of certain strongly relevant traits by the name "god," is to intrude a transcendental argument just when more strenuous phenomenological effort is demanded. There is a certain conceptual laziness in the transcendental argument, which posits a necessary, universal, and hidden condition to account for what *is* encountered, at this juncture, in finite experience.

For a tightly bound Neo-Kantian, the more formal and well-dressed cousin of the postmodern *boulevardier*, such transcendental arguments are necessary and even welcomed. There is a strong logical link between the limitations built into finitude and the requirements, given these limitations, to use a variety of transcendental arguments to escape, however precariously, from these limitations. Both Ernst Cassirer and the young Heidegger (who dedicated himself to the destructuring of Neo-Kantianism) fell prey to the presupposition that finitude was the 'natural' condition of the self, although Cassirer envisioned an opening into the infinite through mathematical physics and the right use of the symbols of objective spirit. On this side of the Atlantic, naturalists like John Dewey, Frederick Woodbridge, John Herman Randall, Jr., George Santayana, and Buchler all affirmed our littleness in the face of a nature that could be partially transfigured to human ends, yet always had the final word.[6]

But what if the twentieth century obsession with human finitude was deeply flawed in ways that must now be probed by a healthy naturalism, an ecstatic and pantheistic naturalism more attuned to the various modalities of the infinite? If the unthought presuppositions concerning human finitude are opened out and shown to be un-phenomenological, then the corollary use of half-blind transcendental strategies is also put into profound question. With a different understanding of the self-in-process, might there not emerge a very different sense of the human passages through finite shells into something non-finite? More formally asked: is ordinal phenomenology itself ready to give way to another dimensionality within its own momentum, a dimension that was first opened out by G.W.F. Hegel in 1806 but without the full grasp of ordinality? Perhaps. And it is this "perhaps" that has become one of the well-lit buoys of my recent thinking. And yet, what of the other two divine dimensions as articulated in *Nature and Spirit*?

Here the prospects are somewhat brighter. If the first two divine dimensions are finite and subject to the surrounding conditions of *nature natured*, then the third and fourth dimensions obtain in a more infinite way, precisely because they are tightly linked to the self-othering potencies of *nature naturing*, which cannot be finite in any ways available to us. The third divine dimension is understood to be sheerly relevant to the innumerable orders of the world, that is, in this dimension god does not alter the traits of any order in any way other than to preserve all orders against absolute nonbeing. This sustaining relation, however, has nothing whatsoever to do with the androcentric and anthropocentric dogma of *creatio ex nihilo* because creation, in its innumerable guises, is always a trait within nature rather than a trait that could be located outside of nature. In general, it makes no sense to think of any trait as being outside of nature as it would have no relevance of any kind to any order of nature. Starkly put—there are no non-natural traits or orders. A god who creates out of nothingness is no god at all, but merely functions as a linguistic artifice to render and secure certain personal and social power structures in an asymmetrical dependency relation.

In its third dimension, the divine is co-extensive with all orders (even if they can never be summed) of *nature natured*. Yet the divine is never co-extensive with the 'greater' infinity of *nature naturing*, which can also be rendered by my recent language as the "underconscious" of nature.[7] Hence, in its third dimension, god is infinite in one respect, the respect in which it always has as much scope as the innumerable orders of nature, while in another respect god is of a lesser infinite than the underconscious of nature which ejected it *into* its sustaining relation. God cannot sustain *nature naturing* yet it can and does sustain the orders of *nature natured*. And here again we see the crunch point first articulated by Neville. Why does *nature naturing* 'need' a divine dimension in order to, by proxy, sustain the innumerable orders of the world? In spite of its infinite scope vis-à-vis the world, is not this dimension of the divine equivalent to Neville's "middling god" that is artificially posited to solve some alleged problems within the generic portrayal of nature—much like the role of Whitehead's eternal entities and the initial aim of god to establish concresive relevance? In retrospect, this now must be seen to be the case. A trait sensed on the edges of the human process, namely that of being held firm against nonbeing, was again projected onto a divine aspect that was itself only a linguistic contrivance.

The fourth divine dimension, also finite and infinite but in different respects, was shaped out of my dialogue with Hartshorne. In accepting his surpassibility thesis, which asserts that god is that than which nothing greater can be thought but is also self-surpassible, I asked the question: unsurpassable in the face of what? Where does this endless and progressive self-surpassing occur? My answer was that it could only occur in the face of the encompassing, a metaphorical substitute for the more technical terminology of *nature naturing*. I was lead to this conceptual move by yet another hidden transcendental argument that was of the form: self-surpassibility must itself have a sufficient reason and that sufficient reason must, following the process line of thinking, be a lure that god itself responds to. Otherwise, why would god 'want' to be even more than "that than which nothing greater can be thought?" Surely, god must be incomplete in some sense.

Therefore it followed that only the encompassing was of greater scope than even the god at the boundaries all thought.[8] In the letter just quoted in footnote eight, Hartshorne was prophetic in pointing to my less than acknowledged relationship with Plato, which has now flowered into a strong affirmation of Plato through the highly illuminating prospect of Neo-Platonism. As I now realize,

I was underway toward the inner light unveiled by Plotinus, which is at the heart of *nature naturing*.

The correlations among the four divine dimensions are worked out in terms of the dialectic between finitude and the infinite, as well as under the purview of the concepts of relevance and identity:

> The divine is fragmented and incomplete in its first two natures, while living as the sustaining ground for the world's complexes in its third dimension. In the fourth dimension, God experiences its own travail in the face of that which is forever beyond its scope. While God can interact with complexes within the world, even though many of them remain recalcitrant to the divine infusion, God cannot become strongly relevant to the encompassing. The relationship between God and the encompassing is asymmetrical in that the encompassing is strongly relevant to God, while God cannot be strongly relevant to the encompassing. That is, God experiences a transformation of its identity and integrity when standing before the encompassing, while the encompassing, by definition, is beyond the reach of any counter influence. Does the encompassing acknowledge God and the divine travail? For good or ill, this question cannot be answered, at least from the standpoint of the human process. When confronting the encompassing the ordinal perspective must acknowledge an ultimate mystery that can only be partially understood.[9]

Contextually, these are valid and compelling arguments, yet they seem to be the result of somewhat hasty and un-phenomenological thinking on the self-givenness of the sacred. While I had opened out a serious unthought 'flaw' at the heart of Hartshorne's perspective, I had failed to understand my own need to shape a quaternity of divine natures that would have a co-implicating circularity combined with some sense of cosmic and human progress. I had allowed the species of history (read in an evolutionary eschatology) to overwhelm the genus (actually, pre-genus) of nature. This mistake compelled me into a decade of sustained rethinking that has now come out on the other side. Intriguingly, as we shall see, the weight of the last assertion from my quoted text has been partially lifted in my passage from panentheism to pantheism.

PSYCHOANALYSIS, SEMIOSIS AND *THE HIGHLANDS INSTITUTE*: A SEA CHANGE

Thus, by the mid-1990s I was more adrift in my passage toward *nature naturing* than I realized. On board with me were middling gods, anthropomorphic projections, and rather vociferous transcendental arguments. In addition, I had Neville's critique, now embodied in a genuine interlocutor, to assimilate and integrate. We were able to sit at the Captain's table to probe into the tensions between our perspectives, especially concerning the issue of cosmic optimism verses an emerging pantheistic sadness, now, thankfully, more ecstatic in attunement. Yet the cumulative effects of living in close confinement among these fellow passengers, with their highly ambiguous messages, would not be felt until after I had reworked the foundations of semiotics (at least a portion of it) and European depth-psychology. On the external front, a novel experience for me, my work with *The Highlands Institute for American Religious and Philosophical Thought*, gave me a place to listen to and talk with fellow spirits who had embarked on a similar trajectory through philosophy and religious thinking (sometimes, even theology). Our underlying commitment to some kind of naturalism (how varyingly defined!) made it possible for me to encounter prospects different from my own, but prospects and perspectives that were to some extent congenial to my lingering panentheism and my nascent pantheism.

If nature is all that there is, can we even use the word "nature" in a philosophical perspective in which the concept of the "non-nature" makes absolutely no sense? This dilemma faced Heidegger in the late 1930s as he struggled with his own mother tongue to find a way past the lingering substantive connotations of *Sein* as it contrasts with things-in-being (*Seinden*). The tension between these two dimensions of the ontological difference, as also entailing our-being-grasped by nonbeing (*das Nichts*), almost always collapsed the first primal dimension of the shining forth of sheer being *into* the *orders* within which the shining appears while also receding in a more darksome way. Heidegger asked: how is it possible to keep the ontological difference, as difference, open while also allowing for the uncanny presence/absence of nonbeing? Entwined within this question was a second: what might enable the ontological difference itself? In his unrelenting and always unfinished quest to answer the first question Heidegger invoked an older term for *Sein*, namely, *Seyn* (which has its 17th century English parallel in the term *beyng*). Combining etymology with this slight iconic shift, Heidegger hoped to jar thought from its habitual pathways of encountering and thinking the ontological difference between being and things-in-being.

By adding the concept/pre-concept of *Seyn* to those of *Sein* and *Seinden*, Heidegger was able to relocate the 'middle' concept/pre-concept of *Sein* in terms of what he called the first (or Primal) beginning of historical thought in the Greek world in which being was rendered as: beings-as-a-totality, that is, as a unity under a first genus. But is Heidegger's proposal/disposal equivalent, for an ecstatic naturalism which rethinks the being-problematic from a deeper pre-giving 'realm' of potencies, to its growing sense that a triad obtains, constituted by: *nature naturing* (improperly equated with *Sein*), *nature natured* (the 'domain' of orders), and yet something else on the fringes of ordinal phenomenology? Is this "something else" related to Heidegger's second question pertaining to the elusive third (not in Peirce's sense of "thirdness" as concrete reasonableness) that supports the eruption of *nature natured* out of *nature naturing*?

Heidegger's second embedded question appears in the triad in a displaced way as ecstatic naturalism shows its *own* evolving momentum in contrast to the being-problematic. For ecstatic naturalism, the question of the third, held to be the mysterious ejective nongrounding ground (*Ab-grund*) of the difference between *nature naturing* and *nature natured*, becomes: what prevails as the Prior (to use a term from Plotinus) to the potencies (presumably plural yet preordinal) and their 'subsequent' manifestation in and as the innumerable orders of the world? Note that the question is no longer that pertaining to what connects the two dimensions of nature, qua middling gods, but moves toward something that may obviate that so-called need. First, some categorial clarification is in order.

The concept of the "world" is a rich one in the history of phenomenology. It denotes that which is always more than the sum of all realized and possible meaning horizons of the human process. Further, it represents that which is always more than the subaltern worlds explored by the various sciences. In this expanded notion the world subsequent to the Big Bang is merely one world among others, not only among other such potential or actualized Baby Universes, but also among any kind of world whatsoever. Metaphysics should not confine its delineations to the world of astrophysics, but must understand that the universe of astronomy, for example, is a subaltern world, no matter how expansive are its spatial-temporal traits. The generic concept of "worldhood," is the pre-genus for any world that is or could be denoted or hinted at in the inexhaustible 'realms' of *nature natured*. Hence, worldhood (as equivalent to "world") is the ultimate enabling condition for any world or order whatsoever, but it is never *a* world.

The concept of the "potencies" is obviously more elusive to articulate. Negatively I have said that the underconscious of nature is the dimension of nature in which the potencies somehow obtain, but that they are also preordinal (that is, they are not yet orders of traits), prespatial, and pretemporal. However, like the phenomenon (or prephenomenon) of worldhood, the potencies are enabling conditions for whatever is manifest in and as a world. They are ejective of actuality and possibility, noting that there is an abyss of difference between a possibility, which is always intra-worldly and tied to a specific trajectory of actualities, and a potency, which has no worldly location except very indirectly through special traces (engrams).

The parallels between the concepts of "worldhood" and "potency" are also important to exhibit. First, neither aspect of nature can be counted or summed, that is, both are infinite, but in different respects. Secondly, these twin features of nature are indefinitely explorable, but again, in different respects. This second parallel has become clearer to me as the wisdom of pantheism has opened up some clearings onto the potencies via a reconfiguration of the concepts of the infinite. Finally, there is a parallel between the ways in which worldhood and the potencies obtain insofar as 'they' both are gathered up into a dialectic of unfolding and enfolding—a reigning dialectic to be explored in the last section of this essay.

There is thus a sense in which the underconscious dimension of the potencies is prior (but not temporally so, as it is pretemporal) to the innumerable worlds and their subaltern orders that constitute *nature natured*. This is a unique kind of priority and does not involve the principle of sufficient reason, which would affirm that for every consequent there is a sufficient rational and causal antecedent. The concept of sufficient reason flounders and splits open at this abyss between *nature naturing* and *nature natured*. But it is not enough to talk of the shipwreck of the principle of sufficient reason. Light must be shed on why this seemingly so unsinkable vessel has broken apart at the fissuring and gifting of the naturalized ontological difference.

The question turns inward yet again. Is this shipwreck of sufficient reason necessitated by the surface drama of the seas *or* by an undercurrent that may be even deeper down than the sea/seed-bed of nature, namely, than its own underconscious dimension? Here is where ecstatic naturalism must appeal to the aid of a reconfigured concept of the infinite, as embodied in its own restructured semiotics, to find some means of access to that which may indeed be prior to the (now second) prior of *nature naturing*. What is the infinite, and how many modes does it have? And in what respects must these modes be semiotic, that is, available in and through signs?

Peirce only got it partly right. His triadic semiotics, with all of its power and sophistication, remains limited to the innumerable domains of *nature natured* and, via indirection through his concept of "firstness," to the surface manifestations of *nature naturing*. He can be seen as the Isaac Newton of semiotics—right as far as he goes within his somewhat limited conditions of signification, but wrong about the more fundamental *how* of nature in its inexhaustibility and infinity. Further, Peirce lived in abjection (desire, fear, and denial) of the depth-meaning of firstness and iconicity, thereby cutting semiotics off from the rhythms of the underconscious of the self and nature, not to mention the Prior of all priors which ecstatic pantheism seeks.[10] The contemporary slavish devotion to Peirce has seriously blunted and even exhausted the movement of semiotics toward its own fore-structures and powers. Where do we go to find our post-Newtonian semiosis?

For me, the answer came at about the same time that I was writing my book on Peirce in which I came to realize just where Peirce had stopped short in his metaphysics and semiotics. My first indication that something was amiss occurred when I realized that Peirce had only the most foreshortened understanding of the enabling conditions for semiosis, and that his concept of the ground relation was little more than a hint, and a bad one at that, of what makes any forms of signification possible beyond the ontological triad of sign, object, and interpretant. I knew that he had grasped what I came to call the "actual infinite" of interpretants, but that he had no sense of other forms of infinity that weave themselves among signs and body them forth in different ways. This deepening sense of Peirce's failure led me, among a number of other motives, to write my fourth book, *Ecstatic Naturalism: Signs of the World*, which was envisioned as the first work in trilogy that was indeed completed with, *Nature's Self*, and *Nature's Religion*. In *Ecstatic Naturalism* I delineated four forms of the infinite (and carried them forward in a new way in *A Semiotic Theory of Theology and Philosophy*).[11]

Briefly put, the four forms of infinity are: 1) the *actual infinite*, as the 'sum' of all realized signs in all of the worlds that obtain at any given time, 2) the *processive infinite*, as the enabling condition for sign *series* as they obtain within given worlds, 3) the *open infinite*, which obtains as the principle of individuation surrounding any *given* sign, and 4) the *sustaining infinite*, which obtains as the sheer prevalence of all forms of actual and potential signification at any possible or actual time. I give a detailed phenomenological description of the way of these four dimensions of the infinite in an analysis of the phenomenon of Stonehenge in the subchapter entitled, *Petroglyphs* in *A Semiotic Theory of Theology and Philosophy*, toward which I steer the interested reader. My contention is that Peirce only understood the first form of the infinite, had a limited vision of the third form (via his ground relation), but because of a privileging of the principle of plenitude over that of emptiness, simply had no grasp of the processive and sustaining forms of the infinite. Peirce did have a strong sense of betweenness (a concept I unfold in Chapter Three of *Ecstatic Naturalism: Signs of the World*), but still tied it too closely to developmental thirdness to show how it also entails emptiness at its heart.

The four modes of the infinite, and surely there are innumerable others yet to be delineated, all point to some of the ways, hows, and forms of scope of the infinity manifest in nature. As these modalities dawned on me, it also became clearer that a new understanding of phenomenological method must be developed that better co-responds to the ways in which the phenomena of infinity appear in their respective forms of presence/absence. Without abandoning ordinal phenomenology, is was clear that I needed to readjust my understanding of the limits and potential goals of phenomenological query into nature. And it is here that the Hegel of 1806 reminded me of the *ur*-history of the phenomenological movement.

In its twentieth century variants, phenomenology clung to the presupposition of finitude, thereby ironically imposing an imperial notion onto the phenomenological process of rendering regnant traits available to human probing and assimilation. This imperialism is manifest in the commitment to the idea that noetic acts of either consciousness or the *Dasein* are the necessary, and even sufficient, condition for the entrance of meaning into the world. Yet such a prejudgment (*Vorurteil*) failed to grasp the fact that phenomena of the infinite may actually probe into and stretch the parameters of the self that is engaged in phenomenology. As Hegel showed, albeit from a Christocentric perspective that is no longer binding on us, each unfolding of the infinite takes place only in and through a widening and deepening of the attending shape of self-consciousness. This co-implicating dialectic has no built-in terminus other than the level of awareness of the self at the end of its trajectory through temporality (and, I would now add, at the end of a given incarnation). If one assumes that the infinite in its modes obtains, then it follows that the very act of attending to and being enveloped by its ways and manifestations renders us less and less finite as we proceed on the pathway of ordinal phenomenology. To mark this insight I now speak of an *infinitizing* ordinal phenomenology. It is "infinitizing" in its *how* precisely because the phenomenological act is grasped and shaped by the unrelenting unfolding of the modalities of the infinite to which it is bound. Put differently, the finite self is slowly infinitized, but only insofar as it can pierce through its pathological psychic armoring—and this is where semiotics and psychoanalysis converge in the domain of psychosemiosis to show just how the infinitizing processes are thwarted and/or accelerated.

The discipline of psychosemiosis completes the semiotic analysis of signification by moving toward those internal conditions of the sign-user that enter into and shape all phenomenological probing into traits of greater semiotic scope and density. The scope of a trait is measured by its sphere of inclusiveness of relevant traits (and their subalterns), while the density of a trait is measured by the degree to which it maximizes the equation of power X meaning. As the density of a trait increases, so does its relevance to the archetypes:

> The conjunction of power and meaning is intensified in the archetypes, which represent a kind of specificity for

the spirit. It is as if the spirit, as the ultimate source for the conjunction of power and meaning, uses the archetypes to clothe itself in particular centers of enhanced power and meaning. To use slightly different language, archetypes live as mobile concrescences of the spirit.[12]

Now the second term of the pairing of "nature" and "spirit" emerges. It is in the phenomenological encounter with the spirit (later, post-2000, I only speaks of spirits in the plural) that the depth-connection of semiosis, naturalism, and psychoanalysis emerges. At no point have I argued that the spirits are extra-natural, or that they have some kind of personal identity with a unique kind of sacred history. Rather, the spirits that emerge in nature are points of energy and concentration that have fully natural gradients that enliven our encounter with signs. The obvious problem is: how do we know which aspect of a spiritual presence is a human-all-too-human projection and which is an emergent that has its own laws and forms of prevalence? The struggle to answer this question moves ecstatic naturalism into psychosemiotics, which always belongs to metaphysics as one of its spheres of query.

Prior to being rendered transparent by the infinite *an sich*, all phenomenological acts involve interpretants as their neomatic correlate, that is, signs that are interpreted out of prior configurations of the 'original' sign/object relationship. Sign series are actually series of interpretants (i.e., signs already modified/interpreted) as there can be no such thing as a first or final sign, only signs in co-implicating series and *in medias res*. In rare and fragile cases, power and meaning are configured in such a way that a spiritual presence is manifest within a sign series, often gathering that series around its own sphere of momentum. The sign-using self is seized in this encounter and must negotiate the underground terrain where projections meet numinous orders of relevance.

After many years of thinking on this encounter I have arrived at the conclusion that phenomenology can go no further into its infinitizing mode until it finds a way of dealing with the concrescences of the spirits that are, by definition, infused with finite projections. Hence there is a dialectic between the movement of infinitizing and the counter-movement (which is actually the *same* movement) to disentangle (de-cathect) projections from their neomatic correlates. For Hegel the counter-movement works through determinate negation in which the essentializing dynamics of an attained shape of self-consciousness is spun around into its opposite energetic field so that a one-sided perspective is balanced prior to a deeper re-gathering on a higher level. Yet this form of negativity (the heart beat of his dialectic) often lacks the intimacy of a more destabilizing encounter with projective fields and their uncanny logic. Projections are much harder to isolate and understand, that is, render conscious, than Hegel realized in his admittedly glorious form of *pansophia* and *das absolute Wissen*. But they are not, dare I hope, beyond the powers of infinitizing ordinal phenomenology.

The most important species of the genus projection is the transference, the wild-child within the projection family. All projections are, by definition, unconscious. This applies to any of the species and their members. The wild-child transference moves with a sharp, direct, and frightening power into a noema (intentional object) in order to clothe it with archetypal colors and textures. The object becomes what the transference says it is. While a given projection may or may not be activated by an archetype, the transference always is. Hence the transference is, by our prior delineations, an agent of the spirits. Put differently: there is no spiritual presence without the transference, and there can be neither spiritual presence nor the transference without an archetype. The three moments belong together in the same. Phenomenology is gathered up into this three-in-one and honors the complex inter-weave of the outward going finite transference, its now infinitized object, and the numinous archetype.

What then is to be done to untangle the pathological forms of this triad? Psychosemiotics, as the semiotically reconfigured form of depth-psychology, works its own uncanny logic into, with, and against the overweening transferences that make the pertinent order of relevance far more "real" than it otherwise is *an sich*. For the transference, its object is always placed into the vertical structure of ontological priority in which its privileged object-choice must have more reality than any of its pale competitors. The principle of ontological priority, a product of projection and the transference, renders nature into spheres of differing degrees of reality. Philosophy, if it accomplishes nothing else, must work over and over again to undermine any form of ontological priority that would render any part of nature more or less real than another. The 'outer' movement of returning all prioritizing schemas to the truer naturalist form of ontological parity, runs parallel to the 'inner' movement of finding and dissolving the transferences that infuse specific orders with unearned numinosity.

In phenomenological practice this two-track strategy involves: 1) finding and deflating those noetic acts, unconscious though they be, that carry with them some form of ontological privileging, 2) disentangling a sign series from the excess field of pseudo-numinosity that surrounds it, 3) pushing the sign-using self back onto its own desire structures to show it how the transference has distorted its phenomenal field, and 4) gently but insistently showing how the commitment to ontological parity (the insight that everything is real in just the way that it is real) frees the self from finite and armored shells that are concrescences of ontological priority. Each armored shell is a muscular, emotional, and conceptual "as if" structure that closes off vast dimensions of the world and in turn does not allow the sign-using self to become open to the rhythms of *nature natured*, not to mention the undercurrents of *nature naturing*. The conjunction of psychoanalysis and metaphysics, through psychosemiotics, produces, through the infinitizing process, which it serves, a seamless whole in which armoring is dissolved and gathered up into the gifting of nature.

Naturalism, which asserts that nature is all that there is, psychosemiotics, which traces all humanly used signs to their unconscious projective fields, and a naturalized pneumatology, all point toward a rejection of the halfway measure of panentheism. Naturalism does not require the "in and above" relationship between a divine being and nature. Psychosemiotics does not require anything other than nature signifying in order to talk about the sign-using self. Naturalized pneumatology does not require any extra-natural agency to define the ways and hows of the spirits. There is thus no need for a god, four-fold or otherwise, in and yet somehow beyond nature.

PANTHEISM—*HEN KAI PAN*

Nature has neither beginning nor ending, no center nor circumference. It has no location and cannot be understood from outside of itself. And yet there remains a tremulous sensation at the edges of our infinitizing phenomenology. We somehow know that there is something else, perhaps fully natural, perhaps not, or perhaps natural in a very strange and overturning way. This unique sensation fills us with a subtle blissful disquiet. It is blissful because we have entered into the momentum that can grant us an exhilerating freedom from our finite boundaries, yet it is disquieting because at the same time it produces the vertigo of groundlessness—the experience of the shock of the *Ab-grund*.

We have circled back again to the primary question: what makes the difference between *nature naturing* and *nature natured* possible (what is Prior to the prior of *nature naturing*)? Or, does there even need to be such a "making possible," as if the ontological difference still demanded something more from thought by way of explanation? Shouldn't pantheism, unlike its highly talkative grandniece panentheism, be less verbose, less inclined to tout its own provenance and legitimation? And, on the other side, haven't almost all thinkers of any stature rejected pantheism especially when they have been accused of maintaining it? Even that canny pantheist Hegel (would he believe me?) tells us that pantheism is not properly philosophical (*Wissenschaftliche*):

> Organization and system remain entirely alien to pantheism. Where it appears in the form of presentation it is a tumultuous life, a bacchanalian intuition, for instead of allowing the single shapes of the universe to emerge in order, it is perpetually plunging them back into the universal, veering into the sublime and monstrous. Still this intuition is a natural point of departure for every healthy breast [*Brust*]. Especially in youth, through a life which ensouls us and all about us, we feel kinship and sympathy for the whole of nature, and we therefore have a sensation of the World-Soul, of the unity of spirit and nature, of the immateriality of nature.[13]

Certainly, this wizened forty-seven year old Hegel, looking back on his own early twenties at the *Stift* warns us; we desire anything other than a tumultuous life (*taumelndes Leben*) with its unending and nauseating revels of diffusion and chaos (*ein baccanalisches Anschauen*). Only the full system of scientific philosophy, itself made possible by phenomenology, can bring us into the sphere of infinitizing knowing! Yet is Hegel being true to his own thought-world here? Is there an irreconcilable tension between systematic thinking and the notion that nature is all that there is? Hardly. The issue is not whether or not we have chaotic intuitions (with their wicked taint of immediacy), but with whether or not philosophy lives in service to both intuition and categorial description within the one nature that is. The ancient wisdom of *der Pantheismus* represents the earliest and yet latest high watermark of speculative philosophy, even if its cooler demeanor, contra Hegel, is so easy to mistake for empty identity and sheer indifference.

Let's have one last moment in which we honor the invisible church of the Adepts of Wisdom. Arthur Schopenhauer, also a closet pantheist, helps us on this current leg of our sea voyage by reiterating how unnecessary it is to even *equate* god with nature, as if this advances thought, "Against pantheism I have mainly the objection that is states nothing. To call the world God is not to explain it, but only to enrich the language with a superfluous synonym for the word world. It comes to the same thing whether we say 'the world is God' or 'the world is the world.'"[14] The latter clause is the only one that a genuine (ecstatic?) pantheist needs to make, even if it takes the form of a tautology. But, contra Ludwig Wittgenstein, some tautologies are more informative than others, that is, the important ones serve as more than mere placeholders of thought around which synthetic a posteriori assertions cluster. To say "the world is the world" is also to say that worldhood is the unfolding granting of any and all worlds, requiring no other world or being (order of relevance) beyond it. In the dimension of *nature natured*, world and worlds is all that there is.

Nature naturing, the lost material maternal of my naturalism, now points us inward one last time. This pretemporal, prespatial, presemiotic, and preordinal, lost object (from the human perspective) is tinged with melancholy and denial. Its transfiguration into bliss and joy (Julia Kristeva's *jouissance*) is always posited away from itself back into the "no longer" and forward into the "not yet." The selving process, carefully traced in several books, is gathered up into this dialectic:

> How, then, do we move from finite frustrations to the
> kind of primal melancholy that puts the *entire* world

into question? The answer is simple: we do not move at all, but *are* moved by the spirit that gives us melancholy as one of its most treasured gifts. The transition from finite disappointments to the infinite power of melancholy is not the product of *nature natured* or any of its orders. It is a gift of the spirit that moves to free us from our absolute dependence on the world, so that we can begin to fathom the abyss of *nature naturing*.[15]

Melancholy pulls us into the great "no longer," the hidden *whence* of our being, while ecstasy pulls us into the spirit (and is pulled by the spirit) into the not yet. But why must I continue to speak of a hidden *whence* and a deferred *whither*? Why indeed if infinitizing phenomenology promises to bring us into the great *now* of the infinite and its modes? Why indeed?

The great lost object of *Nature's Self*, the material maternal, serves as yet another metaphor for *nature naturing*. However, unlike the metaphor of the encompassing, my image of the lost object contains traces of the abjected and distorted maternal, as was noted by Nancy Frankenberry at the time. The ejecting and rejecting material maternal ground of the selving process is a haunting presence/absence dimly luminous as the *vagina dentate*—a devouring castrating force that operates in patriarchal consciousness, no matter how allegedly emancipated. Was my eschatology of the *not yet* an unconscious response to the fear of the vagina with teeth, always threatening to dismember the prodigal son who wove his hero myth into the present world of ecstasies?

I have come to see that this is so, precisely through the process of psychosemiosis, which is unrelenting in bringing the thinker back to the motivational economy of her or his language and its displacements. The human-all-too-human armoring of castration anxiety blind-sided the phenomenological query into the unfolding momenta of the depths of nature. The great maternal had shown only one of its many faces. Another, and deeper more capacious face had yet to show itself before the metaphors and the categorial delineations of ecstatic pantheism could become free from some of the stronger antecedent abjected and finite material. Only a transfiguring experience, on the edges of all semiosis, could make this transition possible. By way of a necessarily *proximate* culmination of this thought work, I will say something about this experience and delineate in a very tentative fashion how it has facilitated the infinitizing process of coming into awareness of the unfolding/enfolding dialectic of nature.

My encounter with the other face of the material maternal, the great chthonic ground of worldhood, took place in the ancient Meenakshi Temple devoted to Lord Shiva in Madurai, India in January 2001. In meditation a warm white light suddenly seized me from my heart chakra. Out of this light a presence appeared that did not speak in words, but somehow managed to convey images and something akin to ideas. The center of this cluster of unfoldings was the unambiguous presence of the Great Mother who is eternally present within, underneath, and throughout nature. The masking of this presence through projection and wayward transferences was instantly dissolved by this pretemporal 'voice,' which showed that there never was a lost object, and that the "no longer" and the "not yet" were real in a different sense than I had thought (for even *Maya* is real in the *way* that it is real—an implication of ontological parity). Further, I realized that the chthonic ground of Shiva/Shakti was only a devouring mother on the surface or edges of experience, never at the center or infinitizing periphery. Like so many others, I had been found by the *nunc stans* in which the tri-dimensionality of temporality is gathered up into the eternal now. This epiphany resolved the issue of finding the passage through to the gifting that is prior to the potencies of *nature naturing*. The potencies, so carefully evoked by Schelling, were themselves in service to something prior to all energized moments of self-othering—beneath heterogeneity lay homogeneity.

Subsequent to this experience, certainly prepared by decades of study of South Asian thought, I have been even more slowly listening to the rhythms of the unfolding of the Great Mother and the enfoldings that are emergent from this Prior of all priors. Note again that this Prior is not prior in the sense of establishing and grounding all consequents through the principle of sufficient reason. The grounding of the Great Mother is a groundless giving of hovering, but fully real, grounds, all of which echo forth the *Ab-grund*, which *is* the Great Mother.

But are we not in the same position as before, only one step back? Isn't this talk of an alleged "Great Mother" merely the result of a Vedantic, rather than *Liberal* Christian, transcendental argument, carefully scripted by the ambiance of the Meenakshi Temple? Perhaps. But I suspect that this "perhaps" is different in kind from all others.

Perhaps I should substitute a starker term for this gifting of the *Ab-grund*. Were I to do so I would speak of the Great Unfolding that is never enfolded or folding. Does this help us along the passage through and with infinitizing phenomenology, from the potencies of nature naturing to the enfolded orders of nature natured and back again to the *hen kai pan*, the great one and all? Perhaps it is best to remain in these still waters a moment longer before proceeding elsewhere, for thought is too quick to move on before its horizon has become clear again.

ENDNOTES

PREFACE

1. *Shambhala: The Sacred Path of the Warrior*, by Chögyam Trungpa, ed. by Carolyn Rose Gimian, (Boston: Shambhala Publications, 1988). p. 114.

CHAPTER ONE

1. My sister reports that at that time my mother was a brilliant actress, under the tutelage of a drama teacher.

2. The complete story of this episode can be found in *The Times of Coral Gables*, Thursday, July 31, 1958 (Vol. 33, No. 27) on page 3.

3. On this issue see, *Moodswing*, by Ronald R. Fieve, M.D. (New York: Bantam Books, 1989), pp. 179-186.

4. The book appeared in 1987 with the title, *The Community of Interpreters: On the Hermeneutics of Nature and the Bible in the American Philosophical Tradition*, (Macon, GA: Mercer University Press). In 1989 the American Academy of Religion sponsored a General Session at its annual November meeting on the book that consisted of four presented papers along with my response. In 1995 the same Press published a second, paperback edition, with a new preface.

5. Various accounts of the divestment struggle can be found in *The Centre Daily Times* of State College, Pennsylvania, starting with March 21, 1986. Issues of special importance are: March 24, 1986 (page 1), March 25, 1986 (page 1), August 29, 1986 (page B 1), October 7, 1986 (page 1), November 8, 1986 (page 1), March 1, 1987 (page 1), and September 19, 1987. See also *The Chronicle of Higher Education*, June 18, 1986, August 6, 1986, and October 1, 1986 (all in Letters to the Editor Page for my debate with the philosopher Sidney Hook). See also, *The Pittsburgh Press*, March 30, 1986.

6. *Nature and Spirit: An Essay in Ecstatic Naturalism*, (New York: Fordham University Press, 1992).

7. *Ecstatic Naturalism: Signs of the World*, Advances in Semiotics, (Bloomington, IN: Indiana University Press, 1994).

8. *An Introduction to C. S. Peirce: Philosopher, Semiotician, and Ecstatic Naturalist*, (Lanham, MD: Rowman & Littlefield, Pub. 1993). This book was written after *Ecstatic Naturalism*, but differing production schedules in the

two presses inverted their order of appearance. The fifth book is *Nature's Self: Our Journey from Origin to Spirit*, (Lanham, MD: Rowman & Littlefield, Pub. 1996). The sixth book is, *Nature's Religion*, (Lanham, MD: Rowman & Littlefield, 1997). The seventh book is, *A Semiotic Theory of Theology and Philosophy*, (Cambridge: Cambridge University Press, 2000). The eighth book is, *Wilhelm Reich: Psychoanalyst and Radical* Naturalist, (New York: Farrar, Straus & Giroux, 2003). Readers interested in an overview of my philosophy can read: "Beyond the Text: Ecstatic Naturalism and American Pragmatism," by Todd A. Driskill in *American Journal of Theology and Philosophy*, Vol. 15, No. 3, September 1994, "Windows on the Ecstatic: Reflections upon Robert Corrington's Ecstatic Naturalism," by Roger A. Badham in *Soundings*, Vol. 82, No. 3-4, Fall/Winter 1999, and *Nature's Primal Self: An Ecstatic Naturalist Critique of the Anthropocentrism of Peirce's Pragmaticism and Jaspers' Existentialism*, Doctoral Dissertation at Drew University by Nam T. Nguyen, 2002..

9. This is the same knife referred to above that she strapped to her leg during the daytime.

10. One of the best books on dreams, written primarily for analysts in training, is *Dreams, A Portal to the Source*, by Edward C. Whitmont & Sylvia Brinton Perera, (New York: Routledge, 1989).

11. *The Interpretation of Dreams*, by Sigmund Freud in a new translation by Joyce Crick (based on the original 1899 edition), (Oxford: Oxford University Press, 1999), p. 113. This edition also contains an important Introduction by Ritchie Robertson.

12. *The Interpretation of Dreams*, p. xviii.

13. *On Dreams*, by Sigmund Freud, translated by James Strachey, from the Standard Edition, (New York: Norton, 1952), p. 57.

CHAPTER TWO

1. *Ion*, from *The Collected Dialogues of Plato*, ed. by Edith Hamilton and Huntington Cairns, (Princeton: Princeton University Press, 1961), p. 220.

2. Mircea Eliade, *A History of Religious Ideas*, Vol. I, (Chicago: Chicago University Press, 1978), p. 368.

3. *Diagnostic and Statistical Manual of Mental Disorders, Fourth Edition*, (Washington, DC: American Psychiatric Association, 1994), p. 332.

4. Ibid, p. 327.

5. Ibid, p. 386.

6. *Practical Guideline for Treatment of Patients With Bipolar Disorder*, (Washington: American Psychiatric Association, 1995), pp. 46-47. This guide for physicians further recommends birth control for manic-depressive women. The actual risk of birth defects from lithium, carbamazepine, and valproate (during the first trimester) is from 4% to 12%, which compares to 2% to 4% in the untreated group. However, the guide does give precise treatment plans for those who choose to have children. Electro convulsive treatment is listed as a good back-up plan when medications are not indicated.

7. He describes this development in his book *Moodswing*, Revised and Expanded Edition, (New York: Bantam, 1989). Fieve combines case studies with rich clinical and medical analyses and data.

8. *Manic-Depressive Illness*, Frederick K. Goodwin and Kay Redfield Jamison, (New York: Oxford University Press, 1990).

9. Readers will be interested in her recent "coming out" book in which she describes, with her usual literary brilliance, her struggles with manic-depression — *An Unquiet Mind: A Memoir of Moods and Madness*, (New York: Knopf 1995). Recently I had the pleasure of hearing Jamison lecture at the 92nd Street Y in New York. Her books and her lecture were instrumental in giving me the courage to write my own book on this subject.

10. *Manic-Depressive Illness*, p. 301.

11. Ibid, pp. 310 & 311.

12. An interesting literary expression of this reality can be found in two fine mystery novels by Abigail Padgett, *Child of Silence*, (New York: Mystery Press, 1993), and *Strawgirl*, (New York: Mystery Press, 1994). Her protagonist, Bo Bradley, does her best detection when she stops taking lithium.

13. *Manic-Depressive Illness*, p. 127. The Kraepelin work to which they refer is, *Manic-Depressive Insanity and Paranoia*, trans. R.M. Barclay, ed. G.M. Robertson, (Edinburgh: E. & S. Livingston, 1921), reprinted by (New York: Arno Press, 1976).

14. Ibid, p. 132.

15. Ibid, p. 137.

16. Ibid, p. 139.

17. The best argument for this claim can be found in, *Touched With Fire: Manic-Depressive Illness and the Artistic Temperament*, by Kay Redfield Jamison, (New York: Free Press, 1993).

18. *Manic-Depressive Illness*, pp. 142-143.

19. In his best selling work *Listening to Prozac*, (New York: Viking, 1993), Peter D. Kramer, uses the analogy of "faulty wiring" to point to the issue of how stress generated brain states may affect such things as rejection sensitivity or a tendency toward aggression. The underlying neurological pattern has its own history deeply related to the unique life history of the individual. Like other drugs in its class, Prozac affects how the brain uses Serotonin.

20. *Manic-Depressive Illness*, p. 146 & 151.

21. *Practice Guideline for Treatment of Patients with Bipolar Disorder*, p. 2.

22. Ibid, p. 2.

23. *Manic-Depressive Disorder*, p. 398.

24. *Practice Guideline for Treatment of Patients With Bipolar Disorder*, p. 3.

25. For example, see *Schizophrenia and Manic-Depressive Disorder*, by Torrey, Bowler, Taylor, and Gottesman, (New York: Basic Books, 1994)

26. *Mood Genes: Hunting for Origins of Mania and Depression*, by Samuel H. Barondes, (New York: W. H. Freeman and Company, 1998). pp. 177-178.

27. See *Manic-Depressive Illness*, Chapters 21 and 22.

28. Lithium was formed very early on when helium joined with some local nuclei, thus making lithium virtually as old as the universe itself, which is variously seen as being between 8 and 12 billion years old. On this issue see, *Through a Universe Darkly: A Cosmic Tale of Ancient Ethers, Dark Matter, and the Fate of the Universe*, by Marcia Bartusiak, (New York: Harper Collins, 1993).

29. *Moodswing*, pp. 211-213.

30. *Moodswing*, p. 213.

31. Jamison describes her own experiences with a lithium suicide attempt in such a way as to discourage *anyone* from trying it him or herself. See her *An Unquiet Mind*, pp. 114-118.

32. This list comes from a fact sheet given to me by my very conscientious pharmacist when I was still taking lithium.

33. Patty Duke has elevated this aspect of lithium treatment to high humor in her moving book, *A Brilliant Madness: Living with Manic-Depressive Illness*, co-authored with Gloria Hochman, (New York: Bantam Books, 1992).

34. *An Unquiet Mind*, p. 95.

35. *Manic-Depressive Disorder*, p. 690.

36. Ibid, p. 691.

37. *Mood Genes: Hunting for Origins of Mania and Depression*, p. 190.

38. Ibid, p. 227.

39. *Touched with Fire*, p. 41.

40. *Manic-Depressive Disorder*, p. 242.

41. Ibid.

42. *Night Falls Fast: Understanding Suicide*, by Kay Redfield Jamison, (New York: Alfred A. Knopf, 1999), p. 192.

43. *Night Falls Fast: Understanding Suicide*, p. 193. In his book *A Mood Apart: Depression, Mania, and Other Afflictions of the Self*, (New York: Basic Books, 1997), Peter C. Whybrow details the activities of the primitive mammalian brain (the limbic alliance) within us and how it is disturbed in manic-depressive disorder producing a kind of "irritable fermentation."

44. *Night Falls Fast: Understanding Suicide*, p. 200.

45. This is well described in *We Heard the Angels of Madness*, by Diane and Lisa Berger, (New York: Quil, 1991), p. 233.

46. *Sanford Meisner on Acting*, by Sanford Meisner and Dennis Longwell, with an Introduction by Sydney Pollack, (New York: Vintage, 1987), p. 15.

47. *A Theory of Semiotics*, by Umberto Eco, (Bloomington, IN: Indiana University Press, 1976).

48. *Touched with Fire*, p. 118.

49. C.G. Jung, *The Symbolic Life: Miscellaneous Writings*, Volume 18 of the Collected Works of C.G. Jung, (Princeton: Bollingen, 1976). The book referred to is, *Wisdom, Madness and Folly*, by John Custance, (New York, 1952).

50. C.G. Jung, *Psychological Types*, Volume 6 of the Collected Works, (Princeton: Bollingen, 1971).

51. One such work is, *Please Understand Me: Character & Temperament Types*, Fourth Edition, by David Keirsey, and Marilyn Bates, (Del Mar, CA: Prometheus Nemesis Book Company, 1984).

52. *The Symbolic Life*, p. 31.

53. Ibid, pp. 31-32.

54. He describes this awakening in *Memories, Dreams, Reflections*, (New York: Random House, 1961). See especially, p. 131.

55. Matthew McKay, Ph.D., writing in Mary Ellen Copeland's *The Depression Workbook: A Guide for Living With Depression and Manic-Depression*, (Oakland, CA: New Harbinger Publications, 1992), refers to the presence of the PIP2 enzyme, which seems to be overactive in manic states. He says, "Lithium turns down the response to any stimulus that depends on the presence of the PIP2 enzyme."

56. *Touched With Fire*, p. 150.

57. While I have not quoted from the following books in the main body of the text, I recommend them highly: *Bipolar Disorder: A Family Focused Approach*, by David J. Miklowitz and Michael J. Goldstein, (New York: The Guilford Press, 1997), *Bipolar Disorder: A Guide for Patients and Families*, by Francis Mark Mondimore, (Baltimore: The Johns Hopkins University Press, 1999) and *Surviving ManicDepression*, by E. Fuller Torrey and Michael B. Knable, (New York: Basic Books, 2002). In the first book, Miklowitz and Goldstein deal with the complex web of family dynamics, especially denial, that can set in when the initial diagnosis of manic-depression is given to a family member. They are especially helpful in showing the concrete clinical aspects of treatment. In the second book, Mondimore gives a very clear and precise analysis of neurochemistry and also talks about alternative forms of treatment, such as ECT and herbs. His parting piece of wisdom is important: "There is no cure for bipolar disorder, only treatment and management. It is a relentless illness whose symptoms inevitably and repeatedly return to torment its sufferers. The only way for the patient to keep it at bay is for the patient to be relentless as well--relentless about getting needed treatment and sticking to it. No other piece of advice I can give is as important as this one." p. 219. In the third book, Torrey and Knable deal with recent research on manic-depression in children. Further, the add their own insights to the correlation of manic-depression and creativity.

59. *Nature's Self: Our Journey from Origin to Spirit*, (Lanham, MD: Rowman & Littlefield, Pub., 1996), p. 1.

CHAPTER THREE

1. See his work, *Strange Brains and Genius: The Secret Lives of Eccentric Scientists and Madmen*, (New York: Plenum Trade, 1998).

2. For those who are skeptical of this strong correlation of genius and manic-depression, I suggest two excellent works, *The Key to Genius: Manic-Depression and the Creative Life*, by D. Jablow Hershman and Julian Lieb,

M.D., (Buffalo: Prometheus Books, 1988, second edition with a new epilogue, 1998), and *Touched With Fire: Manic-Depressive Illness and the Artistic Temperament*, by Kay Redfield Jamison, (New York: Free Press, 1993). The latter book has already been featured in the previous chapter, but other aspects of Jamison's work will come to the fore here. The figure of 3/4 to 1/4 is my own approximation, which is based on an educated guess from the statistics, still rough, for relative frequency. This ratio should be taken with some caution.

3. These three criteria derive from one of the best recent studies of creativity, *Creating Minds*, by Howard Gardner, (New York: Basic Books, 1993). Gardner has been at the forefront of efforts to get us past the kind of simple-minded understanding of creative intelligence found in, for example, IQ tests. His approach combines several disciplines; one of the distinguishing marks of creativity, and helps the researcher become more open to the astonishing forms that creativity assumes in our species.

4. *The Key to Genius*, p. 7.

5. See especially, *Philosophy and the Mirror of Nature*, by Richard Rorty, (Princeton: Princeton University Press, 1979).

6. I have carefully described the irruptions of *natura naturans* in my book, *Ecstatic Naturalism: Signs of the World*, Advances in Semiotics, (Bloomington: Indiana University Press, 1994).

7. For a detailed study of Peirce's semiotics, see my *An Introduction to C.S. Peirce: Philosopher, Semiotician, and Ecstatic Naturalist*, (Lanham, MD: Rowman & Littlefield, Pub., 1993), pp. 141-166. Also, see my articles on the psychoanalytic aspects of Peirce's manic-depressive disorder, "Peirce's Abjected Unconscious: A Psychoanalytic Profile," *Semiotics 1992*, ed. by John Deely, (Lanham, MD: University Press of America, 1993), pp. 91-103, and "Peirce's Abjection of the Maternal," *Semiotics 1993*, ed. by Robert S. Corrington and John Deely, (New York: Peter Lang, 1995), pp. 590-594.

8. See, *The Limits of Interpretation*, by Umberto Eco, (Bloomington, IN: Indiana University Press, 1990.

9. As taken from, *Beethoven: Biography of a Genius*, by George R. Marek, (New York: Funk & Wagnalls, 1969, p. 547. Marek points out that Schindler misnamed the piece that Beethoven was working on from the *Missa Solemnis*. Instead of the Credo, it was probably the Gloria.

10. A well done, if somewhat over-the-top expression of Beethoven's creative process is the 1994 film *Immortal Beloved*. The star, gifted British stage and screen actor Gary Oldman well portrays the manic-depressive heart of Beethoven, even if it is not named as such in the film. The film also deals with the issue of male genius and the *anima* in a rich, if slightly patriarchal, way.

11. From the anthology, *Genius: The History of an Idea*, ed. by Penelope Murray, (Oxford: Basil Blackwell, 1989), pp. 226 & 223.

12. On this issue see, *The Drama of the Gifted Child: The Search for the True Self*, by Alice Miller, trans. by Ruth Ward (New York: Basic Books, 1990).

1 3. *Genius: The Natural History of Creativity*, by Hans Eysenck, (Cambridge: Cambridge University Press, 1995), pp. 7-8.

14. *Origins of Genius: Darwinian Perspectives on Creativity*, by Dean Keith Simonton, (Oxford: Oxford University Press, 1999), pp. 87-88.

15. *Origins of Genius: Darwinian Perspectives on Creativity*, p. 123.

16. *Origins of Genius: Darwinian Perspectives on Creativity*, pp. 44-45.

17. See *Black Sun: Depression and Melancholia*, by Julia Kristeva, trans. by Leon S. Roudiez, (New York: Columbia University Press, 1989).

18. From essay, "Genius and Mental Disorder: A History of Ideas Concerning Their Conjunction," in *Genius: The History of an Idea*, p. 209.

19. *The Duty of Genius*, by Ray monk, (New York: Free Press, 1990).

20. Ibid, p.13.

21. Julia Kristeva, *Powers of Horror: An Essay on Abjection*, (New York: Columbia University Press, 1982), p. 45.

22. *Touched With Fire*, pp. 143 & 146.

23. I heard her make this argument at a recent series of lectures on the French writer Marcel Proust. The lectures were held at Princeton University.

24. The concept of the not yet, more precisely, the not yet being (noch nicht sein), comes from the utopian Marxist writer Ernst Bloch. His major work, in which this key concept unfolds, is *The Principle of Hope*, Vols. I-III, trans. Neville Place, Stephen Plaice, and Paul Knight, (Cambridge: The MIT Press, 1986). The translation is from the 1959 edition, *Das Prinzip Hoffnung*, (Frankfurt am Main: Suhrkamp Verlag). Bloch was forced to remain in West Germany when the Berlin wall was erected, which convinced him against returning to his home and academic post in the East. While in the West he decisively influenced the movement known as the theology of hope, whose chief exemplar is Jürgen Moltmann.

25. See his *Systematic Theology, Vols I-III*, (Chicago: University of Chicago Press, 1967).

26. *Touched With Fire*, pp. 60-99.

27. A break-through study of Newton from the standpoint of manic-depression can be found in, *The Key to Genius*.

28. *The Key to Genius*, p. 42.

29. *The Life of Isaac Newton*, by Richard S. Westfall, (Cambridge: Cambridge University Press, 1993), p. 10.

30. *A Portrait of Isaac Newton*, by Frank E. Manuel, (New York: Da Capo Press, 1990, original edition by Harvard University Press in 1968), pp. 24 & 26.

31. *A Portrait of Isaac Newton*, p. 39.

32. *The Key to Genius*, pp. 43-44.

33. *Isaac Newton: The Last Sorcerer*, by Michael White, (Reading, MA: Addison-Wesley, 1997), p. 61.

34. *A Portrait of Isaac Newton*, p. 64.

35. Ibid.

36. *Isaac Newton: The Last Sorcerer*, p. 261.

37. *The Life of Isaac Newton*, Westfall, p. 45.

38. *Isaac Newton: The Last Sorcerer*, pp. 153-154.

39. cf. *Isaac Newton: The Last Sorcerer*, pp. 226-229.

40. *Isaac Newton: The Last Sorcerer*, p. 132.

41. As quoted in *Isaac Newton: Adventurer in Thought*, by A. Rupert Hall, (Oxford: Blackwell Publishers, 1992), p. 126.

42. As quoted in, *Isaac Newton: The Last Sorcerer*, pp. 248-249.

43. *Isaac Newton: Adventurer in Thought*, p. 219.

44. *The Principia: Vol. I The Motion of Bodies*, by Sir Isaac Newton, translated by I Bernard Cohen and Anne Whitman, 1934), (Berkeley: University of California Press, 1999), pp. 416-417.

45. *The Principia: Vol. II The System of the World* (Book III), by Sir Isaac Newton, p. 794.

46. *Isaac Newton: The Last Sorcerer*, pp. 244-246.

47. *Isaac Newton: The Last Sorcerer*, p. 267.

48. *Opticks*, by Sir Isaac Newton (from 1730 posthumous edition), (New York: Dover Books, 1979), pp. 26-28.49. *Opticks*, p. 402.

50. *Sri Ramakrishna: The Great Master*, by Swami Saradananda (a direct disciple of Sri Ramakrishna), translated by Swami Jagadananda, (Mylapore, India: Sri Ramakrishna Math, 1946), pp. 36-38.

51. *The Gospel of Sri Ramakrishna*, translated by Swami Nikhilananda, (New York: Ramakrishna-Vivekananda Center, 1942), p. 4.

52. *Kali: The Feminine Force*, by Ajit Mookerjee, (Rochester, VT: Destiny Books, 1988), p. 11.

53. *The Life of Ramakrishna*, by Rolland, trans. by E.F. Malcolm-Smith, (Calcutta: Advaita Ashram, 1997). p. 14.

54. As quoted in *Sri Ramakrishna: A Prophet for the New Age*, by Richard Schiffman, (New York: Paragon House, 1989), p. 39.

55. *Ramakrishna Revisited: A New Biography*, by Narasingha P. Sil, (Lanham, MD: University Press of America, 1998), p. 53.

56. *Kali's Child: The Mystical and the Erotic in the Life and Teachings of Ramakrishna*, Second Edition, (Chicago: University of Chicago Press, 1995), p. 66.

57. For a thorough and succinct study of the bhakti form of worship, see, *The Embodiment of Bhakti*, by Karen Pechilis Prentiss, (New York: Oxford University Press, 1999).

58. *Sri Ramakrishna: A Prophet for the New Age*, p. 57.

59. *The Gospel of Sri Ramakrishna*, p. 14.

60. *Advaita Vedanta: A Philosophical Reconstruction*, by Eliot Deutsch, (Honolulu: University of Hawaii Press, 1969), p. 12.

61. As quoted in *The Life of Ramakrishna*, by Romain Rolland, pp. 31-32.

62. *The Gospel of Sri Ramakrishna*, p. 965.

63. *Vivekananda: A Biography*, by Swami Nikhilananda, (New York: Ramakrishna-Vivekananda Center, 1953), p. 13.

64. As quoted in, *Great Swan: Meetings with Ramakrishna*, by Lex Hixon, (Burdett, NY: Larson Publications, 1992). pp. 15-16.

65. *The Gospel of Sri Ramakrishna*, p. 911.

66. See Kripal's *Kali's Child*, pp. 298-299.

67. *The Life of Ramakrishna*, by Romain Rolland, p. 214.

68. I should note that Jeffrey J. Kripal works very hard to maintain a more balanced position between these extremes. His book *Kali's Child* is compelling reading.

Endnotes 227

CHAPTER FOUR

1. As quoted in, *The Enigma of the Oceanic Feeling: Provisioning the Psychoanalytic Theory of Mysticism*, by William B. Parsons, (Oxford: Oxford University Press, 1999), p. 177. Parsons argues, as I do, that psychoanalysis can be regrounded to account for mystical states in a nonreductive fashion and can be used to probe into the genuineness of mystical experience.

2. *The Enigma of the Oceanic Feeling*, p. 176.

3. *The Upanishads, Volume One*, translated with commentary by Swami Nikhilananda, (New York: Ramakrishna-Vivekananda Center, 1949), p. 288.

4. *The Vedic Experience*, by Raimundo Panikkar, (Delhi: Motital Banarsidass Publishers, 1977), p. 50.

5. *Emerson: Essays and Lectures*, by Ralph Waldo Emerson, (The Library of America, 1983), p. 471.

APPENDIX

1. The books are: *The Community of Interpreters* (Macon, GA: Mercer University Press, 1987, new edition with new Preface 1995), *Nature and Spirit* (New York: Fordham University Press, 1992), *An Introduction to C.S. Peirce* (Lanham, MD: Rowman & Littlefield, 1993), *Ecstatic Naturalism* (Bloomington, IN: Indiana University Press, 1994), *Nature's Self*, (Lanham, MD: Rowman & Littlefield, 1996), *Nature's Religion* (Lanham, MD: Rowman & Littlefield, 1997), *A Semiotic Theory of Theology and Philosophy* (Cambridge, UK: Cambridge University Press, 2000), and *Wilhelm Reich: Psychoanalyst and Radical Naturalist* (New York: Farrar Straus & Giroux, 2003). A few of my articles will be referenced in the essay.

2. Justus Buchler's most important foundational work is, *Metaphysics of Natural Complexes*, second expanded edition, edited by Kathleen Wallace, Armen Marsoobian, and Robert S. Corrington (Albany: SUNY Press, 1990).

3. See my articles, "Toward a Transformation of Neoclassical Theism," *International Philosophical Quarterly*, Vol. XXVII, No. 4, December 1987 pp. 393-408, and "Ordinality and the Divine Natures," in *Nature's Perspectives*, edited by Armen Marsoobian, Kathleen Wallace, and Robert S. Corrington, (Albany: SUNY Press, 1991), pp. 347-366.

4. The method of phenomenology becomes *ordinal* when the transcendental perspective is overcome by ordinal naturalism in which the focus shifts to the

self-in-process as it rotates its perspectives in and among relevant orders of the world as they are encountered. The spatial and temporal features of phenomena (orders of relevance) are no longer privileged over, for example, social, economic, historical, religious or other traits, traits that are also self-showing in the phenomenon as it is rotated through its pertinent ordinal locations. Edmund Husserl's concept of the epoche, which brackets out existence claims, is rendered unnecessary by the deeper sense of ontological parity. The concept of the *Wesensschau* is replaced with the concept of ordinal rotation as it acknowledges traits and their subaltern traits. Concerning this shift from transcendental (and even hermeneutical) phenomenology to ordinal phenomenology, see, *Pragmatism Considers Phenomenology*, Ed. By Robert S. Corrington, Carl Hausman, and Thomas M. Seebohm, (Center for Advanced Research in Phenomenology and University Press of America, 1987), my Introduction, pp.1-35.

5 *Nature and Spirit*, pp. 172-173.

6. One of the least successful expressions of American naturalism can be seen in, *Naturalism and the Human Spirit*, ed. By Yervant H. Krikorian, (New York: Columbia University Press, 1944). Buchler told me that he considered this anthology to represent a "dogmatic and narrow" view of true naturalism. This quote comes from, "A Conversation between Justus Buchler and Robert S. Corrington, *The Journal of Speculative Philosophy*, Vol. III, No. 4, 1989, pg. 261.

7. *A Semiotic Theory of Theology and Philosophy*, p. 18. The term "underconscious" is taken from Coleridge.

8. But perhaps my reconstruction of process thought was not as radical as I had thought. In a considerate and well thought out letter to me concerning his reading of my *Nature and Spirit*, Hartshorne wrote, "I write about his [Jaspers] encompassing and why I think mind or spirit is both encompassing and encompassed, and mere mindless matter is a mere fiction, or a mere word for some very low but pervasive forms of mind, sub-animal and sub-cellular. . . Your basic stance overlaps a good deal with mine, as you are aware. . . . Plato's theology means much more to me than it did even to Whitehead. He allowed A.E. Taylor, too close to traditional Christianity, to mislead him, and did not accept Plato's view that the divine psyche, like all psyches, is *embodied* mind and has self-activity or freedom. Whitehead did agree about the freedom. Apparently you're closer to Plato than you know. The cosmos is the divine body. However for Plato the divine psyche encompasses the divine body, and your or my psyche encompasses our body. This is an analogy, which means a difference in principle and a likeness in principle. . . I say [contra Buchler] that if complex has a good meaning then so does simple. This is the principle of Contrast. Everything is complex and everything is simple. There are many kinds and degrees of complexity." October 30, 1992.

9. *Nature and Spirit*, pp. 187-188.

10. On the issue of Peirce's failure here, see my, "Peirce's Abjected Unconscious: A Psychoanalytic Profile," *Semiotics 1992*, ed. John Deely, (Lanham, MD: University Press of America, 1993), pp. 91-103, and "Nature's God and the Return of the Material Maternal," *American Journal of Semiotics*, Vol. 10, Nos. 1-2, 1993, pp. 115-132.

11. My original title for *Ecstatic Naturalism: Signs of the World* was actually *Signs of the World*, but the editors at Indiana changed it in such a way as to cover over its place in the trilogy. In the same way, my original title for *A Semiotic Theory of Theology and Philosophy* was *Principia Semiotica* but the Syndicate at Cambridge, perhaps wary of the obvious historical precedents in Newton, Moore, and Whitehead, wanted something less grandiose and more likely to hit a variety of databases. It is my hope that any later editions will go back to my original titles.

12. *Ecstatic Naturalism: Signs of the World*, pp. 191-192.

13. G.W.F. Hegel, *Philosophy of Subjective Spirit, Vol. 2*, trans. By H.J. Petry, (Dordrecht: D. Reidel, 1978), p. 9.

14. Arthur Schopenhauer, *Parerga and Paralipomena, Vol. II*, trans. By E.F.J. Payne, (Oxford: Oxford University Press, 2000), p. 99.

15. *Nature's Self*, p. 160.

Bibliography

General

Badham, Roger A. 1999. "Windows on the Ecstatic: Reflections upon Robert Corrington's Ecstatic Naturalism." *Soundings*, Vol. 82, No. 3-4, Fall/Winter.

Bartusiak, Marcia. 1993. *Through a Universe Darkly: A Cosmic Tale of Ancient Ethers, Dark Matter, and the Fate of the Universe.* New York: Harper Collins.

Buchler, Justus. 1990. *Metaphysics of Natural Complexes.* second expanded edition. edited by Kathleen Wallace, Armen Marsoobian, and Robert S. Corrington. Albany: SUNY Press.

Corrington, Robert S. 1987. *The Community of Interpreters: On the Hermeneutics of Nature and the Bible in the American Philosophical Tradition.* Macon, GA: Mercer University Press.

_____. 1987. "Toward a Transformation of Neoclassical Theism." *International Philosophical Quarterly.* Vol. XXVII, No. 4, December.

_____. 1989. "A Conversation between Justus Buchler and Robert S. Corrington." *The Journal of Speculative Philosophy.* Vol. III, No. 4.

_____. 1992. *Nature and Spirit: An Essay in Ecstatic Naturalism.* New York: Fordham University Press.

_____. 1993. *An Introduction to C. S. Peirce: Philosopher, Semiotician, and Ecstatic Naturalist.* Lanham, MD: Rowman & Littlefield, Pub.

_____. 1993. "Peirce's Abjected Unconscious: A Psychoanalytic Profile." in *Semiotics 1992.* ed. John Deely. Lanham, MD: University Press of America.

_____. 1993. "Nature's God and the Return of the Material Maternal." *American Journal of Semiotics.* Vol. 10, Nos. 1-2, pp. 115-132.

_____. 1994. *Ecstatic Naturalism: Signs of the World*, Advances in Semiotics. Bloomington, IN: Indiana University Press.

_____. 1996. *Nature's Self: Our Journey from Origin to Spirit.* Lanham, MD: Rowman & Littlefield, Pub.

_____. 1997. *Nature's Religion*. Lanham, MD: Rowman & Littlefield.

_____. 2000. *A Semiotic Theory of Theology and Philosophy*. Cambridge: Cambridge University Press.

_____. 2003. *Wilhelm Reich: Psychoanalyst and Radical Naturalist*. New York: Farrar, Straus & Giroux.

Corrington, Robert S., Carl Hausman, and Thomas M. Seebohm. ed. *Pragmatism Considers Phenomenology*. Center for Advanced Research in Phenomenology and University Press of America..

Driskill, Todd A. 1994. "Beyond the Text: Ecstatic Naturalism and American Pragmatism." *American Journal of Theology and Philosophy*. Vol. 15, No. 3, September.

Eco, Umberto. 1976. *A Theory of Semiotics*. Bloomington, IN: Indiana University Press.

_____. 1990. *The Limits of Interpretation*. Bloomington, IN: Indiana University Press.

Eliade, Mircea. 1978. *A History of Religious Ideas*, Vol. I. Chicago: Chicago University Press.

Emerson, Ralph Waldo. 1983. *Emerson: Essays and Lectures*. The Library of America.

Krikorian, Yervant H. ed. 1944. *Naturalism and the Human Spirit*. New York: Columbia University Press.

Marsoobian, Armen, Kathleen Wallace, and Robert S. Corrington. ed. 1991. *Nature's Perspectives*. Albany: SUNY Press.

Meisner, Sanford and Dennis Longwell. 1987. *Sanford Meisner on Acting*. with an Introduction by Sydney Pollack. New York: Vintage, 1987.

Nguyen, Nam T. 2002. *Nature's Primal Self: An Ecstatic Naturalist Critique of the Anthropocentrism of Peirce's Pragmaticism and Jaspers' Existentialism*, Doctoral Dissertation at Drew University.

Panikkar, Raimundo. 1977. *The Vedic Experience*. Delhi: Motital Banarsidass Publishers.

Parsons, William B. 1999. *The Enigma of the Oceanic Feeling: Provisioning the Psychoanalytic Theory of Mysticism*. Oxford: Oxford University Press.

Plato. *Ion*. from *The Collected Dialogues of Plato*. ed. by Edith Hamilton and Huntington Cairns. Princeton: Princeton University Press, 1961.

Bibliography 233

Tillich, Paul. 1967. *Systematic Theology*. Vols I-III. Chicago: University of Chicago Press.

Trungpa, Chögyam. 1988. *Shambhala: The Sacred Path of the Warrior.* ed. by Carolyn Rose Gimian. Boston: Shambhala Publications.

Manic Depression

Barclay, R.M. 1976. *Manic-Depressive Insanity and Paranoia.* ed. G.M. Robertson. Edinburgh: E. & S. Livingston, 1921; reprinted by New York: Arno Press.

Barondes, Samuel H. 1998. *Mood Genes: Hunting for Origins of Mania and Depression.* New York: W. H. Freeman and Company.

Copeland, Mary Ellen. 1992. *The Depression Workbook: A Guide for Living With Depression and Manic-Depression.* Oakland, CA: New Harbinger Publications.

Custance, John. 1952. *Wisdom, Madness and Folly.*, New York.

Diagnostic and Statistical Manual of Mental Disorders. Fourth Edition. Washington, DC: American Psychiatric Association, 1994.

Diane and Lisa Berger. 1991. *We Heard the Angels of Madness.* New York: Quil.

Duke, Patty and Gloria Hochman. 1992. *A Brilliant Madness: Living with Manic-Depressive Illness.* New York: Bantam Books.

Fieve, Ronald R. 1989. *Moodswing.* Revised and Expanded Edition. New York: Bantam.

Freud, Sigmund. 1952. *On Dreams*, by Sigmund Freud, translated by James Strachey from the Standard Edition. New York: Norton.

_____. 1999. *The Interpretation of Dreams.* translated by Joyce Crick with a introduction by Ritchie Robertson. Oxford: Oxford University Press; based on the original 1899 edition.

Goodwin, Frederick K and Kay Redfield Jamison. 1990. *Manic-Depressive Illness.* New York: Oxford University Press.

Jamison, Kay Redfield. 1993. *Touched With Fire: Manic-Depressive Illness and the Artistic Temperament.* New York: Free Press.

_____. 1995. *An Unquiet Mind: A Memoir of Moods and Madness.* New York: Knopf.

_____. 1999. *Night Falls Fast: Understanding Suicide.* New York: Alfred A. Knopf.

Jung, C.G. 1961. *Memories, Dreams, Reflections.* New York: Random House.

_____. 1971. *Psychological Types.* Volume 6 of the Collected Works. Princeton: Bollingen.

_____. 1976. *The Symbolic Life: Miscellaneous Writings.* Volume 18 of the Collected Works of C.G. Jung. Princeton: Bollingen.

Keirsey, David and Marilyn Bates. 1984. *Please Understand Me: Character & Temperament Types.* Fourth Edition. Del Mar, CA: Prometheus Nemesis Book Company.

Kramer, Peter D. 1993. *Listening to Prozac.* New York: Viking.

Miklowitz, David J. and Michael J. Goldstein. 1997. *Bipolar Disorder: A Family Focused Approach.* New York: The Guilford Press.

Mondimore, Francis Mark. 1999. *Bipolar Disorder: A Guide for Patients and Families.* Baltimore: The Johns Hopkins University Press.

Padgett, Abigail. 1993. *Child of Silence.* New York: Mystery Press.

_____. 1994. *Strawgirl.* New York: Mystery Press.

Practice Guideline for Treatment of Patients With Bipolar Disorder. Washington: American Psychiatric Association, 1995.

Torrey, Bowler, Taylor, and Gottesman. 1994. *Schizophrenia and Manic-Depressive Disorder.* New York: Basic Books.

Torrey, E. Fuller and Michael B. Knable. 2002. *Surviving ManicDepression.* New York: Basic Books.

Whitmon, Edward C & Sylvia Brinton Perera. 1989. *Dreams, A Portal to the Source.* New York: Routledge.

Whybrow, Peter C. 1997. *A Mood Apart: Depression, Mania, and Other Afflictions of the Self.* New York: Basic Books.

Sir Isaac Newton

Hall, Rupert. 1992. *Isaac Newton: Adventurer in Thought.* Oxford: Blackwell Publishers.

Manuel, Frank. 1990. *A Portrait of Isaac Newton.* New York: Da Capo Press; original edition by Harvard University Press in 1968.

Newton, Sir Issac. 1979. *Opticks.* from 1730 posthumous edition. New York: Dover Books.

_____. 1999. *The Principia: Vol. I The Motion of Bodies.* translated by I Bernard Cohen and Anne Whitman Berkeley: University of California Press; originally published in 1934.

_____. *The Principia: Vol. II The System of the World* (Book III).

Westfall, Richard S. 1993. *The Life of Isaac Newton.* Cambridge: Cambridge University Press.

White, Michael. 1997. *Isaac Newton: The Last Sorcerer.* Reading, MA: Addison-Wesley.

Sir Ramakrishna

Deutsch, Eliot. 1969. *Advaita Vedanta: A Philosophical Reconstruction.* Honolulu: University of Hawaii Press.

Hixon, Lex. 1992. *Great Swan: Meetings with Ramakrishna.* Burdett, NY: Larson Publications.

Kripal, Jeffrey J. 1995. *Kali's Child: The Mystical and the Erotic in the Life and Teachings of Ramakrishna.* Second Edition. Chicago: University of Chicago Press.

Mookerjee, Ajit. 1988. *Kali: The Feminine Force.* Rochester, VT: Destiny Books.

Nikhilanada, Swami. tr. 1942. *The Gospel of Sri Ramakrishna.* New York: Ramakrishna-Vivekananda Center.

_____. tr. 1949. *The Upanishads, Volume One.* with commentary. New York: Ramakrishna-Vivekananda Center.

_____. 1953. *Vivekananda: A Biography.* New York: Ramakrishna-Vivekananda Center.

Prentiss, Karen Pechilis. 1999. *The Embodiment of Bhakti.* New York: Oxford University Press.

Rolland, Romain. 1997. *The Life of Ramakrishna.* trans. by E.F. Malcolm-Smith. Calcutta: Advaita Ashram.

Saradananda, Swami. 1946. *Sri Ramakrishna: The Great Master.* translated by Swami Jagadananda. Mylapore, India: Sri Ramakrishna Math.

Schiffman, Richard. 1989. *Sri Ramakrishna: A Prophet for the New Age.* New York: Paragon House.

Sil, Narasingha P. 1998. *Ramakrishna Revisited: A New Biography.* Lanham, MD: University Press of America.

Genius and Creativity

Bloch, Ernst. 1986. *The Principle of Hope.* Vols. I-III. trans. Neville Place, Stephen Plaice, and Paul Knight. Cambridge: The MIT Press; translated from the 1959 edition, *Das Prinzip Hoffnung.* Frankfurt am Main: Suhrkamp Verlag.

Corrington, Robert S. 1993. "Peirce's Abjected Unconscious: A Psychoanalytic Profile." in *Semiotics 1992.* ed. by John Deely. Lanham, MD: University Press of America.

Corrington, Robert S. and John Deely. ed. 1995. "Peirce's Abjection of the Maternal." In *Semiotics 1993.* New York: Peter Lang.

Eysenck, Hans. 1995. *Genius: The Natural History of Creativity.* Cambridge: Cambridge University Press.

Gardner, Howard. 1993. *Creating Minds.* New York: Basic Books.

Hershman, D. Jablow and Julian Lieb, M.D. 1998. *The Key to Genius: Manic-Depression and the Creative Life.* Buffalo: Prometheus Books, 1988, second edition with a new epilogue.

Kristeva, Julia. 1982. *Powers of Horror: An Essay on Abjection.* New York: Columbia University Press.

_____. 1989. *Black Sun: Depression and Melancholia.* trans. by Leon S. Roudiez. New York: Columbia University Press.

Marek, George R. 1969. *Beethoven: Biography of a Genius.* New York: Funk & Wagnalls.

Miller, Alice. 1990. *The Drama of the Gifted Child: The Search for the True Self* trans. by Ruth Ward. New York: Basic Books.

Monk, Ray. 1990. *The Duty of Genius.* New York: Free Press.

Murray, Penelope. ed. 1989. *Genius: The History of an Idea.* Oxford: Basil Blackwell.

Pickover, Clifford A. 1998. *Strange Brains and Genius: The Secret Lives of Eccentric Scientists and Madmen.* (New York: Plenum Trade.

Rorty, Richard. 1979. *Philosophy and the Mirror of Nature.* Princeton: Princeton University Press.

Simonton, Dean Keith. 1999. *Origins of Genius: Darwinian Perspectives on Creativity.* Oxford: Oxford University Press.

INDEX - NAMES

Achilles, 56
Aquinas, St. Thomas, 166
Augustine, St., 74, 153, 166
Badham, Roger A., 218
Barkeley, R.M., 219
Barondes, Samuel H., 220
Bartusiak, Marcia, 220
Bates, Marilyn, 221
Beethoven, Ludwig Van, viii, 110, 120, 126, 223
Bennet, E.A., 96, 97
Berger, Diane, 221
Berger, Lisa, 221
Blake, William, viii, 10, 119
Bloch, Ernst, 224
Bond, James, 48
Bowler, Ann E., 220
Buchler, Justus, 109, 193, 196, 199, 227, 228
Byron, Lord, viii, 100, 119
Cade, John F., 72
Cairns, Huntington, 218
Cassirer, Ernst, 199
Christ, 127, 136, 137, 144, 148, 175, 186
Cohen, Bernard, 225
Coleridge, Samuel Taylor, viii, 119, 228
Copeland, Marry Ellen, 222
Corrington, Joann (sister), 8, 9
Corrington, Murlan S. (father), 8, 9, 11, 12, 34
Corrington, Robert S., 37, 218, 223, 227, 228
Custance, John, 91, 221
De Duillier, Nicholas Fatio, 145, 146
Deely, John, 223, 229
Deutsch, Eliot, 158, 226
Dewey, John, 199

Dickens, Charles, viii, 113, 126
Dionysus, 56, 57, 66
Dostoyevsky, Fyodor, 114
Driskill, Todd A., 218
Duke, Patty, 220
Eco, Umberto, 83, 108, 221, 223
Eliade, Mircea, 57, 218
Emerson, Ralph Waldo, 16, 188, 189, 227
Eysenck, Hans, 113, 225
Feive, Ronald R.,
Freud, Sigmund, 41, 42, 91, 93, 112, 138, 149, 170, 171, 180, 218
Gandhi, Mohandas K., 22
Gardner, Howard, 223
Gershon, Elliot S., 70
Goethe, Johann Wilhelm von, 119
Goldstein, Michael J., 222
Goodwin, Friedrick K., 64, 65, 67, 69, 70, 74, 76, 219
Gottesman, Irving I., 220
Guichard, Jean, 87
Hall, A. Rupert, 142, 225
Hamilton, Edith, 218
Hartshorne, Charles, 193, 196, 201, 202, 228
Hausman, Carl, 228
Hawking, Stephen, 129
Hector, 56
Hegel, G.W.F., 16, 86, 88, 107, 200, 207, 208, 210, 212, 213, 229
Heidegger, Martin, 14, 16, 108, 196, 199, 203, 204
Hershman, D. Jablow, vii, 54, 105, 222

Index - Names

Hixon, Lex, 226
Hobbes, Thomas, 141
Hochman, Gloria, 220
Homer, 56
Hook, Sidney, 217
Hooke, Robert, 138, 147
Husserl, Edmund, 16, 183, 228
Jagadananda, Swami, 226
James II, King, 137
Jamison, Kay Redfield, vii, 33, 46, 54, 64, 65, 67, 69, 70, 73, 74, 76, 77, 78, 79, 90, 100, 115, 119, 121, 219, 220, 221, 223
Jaspers, Karl, 196, 218, 228
Jones, James Earl, 106
Joyce, James, 38, 105
Jung, C.G., vii, 6, 7, 16, 28, 33, 34, 41, 42, 82, 88, 89, 91, 92, 93, 94, 96, 97, 98, 99, 112, 120, 138, 139, 167, 170, 171, 187, 221
Kali, 128, 151, 152, 153, 154, 156, 159, 162, 163, 164, 165, 179, 226
Kessel, Neil, 118
Keirsey, David, 221
King, Martin Luther Jr., 21
Knable, Michael B., 222
Knight, Paul, 224
Kraepelin, Emil, 67, 219
Kramer, Peter D., 220
Krikorian, Yervant H., 228
Kripal, Jeffrey J., 156, 164, 226
Krishna, 151, 155, 161
Kristeva, Julia., 117, 120, 122, 130, 213, 224
Kubrick, Stanley, 27, 103
Lee, Lois (mother), 8, 9, 10, 11, 12, 13, 16, 33, 51, 52, 61, 62, 63, 121, 217

Lieb, Julian, vii, 54, 105, 222
Leibniz, Gottfried, 99, 138, 146, 148
Locke, John, 141
Loman, Willy, 81
Longwell, Dennis, 221
Malcolm-Smith, E.F., 226
Mann, Thomas, 123
Manuel, Frank E., 130, 133, 144, 225
Marek, George R., 223
McKay, Matthew, 222
Meisner, Sanford, 80, 81, 221
Monk Ray, 120, 224
Moore, E.G., 229
Mother, Great, 30, 152, 153, 155, 157, 160, 164, 178, 215
Murray, Penelope, 224
Marsoobian, Armen, 227
Miklowitz, David J., 222
Miller, Alice, 224
Moltmann, Jürgen, 224
Mondimore, Francis Mark, 222
Mookerjee, Ajit, 152, 226
Nebuchadnezzer, 10
Newton, Sir Isaac, viii, ix, 63, 127, 129-149, 155, 163, 169, 173, 183, 190, 192, 206, 224, 225, 229
Neville, Robert C., 194, 201, 203
Nguyen, Nam, 218
Nikhilananda, Swami, 150, 157, 226, 227
Oldenburg, Henry, 140
Oldman, Gary, 223
Olivier, Sir Laurence, 106
Padgett, Abigail, 219
Panikkar, Raimundo, 179, 227
Parsifal, 47

Parsons, William B., 171, 227
Peirce, Charles Sanders, viii, 2, 4, 17, 83, 84, 85, 90, 108, 112, 196, 204, 206, 207, 217, 218, 223, 227, 229
Perera, Sylvia Brinton, 218
Pickover, Clifford A., 103
Place, Neville, 224
Plaice, Stephen, 224
Plato, 16, 55, 56, 57, 183, 201
Plotinus, 202, 204
Plummer, Christopher, 106
Pollack, Sydney, 221
Prentiss, Karen Pechilis, 226
Puri, Tota, 158, 159, 160
Ramakrishna, Sri, viii, ix, 128, 149-166, 169, 170, 178, 179, 192, 226, 227
Randall, John Hermann Jr., 199
Reich, Wilhelm, 180, 218, 227
Robertson, G.M., 42, 219
Rolland, Romain, 153, 164, 170, 171, 226
Rorty, Richard, 223
Roudiez, Leon S., 224
Royce, Josiah, 17
Santayana, George, 199
Saradananda, Swami, 226
Schopenhauer, Arthur, 38, 213, 229
Seebohm, Thomas M., 228
Shakespeare, William, 27, 38, 81
Schiffman, Richard, 156, 226
Shiva, Lord, 151, 176, 215
Sil, Narasingha P., 155, 156, 160, 226
Simonton, Dean Keith, 114, 115, 139, 224
Socrates, 55, 57

Spielberg, Steven, 45
Strachey, James, 218
Storr, Anthony, 112
Taylor, A.E., 228
Taylor, Eduard H., 220
Tillich, Paul, 16, 18, 39, 120, 123, 169, 196
Torrey, E. Fuller, 220, 222
Trungpa, Chogyam, viii, 217
Tutu, Desmond, 21, 25, 182
Vivekananda, Swami, 128, 162, 164, 170, 226, 227
Wallace, Kathleen, 227
Ward, Ruth, 224
Westfall, Richard S., 130, 135, 225
White, Michael, 134, 136, 137, 138, 139, 142, 144, 145, 146
Whitehead, Alfred North, 226
Whitman, Anne, 225
Whitmont, Eduard C., 228
Whybrow, Peter C, 221
Wickens., 139, 145
William, Tennessee, viii, 27
Wittgenstein, Ludwig, 16, 92, 119, 120, 130, 213
Woodbridge, Frederick, 199
Yogananda, Paramahansa, 149

INDEX - SUBJECT

A Brilliant Madness: Living With Manic-Depressive Illness (Duke and Hochman), 220
A History of Religious Ideas, Vol. I (Eliade), 218
A Mood Apart: Depression, Mania, and Other Afflictions of the Self (Whybrow), 221
A Portrait of Isaac Newton (Manuel), 225
A Semiotic Theory of Theology and Philosophy (Corrington), 207, 218, 227, 228, 229
A Theory of Semiotics (Eco), 221
Abaissment du niveau mental, 91
Ab-grund, 196, 204, 212, 215, 216
Actual infinite, 206, 207
Advaita Vedanta: A Philosophical Reconstruction (Deutsch), 159, 160, 226
Alchemy, 67, 129, 135, 136, 138
Alcohol, 1, 2, 11, 13, 18, 26, 27, 31, 35, 37, 38, 78, 79, 80, 177
Allele, 71, 72
American Academy of Religion, 1, 26, 217
Amsterdam, 15
An Introduction to C.S. Peirce (Corrington), 223, 227
An Unquiet Mind: A Memoir of Moods and Madness (Jamison), 219, 220
Andromeda galaxy, 177

Anima, 33, 34, 46, 50, 51, 52, 53, 54, 223
Animus, 34
Anni mirabiles, 134
Archetypal material, 93
Archetype, 33, 34, 43, 45, 46, 47, 48, 93, 99, 107, 128, 144, 208, 209, 210
Atman, 158, 159, 160, 178
Attention Deficit disorder, 12
Autobiography of a Yogi (Yogananda), 149
Avatar, 128, 150, 153, 155, 157
Beethoven: Biography of a Genius (Marek), 223
Being and Nothingness (Sartre), 75
Being and Time (Heidegger), 14
Bengal, 150
Bhakti yoga, 156
Bipolar Disorder: A Family Focused Approach (Miklowitz and Goldstein), 222
Bipolar Disorder: A Guide for Patients and Families (Mondimore), 222
Bi-polar disorder, vii, 62
Bipolar I, 59, 60, 61, 70
Bipolar II, 60, 61, 70
Black hole, ix, 52, 66, 174
Black Sun: Depression and Melancholia (Kristeva), 224
Brahman, 128, 155, 158, 159, 160, 164, 172, 178, 179
British East India Company, 151
Calcutta, 150, 151, 152

Cambridge, 129, 132, 134, 136, 138, 139, 142, 146, 147
Carbamazepine, 72, 219
Celestial mechanics, 127, 133, 137, 138, 142, 144, 145, 148
Center for Cultural Awareness, 15
Child of Silence (Padgett), 219
Church of England, 129, 137, 148
College of William and Mary, 25
Communal testing, 177, 192
Community of Interpreters, The (Corrington), 17, 217, 227
Complexes, 5, 6, 13, 17, 19, 155, 167, 171, 173, 177, 178, 179, 190, 191, 198, 202
Compliance, 6, 63, 64, 74
Confessions (St. Augustine), 74
Corybantes, 55
onsciousness, 5, 6, 31, 38, 40, 42, 43, 45, 49, 51, 53, 81, 82, 86, 87, 88, 89, 91, 92, 93, 95, 98, 101, 110, 115, 116, 119, 122, 125, 145, 149, 151, 154, 155, 157, 158, 162, 163, 164, 167, 168, 169, 171, 173, 174, 177, 183, 186, 189, 190, 192, 208, 210, 214
Countertransference, 162, 170, 190, 191, 192
Creating Minds (Gardner), 223
Creatio ex nihilo, 200
Creative distancing, 177, 178, 179, 180, 182, 188, 192
Creativity, vii, 17, 38, 47, 48, 54, 57, 64, 100, 103, 104, 106, 107, 108, 109, 110, 111, 112, 113, 117, 118, 119, 121, 127, 222, 223
Dakshineswar, 152, 158, 164
Death of a Salesman (Miller), 81
Death mother, the, 31, 33, 34, 51, 52, 53, 54, 81, 124, 178
Decoding, 41, 83, 85, 86, 89, 101
Delphi, 56, 57, 176
Demonic, 39, 47, 123, 124, 179
Denial, 25, 31, 32, 33, 37, 39, 53, 86, 107, 158, 164, 206, 213, 222
Depakote, 6, 32, 75
Depressed stage, 2
Depression Workbook: A Guide for Living With Depression and Manic-Depression, The (Copeland), 222
Dialectic, 5, 86, 87, 89, 90, 93, 98, 113, 116, 121, 125, 126, 156, 168, 172, 174, 176, 177, 179, 185, 186, 188, 191, 193, 196, 199, 202, 205, 208, 209, 210, 213, 215
Dilantin, 12
Divestment Campaign, 21, 23, 46, 182
Doctor Faustus (Mann), 123
Dopamine, 80
Drala, viii, 152, 186
Drama of the Gifted Child, The (Miller), 224
Dream ego, 45, 46, 48, 49, 50, 51, 52
Dreams, 22, 25, 28, 34, 40, 42, 43, 44, 45, 46, 53, 82, 87, 218, 221

Index - Subject

Dreams: A Portal to the Source (Whitmont and Perera), 218
Drew University, 16, 26, 218
DSM-IV, 59, 60, 61, 63, 72
Duty of Genius, The (Monk), 120, 224
Ecstatic naturalism, 26, 38, 188, 193, 194, 195, 204, 206, 207, 209, 217, 218, 227, 229
Ecstatic Naturalism: Signs of the World (Corrington), 207, 217, 223, 229
Enantiodromia, 97
English Civil War, 137
Embodiment of Bhakti, The (Prentiss), 226
Enigma of the Oceanic Feeling: Provisioning the Psychoanalytic Theory of Mysticism, The (Parsons), 227
Epiphanies of power, 125, 154, 198
Eros, 57
Essays and Lectures (Emerson), 227
Existential despair, 32
Extraversion, 95, 97, 98, 156
Father, 8, 9, 11, 12, 34, 130, 131, 137, 145, 148, 150, 151, 155
Fordham University Press, 26
Genetic aspects, 5
Genetic code, 20, 84, 85, 86, 98, 99, 101
Genius, vii, 2, 14, 15, 16, 33, 37, 38, 39, 47, 48, 54, 57, 58, 92, 101, 103, 104, 105, 107, 109, 111-127, 128, 129, 130, 133, 135, 138, 139, 144, 148, 149, 151, 159, 163, 165, 166, 181, 189, 222, 223
Genius: The History of an Idea (ed. Murray), 224
Genius: The Natural History of Creativity (Eysenck), 224
Genius myth, 14, 15, 37, 58, 120
Gestalt of grace, 120
Good breast, the, 121, 122, 124, 130, 135
Gospel of Sri Ramakrishna, (Nikhilananda), 226
Grace, ix, 32, 120, 124, 169, 177, 179, 187, 188, 192
Grandiosity, 61
Grantham, 132
Great mother, the, 30, 152, 153, 155, 157, 160, 164, 178, 215
Great Swan: Meetings with Ramakrishna (Hixon), 226
Greco-Roman, 58
Hen kai pan, 211-216
Hermeneutic circle, 5, 28, 98
Hermeneutic horizon, 66, 82, 99
Hermeneutics, 3, 4, 17, 66, 96, 217
Highlands Institute for American Religious and Philosophical Thought, the, 203
Holy, 39, 51, 55, 56, 123, 124, 127
Holy Grail, 47
Homoeroticism, 161, 164
Huntington's disease, 71
Hypo-mania, 123, 156
Iliad (Homer), 56
India, 149, 150, 165, 176, 215

Individuation, 7, 40, 47, 51, 54, 64, 92, 99, 101, 111, 158, 182, 183, 187, 207
Infertility, 20
Infinitizing ordinal phenomenology, 208, 210
Intervals, 166, 172, 175, 176, 177, 178, 179, 186, 187, 189, 190
Irrational functions, 94
Insomnia, 61, 80, 83, 139
Interpretants, 84, 85, 86, 89, 90, 101, 108, 111, 114, 206, 209
Interpretation of Dreams, The (Freud), 41, 218
Introversion, 95, 97, 98, 140
Ion (Plato), 55, 218
Isaac Newton: Adventurer in Thought (Hall), 225
Isaac Newton: The Last Sorcerer (White), 225
Jnana yoga, 156
Johns Hopkins University, 64
Jouissance, 213
Kali: The Feminine Force (Mookerjee), 226
Kali's Child: The Mystical and Erotic in the Life and Teachings of Ramakrishna (Kripal), 226
Karma yoga, 157
Life of Isaac Newton, The (Westfall), 225
Life of Ramakrishna, The (Rolland), 226
Limits of Interpretation, The (Eco), 223
Lincolnshire, 130, 132
Listening to Prozac (Kramer), 220

Lithium, 1, 6, 10, 31, 32, 34, 35, 40, 49, 50, 51, 54, 58, 62, 63, 68, 69, 72, 73, 74, 75, 76, 77, 89, 92, 99, 172, 219, 220, 222
Logos, 55
Lucasian Chair of Mathematics, 129, 136
Manic-depression, vii, ix, 4, 5, 7, 12, 26, 29, 46, 47, 59, 62, 64, 68, 70, 71, 72, 79, 88, 89, 91, 92, 96, 100, 104, 139, 156, 167, 174, 219, 222
Manic phase, 2, 17, 65, 67, 68, 88, 90, 92, 93, 96, 137
Manic-Depressive Illness (Goodwin and Jamison), 64, 70, 219, 220, 223
Maternal origin, 58
Meenakshi Temple, 215, 216
Melancholy, 77, 124, 183, 184, 185, 186, 187, 213, 214
Memes, 114, 116
Memories, Dreams, Reflections (Jung), 221
Messianic secret, 121
Metaphysics, 193, 194, 196, 197, 205, 206, 209, 211
Metaphysics of Natural Complexes, Second Expanded Edition (Buchler), 227
Missa Solemnis (Beethoven), 110, 223
Mood Swing (Fieve), 217
Mood swings, ix, 5, 12, 16, 27, 33, 34, 35, 43, 54, 68, 75, 97, 99, 103, 175, 177, 182
Mother, 8, 9, 10, 11, 13, 16, 31, 33, 34, 51, 52, 61, 62, 63, 121, 130, 131, 135, 137, 145, 151, 160, 161, 170, 183, 203

Mt. Olympus, 56
Mysterium coniunctionis, 127
Narcissism, 19, 113, 117, 120, 122, 170
National Institute of Mental Health, 64
Natura naturans, 107, 119, 223
Natural grace, 177, 188
Naturalism and the Human Spirit (Krikorian), 228
Nature and Spirit: An Essay in Ecstatic Naturalism (Corrington), 194, 195, 196, , 197, 200, 217, 228, 229
Nature natured, 193, 194, 196, 198, 200, 201, 204, 205, 206, 212, 213, 214, 216
Nature naturing, 107, 193, 194, 195, 200, 201, 202, 203, 204, 205, 206, 211, 212, 213, 214, 215, 216
Nature's Religion (Corrington), 207, 218, 227
Nature's Self (Corrington), 207, 214, 218, 222, 227, 229
Neo-Kantianism, 199
New Jersey, 8, 15, 16, 21, 33
Night Falls Fast: Understanding Suicide (Jamison), 221
Nirguna Brahman, 159, 164
Norepinephrine, 80
Not yet, the, 101, 111-127, 133, 185, 186, 213, 214
Obsessive-compulsive personality disorder, 103, 104
On Dreams (Freud), 41, 218
ʻological difference, 194,
ʻ, 204, 206

Ontological mother, 145
Open infinite, 207
Opticks (Newton), 147, 148, 225
Origins of Genius: Darwinian Perspectives on Creativity (Simonton), 224
Othello (Shakespeare), 106
Ordinal phenomenology, 193, 195, 199, 200, 204, 207, 208, 228
Original sin, 18
Panentheism, 193, 194, 202, 203, 211, 212
Pantheism, 202, 203, 205, 206, 211-216
Pansophia, 210
Paranoia, 10, 13, 29, 122, 137, 138, 141, 179, 182, 219
Parerga and Paralipomena (Schopehauer), 229
Penn State University, 18
Phenomenology, 183, 184, 204, 208, 209, 210, 213, 228
Philadelphia, 9, 33, 83
Philosophy, 13, 14, 15, 16, 17, 19, 26, 55, 120, 145, 183, 197, 203, 210, 212, 213
Philosophy and the Mirror of Nature (Rorty), 223
Philosophy of Subjective Spirit, Vol. 2 (Hegel), 229
Please Understand Me: Character and Temperament Types (Keirsey and Bates), 221
Postmodernism, 4, 186
Postpartum, 8, 61, 62, 145
Potencies, 107, 108, 111, 119, 195, 200, 204, 205, 215, 216

Powers of Horror: An Essay in Abjection (Kristeva), 224
Practical Guideline for Treatment of Patients With Bipolar Disorder (American Psychiatric Association), 219
Pragmatism, 1, 22, 23, 84, 186, 218, 228
Pretemporal, 183, 205, 213, 215
Principia Mathmatica (Newton), 142, 145, 147
Principle of Hope, The (Bloch), 224
Processive infinite, 207
Products (of genius), 181
Projection, 6, 17, 67, 125, 182, 190, 191, 203, 209, 210, 215
Prozac, 35, 69, 75, 76, 220
Psychic inflation, ix, 7, 38, 57, 89, 92, 120, 126, 135, 136, 137, 167
Psychoanalysis, 6, 41, 112, 155, 170, 173, 190, 203, 208, 209, 211, 227
Psychological Types (Jung), 93, 221
Psychomotor agitation, 55, 62, 110
Psychopathology, 56, 58, 67, 91, 97, 111, 118, 128, 145, 149, 167
Psychosemiosis, 208, 214
Psychosis, 7, 8, 32, 71, 79, 92, 99, 157, 188
Ramakrishna Revisited: A New Biography (Sil), 226
Rational functions, 94
RCA, 8, 11
Remission, 7, 31, 32, 60, 62, 73, 86, 119

Royal Mint, 134, 146
Sacred folds, 38, 154, 166, 172, 173, 174, 175, 176, 179, 187, 189, 190
Saguna Brahman, 159, 160
Samadhi, 155, 157, 160, 164, 165
Sanford Meisner on Acting (Meisner and Longwell), 221
Schizoaffective disorder, 9
Schizophrenia, 9, 10, 67, 68, 70, 79, 88, 91, 92, 119, 155, 220
Schizophrenia and Manic-Depressive Disorder (Torrey, Bowler, Taylor, and Gottesman), 220
Self, vii, viii, ix, x, 3, 4, 5, 6, 7, 15, 22, 27, 28, 32, 34, 38, 44, 45, 46, 47, 49, 54, 56, 60, 65, 66, 69, 75, 77, 86, 96, 99, 100, 101, 107, 111, 112, 113, 117, 118, 120, 121, 122, 123, 124, 125, 126, 127, 128, 133, 136, 158, 167, 168, 169, 172, 173, 174, 175, 178, 179, 180, 182, 183, 184, 185, 186, 187, 189, 196, 198, 200, 206, 208, 209, 211, 218, 221, 222, 224, 227, 228, 229
Self-medication, 13, 18, 26, 31, 33, 35, 86, 95, 139
Semiotics, 83, 84, 86, 196, 203, 206, 208, 217, 221, 223, 229
Seroquel, 32
Serotonin, 76, 78, 79, 220
Shakti, 128, 152, 156, 158, 165, 176, 178, 180, 186, 215

Shambhala: The Sacred Path of the Warrior (Trungpa), 217
Shame, 2, 5, 50, 65, 67, 100, 165
Signs, 3, 4, 5, 10, 17, 29, 65, 66, 67, 75, 82, 84, 85, 86, 87, 88, 89, 90, 91, 93, 101, 108, 188, 206, 207, 209, 211, 217, 223, 229
Sister, 8, 9, 12, 33, 34, 50, 52, 162, 217
South Africa, 20, 21, 23, 24, 182
South Dakota, 8
Spirits, the, 35, 57, 107, 141, 147, 154, 159, 160, 179, 183-192, 194, 195-202, 203, 209, 210, 211, 214, 217, 218, 222, 227, 228, 229
Spirituality, 172, 180, 183, 188, 189
Sri Ramakrishna: A Prophet for the New Age (Schiffman), 226
Sri Ramakrishna: The Great Master (Saradananda), 226
Step-mother, 9
Strange Brains and Genius: The Secret Lives of Eccentric Scientists and Madmen (Pickover), 222
Suicide, ix, 4, 5, 7, 26, 33, 35, 60, 63, 64, 70, 73, 76, 77, 78, 79, 80, 81, 82, 86, 124, 126, 174, 185, 220, 221
Summa Theologica (Aquinas), 166
Super-ego, 2, 14, 29, 65, 101, 132
Sustaining infinite, 207

Symbolic Life, The (Jung), 221
Symposium (Plato), 57
Systematic Theology (Tillich), 224
Tardive dyskinesia, 9, 10
Tavistock Lectures: On the Theory and Practice of Analytical Psychology (Jung), 96
Tegretol, 6
Teleological perspective, 43
Temple University, 13
Theater, 3, 8, 52, 53, 95, 103, 126
Theology, 7, 16, 26, 39, 193, 194, 203, 207, 218, 224, 227, 228, 229
Through a Universe Darkly (Baartusiak), 220
Tibetan Buddhism, viii, 152
Torah, 187
Touched With Fire: Manic-Depressive Illness and the Artistic Temperament (Jamison), 219, 221, 222, 223, 224
Tower of London, 134
Transcendental argument, 193, 194, 195, 199, 201, 203, 216
Transference, the, 19, 28, 30, 44, 63, 122, 123, 125, 126, 131, 133, 162, 173, 190, 191, 192, 210, 211, 215
Trauma, 13, 69, 83, 98, 131, 155, 164, 182
Triggers, 5, 61, 69, 78, 80
Trinity College Cambridge, 129, 132
Ultimate import, 167, 169, 171, 172, 173, 180
Ulysses (Joyce), 105

Unconscious, the, 1, 5, 6, 7, 11, 22, 23, 40, 42, 43, 44, 45, 53, 54, 82, 86, 87, 88, 89, 91, 92, 93, 95, 96, 97, 98, 107, 108, 109, 110, 111, 113, 116, 118, 119, 120, 121, 124, 125, 133, 167, 168, 171, 173
Underconscious, the, 201, 205, 206, 228
Unipolar depression, 62, 75
Unitarian Universalism, 39
Upanishads, 178, 179, 183, 190, 227
Valium, 12, 72
Valproate, 72, 219
Vedanta, 128, 156, 158, 159, 160, 163, 165, 178, 186, 226
Vedic Experience, The (Panikkar), 227
Verbindlichkeit, 108
Vivekananda: A Biography (Nikhilananda), 226
We Heard the Angels of Madness (Berger and Berger), 221
Wellbutrin, 32, 35
Wholeness, ix, x, 3, 7, 17, 40, 44, 45, 52, 64, 99, 100, 107, 112, 164, 166, 167, 169, 170, 171, 172, 175, 177, 180, 182, 185, 189, 194
Wilhelm Reich: Psychoanalyst and Radical Naturalist (Corrington), 218, 227
Windhorse, the, viii, ix, 3, 32, 58, 87, 167, 168, 177, 180, 187
Woolsthorpe, 134
Worldhood, 205, 213, 215